MW01518677

The Letters

SallyAnne Grillo Artese

ARCHWAY
PUBLISHING

Archway Publishing books may be ordered through booksellers or by contacting:

Archway Publishing
1663 Liberty Drive
Bloomington, IN 47403
www.archwaypublishing.com
844-669-3957

ISBN: 978-1-6657-0415-1 (sc)
ISBN: 978-1-6657-0414-4 (hc)
ISBN: 978-1-6657-0416-8 (e)

Library of Congress Control Number: 2021904843

Print information available on the last page.

Archway Publishing rev. date: 5/12/2021

For my brother, Peter, who has had faith in me, has supported my effort to publish this story, which would not have happened without his encouragement.

CONTENTS

INTRODUCTION

In 1975, Dover produced an unabridged republication of the book "What is Design?" (originally published by Paul Theobald in 1960) under the title of "Form, Function and Design". As the daughter of Paul Jacques Grillo, the original author, I have endeavored to write the story of his early life and that of our family as we lived it during and after World War II.

Paul Grillo was awarded the coveted *Grand Prix de Rome* in 1937, an honor bestowed on only one recipient each year for excellence in art, architecture, or music. He was also the chief architect for the ski resort of Meribel, France, which hosted the Olympics in 1992, though he never received the recognition due him. He died, destitute, in France, on September 23, 1990.

What I have written is the personal story of who he was as I knew him. And it is the story of a family caught up in forces that would forever shape an uncertain future.

PART I
FRANCE

PART I
FRANCE

– 1 –

THE CHALET

Our families are with us always and are as intimately connected to us as the blood coursing through our veins. We have a shared tapestry, which together we have woven, its many colors and threads creating a singular work of memory in each of our hearts. We have strong bonds, ties of blood and history. I see in my three children that they have this link that comes from facing adversity, adventure, and growing up together to form a common wall of defense against anything that might come in from outside—or inside.

What is this tapestry? Is it a tangled skein of knots woven through the many colors of the warp and weft? Or will I ever decipher an emerging picture of the past as it insists itself into my present?

I'm probably entering the sunset of my life but everything feels new and original—as if I'm going through the doorway of a whole new world, a whole new life. I can look back over the years and it's as if everything happened to someone else—certainly not me—I'm only an observer of my history now.

But how is it that a scent can trigger a set of memories so deeply hidden that when recalled, they overwhelm and surprise—as if this had all happened yesterday? I'd been trimming away some stray oregano that was encroaching onto the driveway, too close to the front wheel of Joe's Lexus. He had just come home, so the engine was still warm.

And suddenly, I was in post-war Paris with my father, on the final leg of the long odyssey that had begun in Paris after I was born, and was finally ending nine years later, in the same place, as the family prepared for the transatlantic crossing at Le Havre. I had felt special because my father had treated me to a lunch of fresh asparagus in a restaurant, like a grownup. I can almost taste the vinaigrette, still sharp on my tongue. The grated hard-boiled egg spills over the stalks in a delicate white and yellow dusting.

The smell of the gas coming from Joe's cooling Lexus catapulted me to a long ago time marked with fear and mystery—a time suddenly crystallized in snippets of memory, of images of my childhood in war-ravaged France. I always remember these pictures of my childhood in black and white, as if color might render them a Walt Disney fantasy.

I had been too small to understand the tension of the adults around me. But when we all had to duck into ditches to escape the strafing, when we had to sleep in hay barns, and when I was so grateful to sleep in a bed with sheets on it, even I had understood that these were not normal times.

We sat out the last four years of the war in our chalet, so close to the Swiss border that RAF pilots often came for shelter as they made their way through the underground and over the mountains into the safety of Switzerland. My father played Bach and Beethoven on his grand piano as the adults sipped Chartreuse, the strong, pale-green alpine brandy, while we children were given a rare sugar cube dipped in the powerful brew.

My parents had become farmers, with sheep and a cow and an occasional pig. Mama was a Wellesley graduate, and a New England Blue-Blood, she used to say with some pride, who learned how to spin wool, make soap, tend the livestock and do all the other complex and timeless work of a peasant farmer. I even had a pet goat—though she eventually became a pair of shoes for me, and rare meat for a hungry family—and today, I use her name as a password on the internet. How ironic are some of the devices we use to recall and reinforce treasured memories.

In most ways, this was an idyllic childhood. Far from the storm of war and too young to appreciate any sense of privation, toys were non-existent so we made up games. Our friends were the *Savoyard* children who lived high on the mountain, our neighbors across the hills.

When my two older brothers, Paul and John, and I finally landed at the chalet, we had a little brother, Pierre, and baby sister Betty, as well. By the time the war ended, Rona came along as the caboose, eleven years younger than her oldest brother, Paul. So we were six, but almost two generations. Paul, John and I have visceral memories of the war, while Pierre, Betty and Rona only know the stories that have been told—almost as legend or folk tale.

September 2007: Joe and I visited the chalet, in celebration of my seventieth birthday. I hadn't seen it since I had left as a child, over sixty years ago. As we drove up the hairpin, one lane road, I wasn't sure I'd recognize it. My memory certainly wouldn't be enough. All I really had to go on was the photograph that hung on the wall at home, a photograph taken about ten years ago by John, on his own odyssey to see the chalet once again. And yet, as we drove, so much was familiar. I even recognized the school where I had to learn to write with my right hand, or I'd get smacked on the knuckles with a ruler.

But then I first heard the sound of the large cowbells echoing with one another across the hills. It was a perfect September day, my actual birthday. The sky was the deep gentian blue of high altitude, in clear contrast to the grassy hills that looked so soft that I would have loved to have run barefooted, as when I was little. I almost expected to see the cherry tree I used to climb to pick the cherries from, hanging the doubles over my ears as if they were earrings. These cherries were so darkly sweet and ripe that they exploded in my mouth like some exotic drink.

As Joe and I approached, the cows ignored the sound of the car and continued to munch the sweet meadow grass, their large bells calling and echoing, as the melody of the mountains.

The chalet seemed thrown onto the side of the hills, yet almost growing out of the land, the rich dark wood of the upper story weathered and worn above the stucco first floor. In a way, chalets all look very much the same, designed to last a very long time.

The chalet was set back from a terrace, which was always where we all played, or where our mother washed endless diapers in a large cauldron, using her gritty soap as she rubbed on the washboard. The terrace was a gathering place where we could drink in the summer air as the sun warmed our backs. The first floor, as with all chalets, was thick stone, covered in plaster or stucco, to withstand the heavy winter snows that could rise to the second floor. The balcony that separated the first from the second floor was used mostly to dry fruit in the summer. The steep roof had a deep overhang, to provide shade in the summer, yet allow the low winter sun to warm the interior of the whole building, as well as to allow much of the heavy snow to collect as insulation in winter, then slide harmlessly down with the warming sun of spring.

The timeless design of these chalets, scattered over the hills like toys, is a function of the land and its people. They all face south, to get the most benefit from the sun; each has a terrace and a balcony for the life and the work of the farming peasants, and the same deep overhanging roof. There is always a cold room for curing meat and cheese. The animals are housed in a barn or stable behind the living quarters, backed up against the mountainside.

Because of the mountainous terrain, all work is done by horse and plow, rather than tractors. In late summer, the hay from the high meadows is scythed and stored in a separate storehouse, a *miche*. This is typically a communal farming life wherein neighbors barter with one another. If one neighbor will help with cutting another neighbor's hay, they may store it in the same *miche*. When it comes time to bring the hay down in the winter, the men will go together with a long saw and cut the hay in blocks, tie it to a wooden sled specifically designed for this purpose, and bring the precarious load of hay down the mountain to the stables. The sleighs go careening down the slope with a brakeman in front and one on either side of the sleigh to slow it somewhat.

Of course, when Joe and I visited in September it was obvious that a whole new industry had replaced the timeless craft of peasant farming. *Samoëns*, the little town below the chalet, is at the heart of Alpine ski tourism and summer sports such as hang gliding. Now, many of these traditional farming homes have become very expensive, very exclusive ski chalets. "*Plus ça change, plus c'est la même chose*"...the more it changes, the more it is the same.

We parked the car in a well-manicured driveway that led to the back entrance of the chalet. The place was shuttered, though it looked occupied. Probably for rent in season and presently vacant, or maybe the owners worked in town and were gone for the day. Typical that the windows would be shuttered, even if someone lived there. As natural as locking the door. Joe had his camera out and continued to document this memorable moment.

I turned from the chalet and looked out over the lush valley spread below. Even at this time of year, late September, I could make out the network of ski slopes among the trees and the emerald hills. Hang gliders, brilliant as kites, floated on air currents like feathers, lazily coming to rest on a grassy field far below.

Papa worked so hard for this, I thought. *But he never got any of the fruit...*

I thought of all the plans he had made, all the ideas he had given away, the vision that was his first—before it was taken from him. Or did he walk away, innocently believing that his partners would honor his efforts and share the eventual reward of the most important ski resorts in France?

But I remembered that when Papa first began to dream of these valleys, the world was in upheaval, consumed and being consumed by an apocalyptic war.

I turned away from the valley below and studied the outbuilding where Rona was born. I was pleasantly surprised to see that it had not changed at all, though of course it was much smaller than I remembered. It was set away from the main chalet, about twenty feet or so, separate but still really connected.

The memories continued to flood me—full-blown, as if the steps I walked now were the same as when I was eight, going to school in my bare feet, a crusty piece of bread with blueberry jam in my hand, my book bag on my shoulder.

I peered in the small side window of the guest house, but saw that it was now simply a tool shed. I could see the shadows and outlines of farming equipment, what looked like a bike, some skis, shovels and such. But what I remembered was superimposed over these shadowy objects. I remembered the big bed and the small night table with a pitcher sitting in a big bowl. There was a small lamp on the other night table, and I remembered several books piled next to the lamp. The room smelled faintly of lavender then, from the bouquets that were hung upside down behind the bed. I could almost see my mother, cozy in the down comforter and the heavy linen sheets with their beautifully faggotted edges.

I remembered that when Rona was born in December, the snowfall had already been very heavy. The path from the chalet to the guest house had been almost a tunnel of snow, piled almost six feet high on either side. The moon had been very full that night, lending a silvery glow to the drifts, even a diamond dust of cold sparkle. *But why was she born here, which had become the guest house, rather than in the main house, in the warmth of the wood stove that always glowed?* I wondered, and realized that this setting would have been an intimate and quiet place, away from the din of family life in close quarters. Mama would have been allowed to enjoy peace and quiet here, with her new baby daughter nestled in her arms. She would have been cozy in the big four-poster bed, piled high with a down comforter and many pillows. I had been allowed to stay home from school that momentous day, a special treat, since my brothers and I wouldn't have to walk down the mountain to the school. We five children stood in awe, gathered around the big bed to meet our new baby sister, cradled in our mother's arms, being tenderly looked after by our father.

6

I turned away from the little guest house finally, lightly running my fingers over the weathered wood, as if in a caress. We got back in the car to continue our odyssey of discovery. We drove on the one-lane road to the next cluster of chalets. This would have been where my neighbors lived. Again, it was obvious that many of the small farms had become vacation chalets. Yet the large cowbells persisted in their deep melodies as the placid cows munched the deep grass; so there was still a thriving dairy community, if nothing else, beyond the tourists who provided such a lucrative base for the local economy.

"Is it everything you hoped it would be?" Joe interrupted my reverie to ask quietly.

"Even more—because I'm sharing it with you…" I was silent, reflecting on my good fortune at being able to experience the dream of a lifetime with the only person who could ever appreciate the depth of my emotions at this moment. Joe was more than my husband, more than the man I had turned to after my divorce, more than a partner and a friend. Joe understood me, loved me, and accepted me in all my difficult moods.

We found the school where I had gone as a child—my first experience in a school. It seemed unchanged from my memory: a solid little building with a steeple, almost as if it had been a church at one time—I didn't know. But I remembered the sound of the bell as it called to the children hiking down the mountain. Most of the students were my brothers and me, with only a handful of others, varying in age from fourteen down to my little brother, Pierre, two years younger than I was. I remembered being rapped on my knuckles when I wanted to write with my left hand.

We continued on until we came to a small parking area at the end of the road. One other car was parked in the shade. A park directory was posted on a big sign, indicating the various trails that led off from the parking area. We studied the map, which showed all the little hamlets that were thrown against the mountain, little clusters of three or four chalets. The overview showed our location relative to the Swiss border, some 40 kilometers away.

"See, Joe? Didn't I tell you we lived close to Switzerland?"

"I wonder why your parents didn't take you over the mountains to the safety of a neutral country…"

"Maybe they felt just as safe, high in the mountains," I shrugged. "Besides, they already owned this chalet." I was beginning to experience emotional overload and was ready to go back down to the village.

"Let's find a different inn for tonight, Joe. I didn't like the place we were in last night."

"Really? I thought it was pretty nice. We sure had a great view of the valley from where we were."

"The food was terrible, and the service was even worse! They didn't even bring my dinner until after you finished yours—and it was cold!"

"Maybe we can stay in the village. That would be fun—a birthday dinner in *Samoëns*. How does that sound?"

In fact, we found an inn where I could also do a little laundry. We were traveling with only a carry-on so I was grateful that we would at least have clean underwear now. *Madame* offered to do the job—for a small fee, of course. I asked about the inn, practicing my French, which was still hesitant and halting.

"The inn is not so old," *Madame* began, "but we have lived here in the valley a long time, especially my husband."

"Are you familiar at all with the Grillo family? We lived in one of the chalets—at *Les Marllys*, above *Samoëns*—during the war, World War II."

"*Non! C'est incroyable!* Unbelievable!" She called her husband over, and gestured toward me. "Madame lived in the nice chalet at *Les Marllys* during the Great War."

"*Mon père*, my father," he said excitedly. "He was the postman here in *Samoens*. He delivered the telegrams to your mother—from her sisters in America. He is still living—ninety years old! A little frail, and in a home now. He remembers your father, and has spoken of him as 'that crazy genius'…but of course, he meant that in the best way, you understand."

"How can it be," I marveled, "that of all the inns that we might have chosen—here we are with a mutual connection to a distant past…"

"And how appropriate that you should get this special gift on your actual birthday," Joe chimed in. He wasn't certain he would be understood, but he had already discovered that, though he didn't speak French, everyone he met seemed to speak fluent English. "SallyAnne is seventy today!"

"*Bonne anniversaire*! Happy birthday! How perfect for you to be here now. Have you visited the chalet yet?"

"Yes, we spent most of the day exploring. It looks much the same as I remembered—except better, I think. There was no one there so we only walked around the outside. We also went to *Chantmerle*, where I went to school. Is it still a school, by chance?"

"Oh, no. We have several schools here in town now. There are many more people here than when you were little."

"Of course…Tell me, is the square still somewhat the same? I remember a very large linden tree. My father did several different paintings of that magnificent tree."

"The *grand tilleul* is indeed still there—older and even more *magnifique*. Please, go spend the rest of this splendid afternoon visiting the square. It is much the same as it's always been. As a matter of fact, there is a farmer's market today that you might enjoy. And when you're ready for your birthday dinner, we can recommend a really nice restaurant that serves very good *Savoyard Cuisine*. It's not too far out of the village. I'm sure you'll enjoy the *fondue*. It's superb!"

The tree was as I remembered it, gnarled as if with the arthritis in my hands, its majestic branches reaching to the limits of its grassy terrace, providing beneficent shade and comfort to the people seated on the low wall that surrounded the ample base. I wanted Joe to take a picture of me here. I wanted the two of us together in a picture, seated as if posing for my father's painting.

"Here, let me take your picture together," the old man said, as if reading my mind. He reached for the camera Joe was holding;

Joe handed it over and told him what to click and how to aim. He squinted into the lens and readied his shot as Joe came to sit next to me, his powerful arm encircling my small shoulders in a gesture of intimacy and protection.

"My father painted this tree—many times," I told the man, in French, as he continued clicking, his weathered face like a wrinkled dry apple. He beamed with pleasure, as if welcoming a long-lost daughter.

"*C'est bon ça, alors*...so, that's good, then. *Bien venue!* Welcome!" He handed me the camera. "Did your father live here, then?"

"Yes, during the war...we lived up there..." I pointed vaguely in the direction of the mountain that brooded over the village.

"Ah! Those were bad days! They shot my brother—lined him up with others of the *Maquis*, the underground—shot them right here in the square!"

"Oh, I'm so sorry!"

"*Bah, c'est la guerre!* It's the war...nothing to be done about it, *n'est ce pas?*"

My first memories are of the specter of war, something I did not understand, but accepted as the norm of my life. But, even as a child, I knew this was a tense and dangerous world. Though my parents were the ones who carried the burden of worry and concern for the family's safety, we children were all touched by what the war represented for every frightened citizen.

I surveyed the village square on this lovely late summer afternoon, a hint of coming fall in the cool breeze that caressed my cheek like a lover's breath. I moved off my perch under the linden tree, and took Joe's hand—as if for reassurance that I was actually here, and that he was with me, bearing witness. My memory of the village was a black and white picture, grainy and somber, as if the war had taken all the color out of everything. But the tree was the same—exactly as my father had painted it, in a whimsical, primitive simplicity. And he had lavished it with broad strokes of color, just as I saw it now. Then, there were no market stalls overflowing with fruits and vegetables. The square had been a place where the farmers brought their sheep to be shorn, bought and traded—but not the best animals, because those would have been appropriated by the occupying army. My brothers and I considered it a rare adventure to be allowed to accompany Papa into the village for the intense trading.

Joe and I wandered to a café at the edge of the square and sat at one of the small round tables and ordered an aperitif and an assortment of cured meats and local cheeses, and a baguette. Joe took my camera to continue the chronicling of this time capsule, new memories being created to overlay the old. Color would now saturate the old black and white images.

Where farmers had traded sheep, they now sold honey and cheeses and sausages and an abundance of fresh fruits, vegetables, flowers. Colorful scarves danced in the breeze. Hats of every description were stacked on tables or hung from the canvas stall covers. Clothes for children, hand-knitted sweaters, were piled on tables in enticing displays. The banter and call of the merchants was a cheerful cacophony of enterprise playing off the melody of laughing children at play. Tourists browsed the stalls and bought treasures to bring back home, while the local women were more serious about bargaining for the freshest vegetables, the most savory sausage, or the sweetest fruit.

We resisted the temptation of buying anything that we couldn't take back with us, or would have no room for in our limited luggage. I almost bought a jar of honey. I brought the open jar to my nose and almost cried at the long-remembered fragrance of Alpine honey.

"We should get something to remember this day," Joe said.
"We'll have our pictures..."
"But didn't your dad always bring back something from his trips? Especially for your mom?" Joe persisted, not to be refused. "You said that to me once. Let me find something for you—from me, to commemorate this day. Besides, it's your birthday! Your seventieth!"

Joe chose a scarf hanging from one of the displays. His love of the water and all things nautical led him immediately to a long and narrow textured silk piece that had the colors of an ocean wave of blue-green foam.

We went to the restaurant *Madame* had suggested. It was farther out of town than we had expected, but the sign was as unmistakable as we had been advised it would be. The giant painted moose loomed out of the dark, its antlers decorated with twirling colored lights. As if we had been transported to an American Southwest rodeo town, I almost expected to hear country music when we entered the restaurant. We were ushered to a table near an open hearth where the fire licked the logs in the fireplace with a snap, dancing with light. The large room was dim, even with the candles placed on each table. It was late in the evening and the dinner crowd was mostly gone, though a small band continued to play in a corner of the room.

As *Madame* had said, the menu was authentic *Savoyard cuisine*, hearty in its simplicity. The *fondue* we shared was rich and complex in its cheesy goodness. We got a little tipsy as we finished a bottle of Alsatian wine that was like biting into a crisply cold and fresh apple.

Everything about this day was linked to my childhood—and yet it was all completely and utterly different. I felt like an observer of someone else's memories, absorbing each small moment, each impression to make it newly my own.

Reluctantly, we left *Samoëns* the following morning. As much as I wanted to linger, I knew that if we didn't leave, the crucible of my memories would burn me to an ember. It was too much.

From the high Alps, we continued our odyssey south and west. As we descended the *Corniche*, the Mediterranean glittered like a blue sapphire. Dotted with little boats, which in reality were one hundred to three hundred feet in length, the scene was surreal in its perfection.

We drove west along the Mediterranean coast, stopping for lunch at a little seaside restaurant between *St-Rafaël* and *Fréjus*. The restaurant overlooked a small beach, nearly deserted this late

September day, though Joe felt compelled to take a picture of the bare-breasted woman sunning herself. "Joe, that's not polite," I scolded, "you look like an American tourist!" He sheepishly put the camera away.

How could it be that this was so familiar to me? I knew that this was a place I had never been to, but this was, in fact the heart of *le Midi,* where I had lived as a very small child. And if it had been springtime, I would have smelled the mimosa and would have known that this place was registered in the deepest part of my hard drive. I would know that it was from here that my memories began. And, in fact, this was the beginning of the history. The ghosts of my ancestors gathered and whispered and called out all around me.

— 2 —

LIV

Sunday dinner, as always, was a somewhat formal affair, with the good silver and china properly laid out on a crisp and snowy white cloth. Gaga had already placed the roast on a large platter, the bone-handled carving set on the silver knife rest next to the platter at the head of the table.

Betty and Steve were the first to come in, properly serious as was fitting for the eldest of the children. They were expected to set the example. Betty, at ten years old, was already conscious of her role as the model for her two younger sisters. The large satin bow rested on her head easily, but her hairnet wasn't sufficient to contain the dark curls that framed her face. Betty was already tall, no longer a little girl, somewhat self-conscious of this new body that was forming under her prim white dress. She took her place at her chair, to the right of her father's seat and stood waiting.

Young Steve was taller, though two years younger. He already had the bearing and stature of the Meeker side of the family. His serious brown eyes belied the mischief that twitched at his full mouth. He moved to the chair at his father's other side and also waited, standing straight and tall.

Gaga came in, holding Barbie's small hand and gently guiding five year old Livie to her place next to her older brother. Barbie was still too small to sit in a grown-up chair and Gaga lifted her into the wooden high chair next to her own seat. She swung the tray down over her head and secured her in place. Gaga sat and the other children followed suit, picking up their napkins and placing them in their laps. They sat, hands folded on the white cloth napkins and waited for their father's entrance.

Stephen Miller walked in, tall and lean in his impeccable grey suit; his hair was severely combed back over his high forehead, a small pair of eyeglasses perched on his long thin nose. His generous mouth relaxed in a small smile of appreciation, as he surveyed his well-mannered family. Still standing, he picked up the carving set and began to slice the roast, as Gaga rose to bring in the side dishes from the kitchen. Betty followed to help her as she had been instructed. Soon Livie would join in for these little jobs, but for now, she was still too small.

Young Steve took the plates from his father as he served and passed them around the table. By this time, all were busy spooning mashed potatoes and peas onto their plate, passing the hot steamy biscuits and the bowl of gravy. The children all began to chatter at once until Father harrumphed for silence and they all looked toward him, even little Barbie, sitting primly in her high chair.

They all bowed their heads as he murmured a quick blessing. As everyone began to eat, he paused, turning to Gaga, "thank you Mother. This looks delicious, as always." He smiled in appreciation, breathing in the savory fragrance of the well-seasoned rib roast.

"I gave you all a word this morning," he continued, looking at his children. "Your daily word to define and spell and use correctly in a sentence. Livie, do you remember what that word was?"

Livie flushed at the attention, but raised her head proudly. "Yes, Father. The word was perihelion. Shall I spell it?"

"Yes, please do," he answered.

She cleared her throat, put down her knife and fork, and clearly spelled the word.

"And do you know what it means?" he continued.

"The point in a solar orbit where the orbiting body is closest to the sun," Steve interrupted.

"That's very good, Steve, though you spoke out of turn," Father smiled. "Now, can you explain that so that even little Barbie might understand?"

Steve flushed and stammered, "But she's so little, how can she understand?"

"Try," Father coaxed gently. "Try describing it."

Steve looked at his father, then at Barbie, wide-eyed in her high chair. "Okay, Barbie. Say you have two balls. A big one and a really little one. And the little one is always going around the bigger one, but as it goes around, it sometimes gets closer than other times…"

Barbie laughed and clapped her hands in delight, enjoying this little game that made no sense to her.

"Betty," Father turned to his eldest, "can you use the word perihelion in a sentence? That might make more sense to everyone."

"I read in the paper today," she began, "that we might be able to see Halley's Comet really well tonight, because as it's going around the sun, it passes it most closely tonight. Tonight is its perihelion."

Father smiled broadly and clapped his hands in pleasure.

"Good explanation, Betty," he said. "I was hoping that one of you very bright children might understand why I chose this particular word for today's exercise."

Not to be outdone by his older sister, Stephen said, "It's only visible once every 75 years. It's named after an astronomer named Halley. I read that same article. And actually, the point of perihelion was a month ago, but tonight, the earth will pass through the tail of the comet. Some people think it means the end of the world."

Father smiled with pleasure at his children, so bright and curious. "You're right, Steve. But surely you don't believe it's the end of the world, do you?"

"Of course not, Father. But I *am* looking forward to seeing the show!"

"Absolutely. But dinner and help Gaga with dishes first. The show will go on all evening. I understand even President Taft will be watching from the Naval Observatory. We may not even need the telescope."

Barbie was wide-eyed with wonder and incomprehension, while

Livie was finishing her dinner as fast as she could, not wanting to miss any part of the show, once the sun went down and the sky would be filled with stars—and the tail of the comet. Betty and Steve, in contrast, attempted a show of bored sophistication. After all, they knew all about it. They had both been following the steady stream of observations by astronomers.

May19th, 1910 and the earth would be passing through the comet's tail at its closest point with the earth. For days, newspapers had a steady stream of comet stories: the tail had a noxious gas that would kill; the comet was a harbinger of disaster; the comet was being called the Vagrant as it traveled outward to unknown distances beyond. The sky had an eerie light throughout those days, suffusing the clouds with an odd luminescence. And now, the best viewing time seemed to have come. Between 8:30 and 10:30 in the evening, the comet and its glorious tail would be visible with the naked eye.

It seemed an ordinary spring evening, the air soft and redolent with the scent of early blooming roses, star magnolia and even an occasional jasmine. It was a soft May evening, the sky turning a deep indigo, the sun having set without a show, simply sinking behind the tall trees to disappear until the morning. All up and down the street, families were gathering quietly, their voices hushed as they waited for dusk to turn to full darkness with the hope of seeing a sight that would not reappear for another seventy-five years.

Father set up the telescope on the highest part of the sloping lawn, pointing it to the sky through a clearing in the tall trees. He squinted through the eye piece, making small adjustments, evidently not certain where the best of the show would actually be. He had also been following the reports, waiting until this evening, knowing that this was a memorable moment for all his children. They would not likely ever see the comet again in their lifetimes. He surely would not.

He thought how he would have loved to have been able to share this moment with his wife, with Lulu. They had promised each other that they would share this with their children, ever since they became aware of the impending passage of Halley's Comet. He sighed and shook his shoulders, shrugging off the thought of what could never be.

Stephen Meeker Miller wore his grief like a heavy cloak about his stooped shoulders, as if the death of his wife three years earlier had only just happened. He could shake his shoulders and stand erect, tall and imposing, but inside was only a crushed ember where his heart had once burned with love. He poured his life into his children now, each one reminding him, by a chance smile, or a slightly cocked head, or in the blue eyes of his precious Livie, that his wife still lived through each of them.

Laura Hamblett Jones, "Lulu", had been slight, petite and as lovely as a fragile porcelain doll. Stephen was enchanted, losing himself in the still depths of her blue eyes, like a deep northern lake of great mystery. Her dry sense of humor and keen intellect surprised and fascinated him. He felt clumsy and even inept in her calm presence.

They were married at the close of the century, a time of tumult and great change. William McKinley was President. Aggressively pro-business, he instituted high tariffs to protect American industries, and was able to lead the nation out of a desultory recession into robust economic growth by the time he was reelected in 1901.

The surge in the economy was particularly welcomed by Stephen Miller, now sole proprietor of the foundry of D. M. Meeker & Son. With over 150 employees, the foundry forged and shipped, iron, steel and bronze to places as varied as Australia, South America, Mexico, and even Germany. The foundry was begun by his grandfather in 1843 and carried on continuously by the Meeker sons. At 35, Stephen Meeker Miller assumed the august responsibility of husband, father and provider for his family, as the steward of a venerable and respected company in New Jersey.

He was desperately in love with his new bride and established her in a fine old home with a porch that wrapped around three sides, with comfortable white wicker furniture that would invite iced tea in the afternoons. The many rooms were cool and dark, with heavy draperies drawn to keep out the hot afternoon sun. The stately frame house was set back on sloping lawns dappled with the shade of many elms, their slender, graceful branches reaching out like umbrellas.

He found a housekeeper for her, interviewing her at great length to assure himself that his bride would have the kind of capable help she would need to manage a large house, to be able to entertain his business friends, and mostly, that she would have help when children became part of their future.

1901 and McKinley was President of the United States. As a staunch Republican, Stephen had voted for him then, but also because he knew this president would be a friend to business.

Laura Elizabeth, his wife's namesake, was born two years after they married. Petite as she was, her first pregnancy was surprisingly uncomplicated, even as her doctor had expressed great concern and suggested bed rest for the last three months. Not to be held back, she sailed through with grace and good humor, overjoyed with this precious gift of a beautiful little girl.

Stephen was solicitous to a fault, hovering over mother and baby as if each would break if he left their sides. He immediately began calling his new daughter Betty, a name which suited her round little face and button eyes, her cupid mouth always in a little bow of surprise. Soon, the household settled into a pleasant rhythm as Lulu's mother, Gaga, eventually moved in to help mother and child.

Phineas Jones, a soldier in the Revolutionary War, married Hannah Phillips in 1798. Of their fourteen children, only the youngest, born in 1819, survived. Phineas Jones Jr. was a tall, imposing figure who carried himself with an air of supreme confidence. So when he fell in love with the lovely Laura Jane Hamblett, he was not at all concerned that she was twenty-two years younger, barely out of her teens. In fact, given that he was the sole survivor among his thirteen siblings, he surmised that her youth would surely improve their chances of having a healthy brood of children. In the days when a large family assured a better future for those who survived the high mortality rate among children, his was a commonly held view.

His mother, Hannah Phillips, was well known in Watertown, Massachusetts, as her great grandfather. George Phillips had been one of the founders of Watertown in 1630. Together with some one hundred or so Englishmen, they had come to the banks of the Charles River to settle and farm their plantations. George Phillips was the pastor of the original community.

It is an odd coincidence that Hannah Phillips Jones died the same year (1841) that Laura Jane Hamblett, Phineas's future bride, was born.

Phineas and Laura Hamblett Jones left Watertown after they were married. Phineas chose to join the burgeoning industrial revolution and leave farming to others. He maintained large holdings in Watertown but he and Laura moved on to New Jersey to begin their family. They bought a large home in Newark, to accommodate the family they hoped to have.

Laura Hamblett Jones, Gaga, had been a widow for seventeen years. She was forty-three; Phineas was sixty-five when he died in 1889. They had shared a rich and full life, though all too brief. Their home sang with the laughter and joy of children, three lovely daughters and a son, Phillip. Laura's light artistic touch brought grace and soft color to a home that might have otherwise been dark and somber. She eschewed the heavy velvet draperies of the time in favor of lighter, more airy pastels. She planted a garden of fragrant flowers which she brought into the house in generous bouquets. She directed the gardener they hired to plant a large vegetable bed in the back of the house where the sun shone all day. She even had a kitchen garden, like those so common in France, for her lettuces and herbs.

She was a vibrant force in the community, involved in the local

Presbyterian Church, leading the way in social causes that might better the lives of the poor, the disadvantaged, orphans and widows. And then, she was a widow herself, suddenly surprised that she was somehow unmoored. Her husband had always been in charge of everything that mattered: the roof over her head, the food on the table, the welfare of her children.

Laura was only forty-three when her husband died. Their children were still young, and though he had left her financially comfortable, she faced an uncertain future, alone to make the family decisions that had always been his to make.

When young Phillip caught a cold that seemed to linger on too long, she fretted and worried. He developed a hacking cough and lost his appetite. His shoulders drooped in fatigue, and his youthful rosy cheeks were pale and sallow. A visit to the family doctor was troubling, as he considered the possibility of tuberculosis. Bed rest, a lot of fresh air, good nutrition…not much else could be done. They would wait and see, and hope for the best.

But Phillip didn't get better. He grew more listless and weary, dragging around the big house, following his mother, coughing and sighing. The White Plague, as tuberculosis came to be called, swept through towns and neighborhoods touching many who came in contact with someone already infected.

Sanatoriums began to appear, places where those infected might be cared for, might even be cured over time, or would eventually die. Those fortunate enough to be able to afford the expense lived out the remainder of their brief lives in places like Pine Ridge, a new sanatorium in Virginia. They hoped for a cure, made lasting friends, carried on as they could, lived with the pall of death all around them, and waited for their own turn.

Heartsick, Laura couldn't bear the thought of leaving her son in a place where he would be all alone, away from his family, his sisters, his mother. At fourteen, he was too young to understand how desperate his situation was. He would get better. He would overcome all of this and be well again.

But he didn't get better. Alone in his room, the windows open winter or summer, he read his books and wrote in the journal that his mother had given him. He walked in the nearby park until he grew too tired, and then curled up in his room again, to sleep away the ever present fatigue that sapped all his youthful energy.

And finally, perhaps mercifully, Phillip gave up. He was barely twenty-two. Laura found him, that early morning, as she brought his breakfast tray in to his cold bedroom, a soft breeze blowing the curtain to brush his face, a look of peace finally softening his young features. Laura thought he was more beautiful than she had ever known, even more beautiful than he had been as a cherubic baby. Her son, her treasure was gone.

Laura turned her attention to her daughters, especially her youngest, Laura, "Lulu". When Stephen and Lulu were married, Laura was there to advise and counsel her daughter as she embarked on this great adventure of her life. She liked and respected Stephen and could see that he would cherish Lulu as much as Phineas had cherished her all the years they had been married. She felt a peace that gave her a strength she needed but had never known until then.

And now, she had a new purpose. She had lost her husband and her son. Her older daughters had established fruitful lives of their own, but her youngest daughter, Lulu, needed her now as she began her new life as not only a wife to Stephen, but a mother to his children.

Stephen was born two years later, pleasing his father immensely, as he had visions of a future in which the foundry would be renamed Miller and Son. But this time, Lulu was a little slower in her recovery, becoming tired more easily and putting more responsibility on Gaga, her mother, so named by little Betty when she couldn't say Grandma. Lulu bore each of her pregnancies with stamina and grace, always with a smile even as her legs swelled and she developed painful varicose veins that seemed to create ugly mountains and ridges along her calves. Her long skirts allowed her to keep the painful disfigurement to herself.

Two years later, Olivia Gardner was born, on June 14th 1905,

Flag Day, a memorable event that had been celebrated by Act of Congress since 1777, to commemorate the first time the flag was flown. In the beginning, while still a child, when she saw all the flags flying from each house in the neighborhood, she thought they were flying just for her. She was the baby in the family, relishing her place of care and attention as a toddler until the news came that there would be another baby.

By this time, Lulu heeded her doctor's pleas, and took to her bed for the last two months. Her husband worried and fretted and Gaga kept the children away from their mother, so as not to tire her unduly. But even with all the care and precaution, the delivery went badly and Lulu was in labor a very long time. The doctor came and went from her darkened room, urging Gaga to bring more cloths, more hot water. Stephen paced outside the door, distraught and frantic with a terrible foreboding.

When the doctor emerged finally, with little Barbie wrapped in her swaddling blanket, his face was somber.

"Stephen," he sighed. "Here is your beautiful new daughter, healthy and sound. But Lulu has had a very difficult time. She's lost a lot of blood. She's exhausted, and is asking for you."

"May I see her?" he asked desperately.

"Please do," the doctor replied gently. "But only for a few minutes. She really needs to rest. I gave her a sedative to help her sleep."

Stephen went into the darkened room and closed the door softly behind him. A heavy stillness settled over the house. Even the other children were quiet, aware that something was very wrong.

And there came a mortal cry, a mourning whimper, from behind the closed door. The doctor quickly entered the darkened room to find Stephen collapsed on the floor, his hands clutching Lulu's limp arm over the side of the bed, his face buried on her still breast.

"She's gone!" he cried. "She's gone…"

The doctor moved quickly over, his stethoscope already in his ears, a look of horror on his face.

"How can that be? She was smiling, when I left; tired, but smiling…"

Three years ago, but it was as if only yesterday. He loved his little Barbie, Lulu's final gift to him, but could not look at her without remembering. Barbie, even so small, bore a striking resemblance to her mother, with her round little cheeks and bright blue eyes that laughed with carefree joy.

He was a good father, attentive, firm yet gentle with his four children. The older ones bore the brunt of his grief and followed him with sober and careful eyes, fearing something they might say would cause him to break into pieces. Livie, with her quiet demeanor, seemed to always have a way of reaching him, warming his heart with her gentle optimism. He called her his Pollyanna, and when she was eight, he gave her the book so that she could understand for herself why he had come to name her so.

In a way, the loss of her mother was hardest on Livie, as she had been only two on that dreadful day. She didn't understand, couldn't understand why Mommy was never coming back. Betty and Steve were quite a bit older and carried their sorrow inwardly, not allowing themselves to show how much they too missed their mother. Livie turned to her younger sister, Barbie, for comfort and companionship. The two sisters were like little puppies as they played together and even made up an imaginary language that only they could understand.

Now, tonight, they would all be gathered as a family, Father at its center, a towering figure of comfort and security. Gaga would be at his side, the faithful grandmother, his mother-in-law, who could never do more for this man who so mourned the loss of his wife, her precious daughter, Lulu. He didn't need to know the depths of her own sorrow. One by one, she had lost the treasures of her heart. First, Phineas, her loving husband. When Philip died after his long battle with tuberculosis, she thought she might be able to move on. After all, she had her three beautiful daughters. And when Lulu married Stephen, she almost felt as if she had regained the son she had lost. She adored the children and cared for them as the gifts from her daughter. She was firm; she was gentle; she gave of her time and her heart in full measure, doing her best to raise her grandchildren the way she had taught Lulu to care for them and guide them.

Now, she carried an old quilt over her arm, ready to place it on the soft green grass wherever Father suggested they would settle. Livie held Barbie's hand, almost stumbling as they ran to catch up to where Father was standing with the telescope. Steve and Betty were already by their father, eager to be the first to look through the eyepiece for an even better view than what they could already see with the naked eye.

The late spring sun had truly set now and the indigo sky was filled with stars. The Milky Way sprayed across the sky with a wash of millions of stars, pinpricks of sparkling, silent light. As if the heavens had thrown down a spinning ball of its pure essence, the comet was visible across the entire sky, its tail now seeming to be forked in two phosphorescent trails.

They stood transfixed, silent in the holy sight of an awesome splendor. The deep, velvet vault of the sky expanded infinitely, silently, holding in the diamonds of stars. As if they were in church (for surely they thought they might be), they whispered, almost afraid to break the silence of the stars.

— 3 —

PAUL

This is the story Mama used to tell us when we pleaded with her to recall her fascinating history—our history as well.

"Your father lived in Bois Colombe, a suburb of Paris," she began, and through her skillful story-telling, we were immediately transported to the world of my father as a child. "And though his parents had quite a lovely home there, this was only occasionally their *Pied à Terre*, their home base. You see, his father, your *Grandpère*, was a government functionary, a minister of the Treasury, and as such, he was sent to Africa, to the French-Belgian Congo, as the colonial secretary of the Treasury; so Papa also grew up in a strange and exotic land." I remember she turned to me then, to include me in this strange world she was about to describe.

"When we left France after the war," she continued, "you were almost nine, about the same age as Papa was when his family went to the Congo. Like you, he could only speak French, but he wanted to learn the language of the little black boys he played with. And he wanted to learn to play their strange instruments, like this one."

She had begun her story because Miqué, my oldest brother, wanted to know the history behind the little wooden instrument in her hand. She plucked at one of the four pieces of metal that were attached to one end of the wood base to make a kind of melodic clicking sound. "Papa called it a *Thumb Piano*," she said.

"Some of Papa's early experiences were with the children of the servants," she went on. "Because *Grandpère* was an important man, he had a lot of servants to help *Mamette,* your grandmother, with the housework and the preparation of some of the lavish meals that were served for the many guests who came to dinner. And if you look at the pictures that were taken at the time, it really looks as if they had a plantation in the jungle—if you can imagine that!" She laughed at our wide-eyed astonishment. We had always thought we had a fairly unusual childhood, but it was clear that Papa had us beat.

Papa told us stories too. He made monkey faces when he told us of the monkeys that scampered into their house through the open windows, climbing the heavy draperies, where they threw bits of things onto the heads of people below. Was this a true story or was he teasing us with his lively imagination? I never knew; though I can imagine that my grandmother, *Mamette,* would have chased a pesky monkey out with her trusty broom, scolding loudly as she did so.

I have a few artifacts that were brought back from that period, and though I know there is an interesting history in each piece, I am clueless, and can only appreciate the unusual artistry and character. One is a little brass elephant that has what looks like a candle holder on his back. Sometimes I've put him in my garden and for now he stands on a small shelf in singular majesty, waving his trunk. I have what I suppose to be a fertility goddess or why else would she have such enormously prominent breasts. But it's also possible that this was a spirit doll, though I can find no image that looks quite like my lady.

When Mama died, we carefully tried to divide these wondrous things we had grown up with. But with six of us, there wasn't much to divide and it all has become a precious legacy for our own children. But will anyone care as much as we did when we listened to Mama pass on the lore of our history? With every generation, the immediacy of time fades a little until it all becomes a folk tale except for the tangible artifacts that have become scattered. And as new families form, each brings a new narrative to add to the mix until the potpourri of shared history is a complex and exotic brew singular to each family.

My younger sister Betty and I have spent many an afternoon combing through the boxes of photographs and papers that are the remnants of Papa's childhood. With no one to fill in the blanks, we have been left to guess the full story of that mysterious and distant past. One picture shows *Mamette,* our grandmother, feeding chickens in a courtyard, wearing the typical bibbed French apron and the felt espadrilles I remember she always wore. She is surrounded by the chickens, pecking in the dry earth around her. There is a huge tree in the background, maybe a mahogany tree or something—who knows? Another picture is clearly of Papa and his older sister *Marguerite.* Both are in immaculate white, he in knee length pants and long white socks, and a very white shirt; she is wearing a simple white linen dress with the dropped waist that was the style in the 1920's. They are standing in a clearing, again with the giant trees in the background. In one of the photographs of that Congo period, a large group of people is seated at a long table, enjoying some kind of feast. Standing behind them are the black faces of the servants, almost indistinguishable from the forest, melting into a kind of ghostly apparition.

I found a hand-drawn map that Papa did. The flimsy paper is about five inches wide and is folded accordion style. When I carefully unfolded it to show Betty, it turned out to be well over three yards long, carefully taped on the back to extend its length. *"Carte du Chemen de Fer du Congo Belge",* "Map of the Railroad of the Belgian Congo", the cover said. He had drawn all the little villages, the rivers, even the topography of the entire length, with all the names of each place along the way. The railroad was a thin red line that laced through from beginning to end. It was my first inkling of the whimsy, the artistry, the attention to every detail that would always be characteristic of my father's work.

But the questions remain...did he travel the length of this railroad? Was this the Cape to Cairo line that was envisioned by both English and French colonialists at the time? What was his life truly like as a young boy in a strange and foreign land? When we are children we are only interested in learning about the world immediately around us. We pay no mind to events or circumstances which may shape our history or the roots of how we got to be where we are now. And now, when it's too late to ask, I have these questions. "Papa, what was it like when you were a child? How did you come to be where you were, and who you were, before you became my Papa?"

The family moved to Africa at the close of World War I, when his father, Marius Grillo was assigned to the post of Colonial Secretary-Treasurer of the young colony of the Republic of French Congo.

Marie Louise Dorland, "Lucie", his wife, went with him, along with their two children, Marguerite, fifteen at the time, and Paul Jacques, who was ten.

The family saw this as something of an adventure, an opportunity to live in a world in which they would have absolutely no frame of reference; nothing would be familiar, with the possible exception that this would be, after all, a French colony, a distant outpost very far from Paris.

Lucie grumbled a little, "this might as well be Mars!" she thought with some disdain. But she would make the best of it. She oversaw the packing of the many trunks of belongings, the cataloguing of the furniture they would bring with them—including the piano, of course, so that she could continue teaching Paul to play not only the violin, but the piano as well. She made certain her fine linens were carefully packed, her silver and crystal and china. And of course, she would choose a good sampling from her extensive cellar of fine wines, gathered over time from her heritage as a fine vintner. They might be going to live in the jungle, but they would not leave civilization and the finer things of French culture behind. She oversaw the inclusion of their very fine library, so that both Marguerite and Paul could continue their studies as they must.

Lucie was a very determined woman, the third of six children brought up by a single mother, Louise Ruet Dorland. Madame Dorland had a wine business, a purveyor of fine wines from the region in Northeastern France, managed by her family from as early as 1725. No doubt, Lucie's heritage played into her resolve to bring many of the finest wines she had in her cellar to the heathen wilderness of the "Dark Continent".

They lived on the outskirts of Brazzaville, in a compound set aside for the French dignitaries who would be charged with taming, and ruling this newest outpost of the French colonial empire. In fact, most of the work would be the establishment of a bureaucracy of government agencies. Marius Grillo would be in charge of the treasury. This was a land that was rich in natural resources, ripe for exploration—and exploitation. This would be a benevolent government, so the natives seemed satisfied with the arrangement, having been assured that their lives would be immeasurably better as they would be fairly compensated for all resources taken.

Marguerite and Paul were enrolled in the French schools in Brazzaville, so that they could continue their rigorous studies— even in this barbaric outpost, Lucie thought.

While Marius was away in Brazzaville, Lucie ruled her own domain at home. She had servants, black as night, with eyes filled with wonder at the marvels she had them begin to unpack from her many trunks. At first, she could only point and gesture to them, but they were eager to learn and were soon speaking a halting, minimal version of French."

"They're like children…" she thought in amazement as she noted two women trying to decipher the purpose of an iron, or an egg beater. Lucie began to teach them her French ways: how to set a table, how to make a bed, how to make a proper *Sauce Bearnaise* or *Aioli*. And they taught her as well. They showed her how to properly care for her chickens, letting them roam on their own to hunt and peck for bugs, to allow them to peck at little stones to help the digestion in their craw. They led her to the river bank, where they did their laundry on the stones. But here she drew the line. Her fine linens would not be washed on stones in a river!

As every family must, when faced with strange circumstances, they all began to adapt, if not adopt the ways of the land they would call home for five years. Marguerite studied hard, preparing for a future in medicine. She wanted to be a doctor of pediatrics. When they returned to Paris, she would be ready. Paul, under Lucie's firm hand, became more and more accomplished at playing both the violin and the piano. In addition, he filled copious notebooks with sketches and ideas. He was particularly fascinated with the ways the natives invented and developed tools and ways of better managing their difficult environment.

And, for this whole European family, the environment presented them with their greatest challenge. At first, Lucie wanted to plant a kitchen garden of lettuces and herbs. The women laughed in delight when they saw the pictures on the seed packets. But of course, the lettuce rotted in the humid heat and the rosemary and lavender didn't even try to grow. They introduced her to plants that did well in the climate, like cucumbers, melons, peppers, yams. They even introduced her to native foods and dishes, including spices that she would have never thought to use but came to savor and enjoy their unique taste and fragrance.

It was hot. It was humid. Everything grew to gigantic proportions. The jungle seemed to want to devour them all. They lived in a European styled house, somehow adapted to the climate. Airy and open to catch even a whiff of breeze, insects and crawling things were part of the package. Mosquito nets were critical over beds to prevent the malaria mosquito; snakes and lizards could be found crawling at every step; beetles grew almost as big as a hand.

For young Paul, this was a wonderland, a phantasmagorical world of everything weird and strange. His *copains,* his gang of black friends introduced him to ways and oddities he would never tell anyone, but which fascinated him. They also took him tracking with them, following the spore of small and large animals, sometimes spearing snakes as they crossed the path, or shooting at bats with their slingshots, as they roosted in the tall canopy. He came to identify some of the birds, enthralled by their bright plumage. And of course, the monkeys were his endless delight. He learned to call to them out of their hiding places in the trees. And when some would actually come into the house and tease his mother, he could only chortle with pleased mischief.

They stayed in the Congo for five years. But then it was time to return to France. Marguerite needed to finish her medical studies, and Paul certainly needed to be tamed from some of the wild ways he had adopted. It was time to come home to all that was comfortable and familiar, to a civilized world that boasted of a culture that spanned the millennia.

Paul was ready to begin some serious study. At fifteen, he was ready to enter the *Lycée*, his last three years of high school. He already knew what he wanted his continuing education to look like. After sitting the *Brevet*, the *Baccalaureat* exam, he would enter the college of *Beaux Arts*. He would be an architect. Fascinated by what he had seen in the Congo, he wanted to take some of these simple village housing solutions and adapt them to the modern world. Enough of the grand edifices of the past. It was time to build for a new future, a time for new adaptations to an ever-evolving environment.

Among the photographs that Betty and I found, there is one of Papa when he was a student at *l'Ecole des Beaux Arts*, with his *copains*, his friends and classmates. In one, he's leaning against a wrought-iron fence, one arm languidly draped over the shoulders of a boyish young man, both grinning as if they had just heard a good joke. In another, he's with many young men in a kind of dormitory where they are all lounging on a row of beds.

Mama used to tell us, somewhat disapprovingly, that they had "bacchanals", wild drinking parties that could get out of control. I guess that's not much different from fraternity parties on American college campuses. Excesses of youth, or just letting off steam when the studies get too intense, could be universal, after all.

Once the family returned to France, to Paris, to their stately home in Bois Colombe, the five years they had spent in the French

Republic of Congo began to take on a mythic quality, especially for Paul. He was barely ten when he stepped into that strange world, so utterly different from anything he had known in his short life. Now, at fifteen, he found that he had to make an equal adjustment as he reentered the Parisian life of a young French teenager. He found that his childhood friends had moved on, or changed in ways that were unfamiliar. They were at first fascinated to hear of all his adventures, but since they really had no idea what his life had been in Africa, they soon got bored with his tales, as they all went on being French teenage boys discovering girls for the first time.

Paul had difficulty adjusting and turned inward, masking his shyness by delving deeply into studies he hoped would open windows of fresh enlightenment in his chosen field of architecture. Even before he entered the *Lycee* (high school), he knew this was his passion. His mother, Lucie, had other ideas. Recognizing his musical talent, she enrolled him in a special high school focused on the arts, music and fine art, to prepare him for an eventual enrollment in *l'Ecole des Beaux Arts*.

He felt awkward and clumsy around girls and put on a show of blasé sophistication. He was relieved to have an excuse for his apparent rudeness. He was cramming, after all. In truth, going to school in Paris was a daunting challenge compared to the freedom of his previous educational experience in the Congo—even in the capital city of Brazzaville. He was testy and impatient at home and in school, and found that he could lose himself a little when playing the piano. He had been carefree in the jungle with his black friends; now he was quiet, subdued, and serious, carefully guarding his emotions.

But Marius could see what Paul had yet to realize about himself. He had watched as his son began to flourish in self-discovery. Always a loner, Paul could, like a chameleon, adopt the ways and mores of wherever he was, while still remaining entirely himself. He had always been well-liked, respected and even admired by his friends, despite his attitude of supercilious superiority. And Marius had listened when Paul described some of his ideas for a future that was entirely in his own head, in his imagination for what could be. He realized that such passion could be harnessed into a vision, which in turn could become a force for change in a field venerated over the centuries. Paul could have a brilliant career as an architect.

Marius and Lucie were very proud of their two precocious children, but there was friction and disagreement between them when it came to the goals they voiced to each other.

"But Marius, what about his piano, his violin? His exquisite music? He can compose; he can conduct; he can play like an angel—"

"Yes, yes, I know. All very true. But have you listened to him? Have you really listened beyond your obsession to see him excel in music? Have you listened to some of his ideas? Lucie, he's an original thinker. The world needs such men as he will be!"

"Pshaw! You exaggerate. I know. I've seen his notebooks—and I agree that he has some very clever ideas, but…his music—I am transported when I hear him play. He has a singular talent!"

"Well, it must be his choice," Marius finished. "And he has clearly told me he wants to go to be an architect. That is his decision and that's final."

Lucie didn't respond; simply shrugged her shoulders and walked out of the room. But she would see to it, she thought to herself, that Paul would never forget his music.

Marguerite's path had always been clearly defined, so there was no issue. She would be a pediatrician, at a time when few women could aspire to becoming a doctor, much less a specialist. And Paul would be a renowned architect, changing the way people thought of buildings and how to live in them. Marius applauded Paul's choice and enrolled him at the most prestigious and venerated *l'Ecole des Beaux Arts*. And to make the experience completely whole and fulfilling, he insisted, over Lucie's objections (he's too young, he should stay home, what about his piano?) Paul would live at the school for a total immersion in scholastic life.

When Paul entered school, at the top of his class and with all the attendant honors of an impressive *Brevet* at his *Baccalaureat*, he was eager for the change that would be his opportunity to prove himself to his mother. Lucie could not give up her dream of seeing him on a concert stage; after all, had that not been the point of all those hours of practice on a piano that she had shipped to that dark continent—and brought back to Paris five years later? Paul had his own vision...and she remembered his notebooks, his careful sketches.

And of course, this was also the dream of his father, Marius. He would have much greater opportunity for a successful career as an architect, rather than the dubious chance of becoming a great concert pianist. Besides, Marius thought, Paul simply didn't have the temperament for a life of fame. He was too condescending of anyone who could not share his understanding of the way of things. He was too easily impatient with others, as if they simply couldn't possibly understand big ideas. Marius worried that such haughtiness needed tempering, even some taming. Living with other young men his own age might be good. As for Paul, he viewed this privileged opportunity as his due. Singularly gifted, he knew his path to greatness and expected nothing less than the best from his parents who, of course, would do whatever it took to fulfill Paul's needs and desires.

He was barely eighteen when he first walked into the impressive courtyard of the institution that had launched artists and architects since well before the days of King Louis XIV.

Paul set his sights on ultimately winning the *Grand Prix de Rome*, which would be the culmination of six years of post-graduate work and a singular achievement awarded to only one student each year. He would be almost thirty years old by the time he would finally make his entry into the grand competition. And indeed, he won the prestigious *Grand Prix de Rome* in 1937, married and with three children.

— 4 —

LIV

Growing up without a mother didn't really seem so strange to Liv. After all, she had never really known what that might have been like. She and her younger sister, Barbie, could think that Gaga was their mother, even though Steven and Betty insisted that she was their grandmother. A generous lap and a big embrace always brought them the comfort and love they needed and sought when they came crying with a scraped knee or a bruised heart. Their older brother and sister both remembered what it was like to really have a mother, but even Steven and Betty came to treasure Gaga's ample love and attention. Father tried, but the very fact that they all addressed him with the formality of "Father" removed him from that easy love of a whole family.

He was stern; he was firm; he was removed. But he did the best he knew how. He had high expectations for each of his four children, guiding them to achieve and even excel in all endeavors. Of course they would all go to college and Steven would eventually join him in the running of the Foundry. That was the legacy, after all.

Liv especially loved the word game he played with them every day. Each morning, a new word was posted on the bathroom mirror. Before the end of the day, and without helping one another, without telling one another, they were each to know the definition, the spelling and the proper use of the word in a sentence. The words became more and more challenging as they competed with each other to be the first to impress Father with their victory.

For Liv, this was the beginning of a lifelong love and fascination with language. She came to excel at finding the root of a given word and its origin. Words were fascinating. Words spoke of worlds she couldn't begin to understand or know. She read. She devoured books.

It began with the secret language that she and Barbie developed together when they were very little. The secret language became an imaginary world, peopled with strange and wondrous creatures of their fantasies. Barbie eventually moved out of this secret place, but Liv never quite closed the door.

Liv was shy and felt painfully awkward in the real world. Compared to her sisters, so healthy and robust, always with a ready smile, self- confident and self-assured, Liv was all arms and legs, hair always in her face, her clothes never seeming to fit her tall, gangly body in the shapely way her sisters carried themselves. She retreated into her world of books even more as she grew through the clumsiness of adolescence. When she looked at herself in the mirror, all she saw was a skinny girl with thin, "dishwater blonde" hair falling in her face. She had terrible acne that she came to think would disfigure her forever. "Not that I'm anything to look at in the first place…" she thought with chagrin.

Her father enrolled her in Wellesley, following in the footsteps of her mother as a legacy student in the women's liberal arts school. Maybe she would "find herself" in this milieu of progressive women.

In fact, Liv flourished at Wellesley. For the first time in her life, she began to feel as if she belonged somewhere. She even joined a sorority and loved the support and camaraderie of her sisters in the school. She was respected, accepted, recognized especially for her linguistic talents. She thought maybe she could be a writer. Father would have been very proud…had he lived.

His death was sudden and unexpected. He developed pneumonia soon after she went off to college and she never saw him again. She lost herself in her studies and tried to focus on how proud he would have been to see her grow and bloom, even as she felt cast adrift in a world that was suddenly so much bigger than it had been in the safety and sheltering shadow of her father.

"How odd," she mused. "I'm an orphan now. I barely knew I had a mother, and I've just begun to know who my father was—and now he's gone too."

On a perfect June day in 1927, a soft breeze bringing the scent of roses, Liv graduated with the rest of her class of young women, ready to move on to the next chapter in her life. Her sisters and her brother were there to congratulate her and wish her well as she prepared for an internship in a New York publishing house, where she would hopefully begin to make her mark as a serious writer.

With the stock market crash of 1929, she, along with countless others, lost her job. The Foundry in New Jersey seemed to weather the worst of the downfall so Liv went back to the family home, not certain where to go from here. Her Aunt Eleanor suggested she come to Europe with her. She might be interested in staying at a *pension,* boarding house, in Paris, and perhaps take some art or history classes at the *Sorbonne.* Maybe even some French classes to hone her linguistic skills.

Feeling adrift and aimless, with no clear path before her, Liv accepted this most gracious and generous invitation and began the necessary preparations. She would spend the summer in Paris, and then maybe tour Italy with her Aunt Eleanor. Her expenses were covered by the magic wand of her favorite Auntie.

— 5 —

THE ENCOUNTER

She appeared one late afternoon, quietly standing at the door, trying to be invisible so that he might not be distracted from his playing. She was tall and slender, almost wraithlike, the soft folds of her dress fluttering in the light breeze that came in with her. Her fine hair was already beginning to brush her cheeks and she raised her hand impatiently.

Paul abruptly stopped his playing and turned to see who might have had the audacity to interrupt him. Everyone at the *pension* knew better than to distract him.

"*Pardon…*"she apologized in French, though her accent was the unmistakable inflection of an American. "*Je suis désolée…*"

"I speak English, a little—probably more than you speak French!" He grimaced, and then caught himself. He stood and bowed formally in greeting.

"I didn't mean to have you stop. Please go on," she protested. "You play so beautifully, with such passion…"

"No. I'm probably finished for today. Where have you come from? Are you staying here too?"

She nodded timidly.

"Well, you must know my rule, then. I don't like distractions while I play. What are you doing here? In Paris, I mean?"

"I'm taking an art appreciation class at *la Sorbonne*…just for the summer. Then I'll go back home…after I visit Rome with my aunt."

He was silent, as he examined this new creature who had dared to interrupt his playing. His eyes bored into her until she looked away uncomfortably. He was no taller than she was, lithe and powerfully built, but graceful and very sure of himself. He exuded an authority that was intimidating.

"I'm sorry. I'll leave you alone. And I'll remember your rule... Are you a student at *la Sorbonne?*"

"No. A *l'École de Beaux Arts*. In architecture. For almost five years now, though I am finally finished with the undergraduate studies. Now I have been working on an important *concours--* competition. I will win the *Grand Prix de Rome.*"

His tone was curt, even dismissive as he politely introduced himself, a little awkward in an unfamiliar language.

"Oh, my! But that's wonderful! That sounds very ambitious, I think. But I would have thought you were a concert pianist...you play beautifully..." she stopped, realizing she was being too forward with him, then stumbled on, "I mean, it sounds so—exciting somehow. What led you to want to become an architect?"

Her interest caught him off guard. He hadn't expected to have to answer such a broadly nebulous question. "The way we live..." he hesitated, "the way we could—or should live. We are a society used to accepting very bad taste."

"Yes...I suppose you're right about that." She paused, and then persisted, "But I would have thought you must be a concert pianist. You play magnificently."

He shook his head impatiently. "No, no. I thought about it. My mother wanted me to do that. But I had to decide. I could do either, I know. It's the challenge of being gifted. Which gift does one choose to pursue?"

She was surprised at such frank ego. She introduced herself. "My name is Olivia. But I have always been called Liv, or Livie, thank goodness." She grimaced. "Olivia is such a dreadful name..."

He bowed. "Paul. *Enchanté.* I agree that Liv is a much more suitable name for you." He said with a smile, appraising her coolly. "Now, please. I need to continue. I'm sure I will see you again."

She blushed at his abrupt dismissal. "Yes. I'm sorry I interrupted you. Perhaps I will see you at dinner?"

"Perhaps." He turned from her and went back to the piano.

So began a tentative, sporadic friendship that included hiccups of misunderstandings, strong opinions and the complete differentness of their backgrounds. Though both had grown up in privilege, there was no other commonality. Liv could appreciate art, but had no talent of her own. As she discovered in her first encounter with Paul, his ego could be fed by her recognition of his talent as a multi-faceted artist. He was flattered by her attention, and found her to be an intellectual equal and a sincere critic.

It began with conversations in the dining room, with the other boarders. Soon, they were continuing their discussions in the garden. She listened quietly, with evident admiration, as he played the piano for her. He began to describe some of his dreams to change the course of the way people live, to put aside the mediocre in favor of a new level of excellence; she commented with comprehension, as if seeing his world as he saw it. He showed her his Paris, taking her into neighborhoods that were far from the tourists. They found that they had many touch-points, even though they were as unlike as if they were from different planets. She learned to speak French fluently—her gifts were linguistic and literary. He came to appreciate her mind and her quiet poise, and began to see her beauty in a way he would want to paint.

She was painfully shy and a naive innocent, having had no experience with men, though she was nearing thirty. And he seemed to have no knowledge or understanding of women, since he had been so focused on his studies. It never occurred to him that their friendship would ever become anything else. But gradually, Liv Miller realized, to her amazement, that she was inexorably falling in love with Paul Grillo.

And in his turn, Paul found himself powerfully drawn to this interesting person who seemed to occupy so much of his thoughts. He was baffled, and even a bit afraid. This was new. He had never been interested in spending any time with a woman. Mostly, he didn't see women. It was as if they were of such small consequence as to be almost invisible. He only knew two women: his mother and his sister. He felt safe with them; but this? Liv was easy to talk to, almost like a man. She seemed truly interested in his ideas, his dreams for the future. He was comfortable with her, in a way he had never imagined would be possible. He mentally repeated his mantra; there are only two women he can trust: his mother and his sister.

So it was that their budding relationship came to an abrupt halt a few weeks later, as they were walking back to the *pension* together.

"Mademoiselle," he began formally, hesitating to find the right words, but his mind was made up. "I think I need to tell you to not become involved with me…I have no time…" He looked away uncomfortably, as if afraid that she might dissuade him from his firm decision.

"Oh, well. It's been nice…" she stumbled awkwardly over her words. "I should have expected—that is, I know you can't be distracted. And besides, I'll be going home to America soon. But you've shown me so much! I know Paris a little better now…I can't thank you enough!"

"Yes, I have enjoyed our times as well. But you must understand how impossible this all is—I'm sorry if you misunderstood at all…"

"Not at all. No, not at all. Please—don't trouble yourself. I received a post card from my aunt. She wants me to join her in Rome. So you see? I would be going anyway."

Paul sighed heavily, relieved that this was going to be an easy parting of the ways. He would go back to his work, his life, and look back on this episode as an interesting interlude, nothing more.

"I will miss our walks, our conversations—our friendship…" She was stumbling now, careful to not reveal too much of her feelings. "I will be back—but I don't know when. Can I write to you?"

"Yes, you can write, but I will probably be too busy to answer." He was abrupt, as he attempted to put on a mask of indifference.

Liv shrugged, hurt by his cool rebuff. She raised a hand to her hair, brushing it back in her familiar gesture of impatience. Her blue eyes were soft, beginning to well with tears and her chin trembled a little. She shrugged impatiently, trying to compose herself.

"Well," she continued, "maybe I will see you again—and maybe not. I have enjoyed getting to know you." She turned and walked into the *Pension,* leaving him alone in the courtyard. She would make her preparation and take the train to meet her aunt in Rome. Deflated by his cool detachment, she resolved to put him out of her mind and go on with her own life. This had been an interesting adventure, but nothing with any future, obviously.

In time, Paul began to realize how much he missed his American friend. He had never known anyone who could grasp his vision as she did. He still wanted to paint her. He enjoyed playing for her; she so obviously loved the music that flew from his fingers. It had been fun to show her Paris and to see her excitement, even with little things. He was fascinated by her fresh innocence—like a child. Reluctantly, he began to think that he really wanted her in his life. In fact, he realized with surprise, he was consumed with a longing to see her again, to know her better.

And she, in her turn, realized that she could not so easily forget Paul. Her Auntie finally had enough.

"Liv, I can see that your heart isn't in the wonders of Rome..." she suggested one day when they were touring the Coliseum. "Are you still thinking of that young man you met in Paris?"

"It's just that I know that if I were seeing Rome with him, he would be taking me on a walking tour through splendid neighborhoods—and he would bring everything to life with his marvelous descriptions, his knowledge of everything around us."

"You haven't learned some history, or seen architectural wonders with me?"

'Oh, I don't mean to belittle any of what we've done together. It's been a marvelous trip—I'll never forget seeing the Fountain, and St. Peter's and the museums! But..."

"I know. I'm just your Auntie. Why don't you send him a little postcard? Tell him when you'll be returning to Paris. Maybe you can see him once more before going back to America."

"You don't think that would be too forward of me?"

"Don't be silly. What can you lose?"

In time, Paul received a cryptic postcard:

> Returning to Paris August 16th, before going home to America. Would love to see you again. Liv

On August 16th, he walked to the train station and waited for the trains from Rome. He waited and watched. He had no way of knowing that her train had been delayed, that she had taken a much later train, that in fact she would finally come limping in at 2:00 in the morning of the next day.

He saw her, finally, as she disembarked, picking her out of the milling crowd by her characteristically fluid movement. She wore a hat, rakishly perched at a coquettish angle that shadowed her eyes. Her full mouth broke into a wide smile when she saw him as he hurried toward her. Then, shyly, he took her hand and kissed it, more a gesture of tenderness than of decorum. They stood together, alone in the hurrying throng that passed around them, as a river winds past immovable boulders. In her high heels, she was equal in stature and looked directly into his eyes, for the first time seeing an unabashed yearning.

– 6 –

BEGINNINGS

Paul and Liv were married a year later, in the spring of 1932, in her ancestral home in New England. Everyone agreed that she had made a very good catch: he was handsome, charming, and very French; Paul would go far, they all agreed. He was so smart, so accomplished. They were a striking couple as they stood together in her parents' country garden, she in a shimmering dress of ivory charmeuse, falling to the grass in a fluid waterfall of silk, the long sleeves brushing her wrists; she cradled a large bouquet of daisies that they had picked together that morning. He was equally striking in his impeccably tailored suit, hands in his pockets in nonchalant ease.

He whisked her back to France to begin what they both hoped would be an exciting career as a pre-eminent artist, architect, writer and musician—a Renaissance man, as Liv always loved to point out. He was captivated by her enormous faith in his abilities, so that he too could believe that anything was possible.

Like the male Bower Bird, who prepares an extravagant and ever-evolving bower to attract and keep the female, Paul had acquired a rustic mountain chalet, high in the French Alps and had prepared it for his aristocratic American wife. He installed a functioning toilet, rudimentary electricity, even a lavish copper tub for taking luxurious baths—though there was no available hot water. His grand piano was later laboriously brought up the hairpin turns of the narrow road to the chalet, so high in the mountain, so that he could serenade his bride. He placed a giant four-poster bed in the single room that was the main room. "She can make some curtains to give us privacy when we want it," he thought.

They spent their first summers together in his "Bower", escaping from the heat of Paris. He played his violin for her, as his piano would not come for several more years; he was inspired by her deep appreciation as he drew lilting melodies or profound fervor and expression from Mozart or Beethoven or Brahms. He loved her and played her body with tenderness. She responded with a passion so deep it surprised her. They took long hikes in the mountains, stopping to rest in a high meadow with a picnic to share between them.

They dreamed their dreams of a future in which he would become a leading thinker and architect, in which his paintings would be sought after, a future that would bring important people to them to discuss all manner of life-changing ideas. They dreamed— innocently oblivious to what their actual future might become.

They started their family. Paul Jr. (Miqué) was born in August of 1934. Liv made the Atlantic crossing alone, back to New England. She wanted her first child born as an American. Besides, she missed being home, spending time with her sisters, surrounded by people who didn't speak French. She stayed in America until she could no longer stand being away from her husband, and his longing for her grew with each letter they exchanged.

They left the chalet behind, ready to return when they could. But Paul needed to finish his studies. They could no longer be on holiday. He was striving for the grand prize, the *Grand Prix de Rome,* which could, would successfully secure his future. So they stayed in Paris.

But after 1933, with the ascension of Adolf Hitler as chancellor of all Germany the rumblings of war were a threat and a contagion throughout Europe. In Paris, they thought this would be far enough away from the creeping madness. After all, this was mighty France, which could withstand the juggernaut that was advancing from Germany, gobbling everything in its path. Life could go on quite normally. There might be some small inconveniences, but the spirit of France would always prevail.

John (Jean) was born a year later, in September of 1935. Again, Liv made the transatlantic crossing so that he might be born an American.

— 7 —

SPECTER OF WAR

And in 1937, Mama was pregnant again—this time it would be my turn. The summer of 1937 would be her last trip home to America, she knew. Again, she left alone. Papa would stay behind, with Miqué and Jean. They would stay with his sister in Paris. Mama would return before Christmas, because in the years they had been married, they had never missed this holiday together. Neither was overtly religious, but both loved the liturgy and the music of the season. And now, Papa enjoyed telling Miqué and Jean about "*Père Noël*" and what treasures he would bring in his sack.

Papa realized, more keenly than ever before, that he needed to keep his family safe. I was born in September. The Great Depression dragged on in America, FDR was elected for a second term, and the Golden Gate Bridge was completed and opened to connect Marin to San Francisco. In Europe, Hitler was growing in belligerence and greediness, poised to take Austria first, then Poland and Czechoslovakia

When Papa successfully completed his studies, securing first place not once but twice in the *Grand Prix de Rome*, it appeared that they could look forward to a full and prosperous future. He accepted a position with an architect in Brussels and the family moved north, full of hope and promise.

They were blissfully in love and he devoted tender attention to his small children in ways his own father never had. Mama learned to cook and became inventive in the meals she prepared in their tiny kitchen. She shopped carefully, stretching the meager budget creatively. They continued their habit of taking long walks through interesting neighborhoods, pushing the baby carriage together, the two boys skipping alongside.

It wasn't as easy as they had dreamed it would be. The architect he worked for embezzled funds from the company and Papa was left with nothing. They returned to Paris, subdued and crestfallen.

To Mama, it seemed as if Papa was always busy, deeply involved in writing articles about how to conserve water through ingenious irrigation, or how to better insulate homes using techniques as old as civilization, or the benefits of lycopene from tomatoes to avert diseases of the eye. Some were published, though most paid very little. He painted, going into the countryside with his paints and pastels. He took his work to galleries, which were glad to show for him, though little was sold. They celebrated and spent the proceeds too quickly. His sister, *Marguerite*, lent him the money to buy a concert grand piano for the bargain price of simply hauling it away. He had a few students, too, often growing impatient with their inability to play the exercises he gave them. But he persevered because this all helped fill the hungry mouths of his growing family. And Mama had what she called her "Fort Knox", the generous inheritance she had from her father's foundry in New Jersey. But bringing anything into France was becoming increasingly difficult as the borders began to systematically close down. She wrote urgent letters to her sisters, who did their best to help.

And through it all, they waited for his number to be called. Full mobilization seemed imminent. Even with a growing family, young men all over France were being conscripted. Like a leaf tossed by an errant wind, he was helpless to form any kind of future. There was no work in Paris. They might as well return to the chalet where they could farm like their neighbors. At least that would put food on the table and a roof over their heads. His family could wait out the insanity of war in the refuge of the forbidding high Alps

He would use the chalet as a base from which he could travel in his continuous search for meaningful work. He wrote a comprehensive proposal for refugee housing, including plans for modest structures that could be built with a minimum of manpower and materials.

And Mama was having another baby. In 1939, the dream of having another baby in America was simply that: a dream.

I can only think that they were extremely optimistic about their future, or more likely, incredibly naïve. And Mama loved having little baby bottoms to hold in her hand, as she loved to say with a smile when we were grown up and hearing her stories.

By March of 1939, not only Austria was gone, but now Czechoslovakia fell to the Nazi juggernaut. It seemed inevitable that France would enter the war, allied with England against Germany and Italy. Losses in World War I had left France woefully undermanned, so conscripts would fill the bulk of "soft" defenses while the regular army mobilized for what might come. After the experiences of the static lines of combat in the first war, some military minds felt a fixed fortified border with Germany would be the best defense. Named after André Maginot, the French Minister of Defense, the Maginot Line extended the length of France's border with Germany. France's borders with Belgium and Switzerland were relatively open, but it was felt that if regular troops could defend those lines, France would be safe.

For Papa and Mama, this was a difficult time.

He finally connected with a group willing to finance his plans for refugee housing. But he would have to go to *La Sarthe*, northwest of Paris, far from the chalet, to oversee the project. He would have to leave her behind with the children. She would have to run their small farm by herself.

Mama, the eternal optimist, rose to the challenge before her. If her neighbors could do this, she would as well. After all, wasn't her Wellesley education worth something?

When he wrote to Mama, he talked of the impossibility of finding basic construction materials. "We don't even have enough nails!" he would cry impatiently. "The pipes don't fit, and there's never enough lumber! It's an impossible task!"

When she read his letters, she struggled with the incongruity of his complaints as she did the work of the farm, her three small children around her and her fourth baby growing bigger in her belly.

He came back to Mama and his children as often as he could get away.

Despite his travels, or maybe because he was gone so much, he and Mama nurtured a deep and abiding love and respect for each other. And when he came home, he was devoted to his little family, always sure to bring something back for each of us. He found a brooch for Mama, of two lovebirds entwined in a circle. "Because they represent our love," he said. He found wooden blocks for Miqué; "He can play with Jean that way," was his pronouncement. And he played sweetly with them when he could. He painted a portrait of Mama, in profile, as if she were a medieval Princess Guinevere, and one of each of his children, all with big serious brown eyes staring out of the small canvas as if we knew what was coming next.

Over the next two years Germany gobbled up Norway, the Netherlands, Denmark, Belgium, and finally France, promising peace in the southeast as a German protectorate: Vichy. *"la Drôle de Guerre"* was France's brief and futile effort to withstand Germany's *"Blitzkrieg"* that smashed around both sides of the Maginot Line, completely overwhelming French forces. The soldiers fought valiantly against tanks and air armament with World War I guns and faulty ammunition. All effort had been put into the fortress bunkers of the Maginot Line, at the expense of any other measures of defense. When the German forces marched through Paris's *Arc de Triomphe*, on June 14th, 1940, Mama's 35th birthday, the city mourned, and then turned to resistance under the rallying cry of Charles de Gaulle.

— 8 —

REFUGEE WANDERINGS

Mama was alone when she had her fourth baby, my brother Pierre. She left the three of us in the care of the teenage girl she had hired to help her with the housework, and went off to *Albertville*, by train, to await the impending birth in the Catholic hospital. To her, it was the only sensible solution to an impossible situation. Papa would come as soon as he could, he wrote to her. And in fact, he arrived the day after Pierre was born.

"I can't do this anymore," she cried out to him. "I can't do the work of the farm and care for these four small children of ours by myself, while you're off doing what you do. Lisette is a big help, but she's just a young girl and will probably leave with the first young man she meets. How will I care for this sweet new baby? And I'm afraid…"

"Afraid?" Paul took her hand and kissed it. He caressed her flyaway hairs away from her face and tucked them behind her ear. He leaned toward his new son, asleep in his mother's arms and lightly kissed him. "What is there to fear when we are together?"

"But we're not together. You are on the other side of France while I am alone with the children in the mountains. The chalet is so close to Italy…and even close to Germany…And I'm an American. What if someone—what if I'm arrested because I don't have proper papers?"

"I'm so sorry, Liv. I've been so preoccupied with my own

problems, I haven't even thought about what all this upheaval means for you."

"Wouldn't it make sense for us all to be together, there where you are working? Why we might even be able to stay in the refugee housing you are building."

"Well, that's not possible of course—because nothing is built yet. I've told you of the difficulties we've had…"

"But surely, in town, where you are. I'm afraid, Paul…" she said again, her voice beginning to tremble as her eyes welled with tears.

"You're right," he said with a sigh. "We'll pack the Renault with as much as we can carry, and we'll go. But you must wait until little Pierre is a little bigger. It will be a grueling trip as it is. And I must plan the move carefully. You have no idea what it's like out there—you're probably safest in the mountains, but you're right. We need to be together."

It would take almost a year for the planned move to finally occur. The refugee housing project was stillborn. Only one model was ever built before all work stopped as France was consumed in war. Mama wrote one of her last letter home to her sisters in May of 1940, just before they left the chalet, before full censorship made it impossible to send or receive news.

Letter to Sister - May 29, 1940

Dear Family,
  This may be the last letter I can send. Censorship of real news is coming down like an opaque curtain but I think everyone guesses that things are not what the news tries to claim.
  There is not a nation on earth that is more realistic than the French. They certainly have cause to be. We are pawns being moved by forces beyond our control… Resignation or resistance? What is the difference for the little families huddled together in terror of the unknown? Each family unit gathers for mutual support to live its existence of self-preservation one day at a time.

This afternoon we were supposed to hear the radio news every hour but because there were planes overhead it was canceled. Radio helps the planes pinpoint their targets so we heard nothing except from the Italians who gave reports of German victories in Holland and Belgium. The bad news is fairly well censored on French radio and the Italian news is very partial to Germany. I will continue writing. Perhaps letters to you get through, though we may receive none.

Dearest love to all.

In a letter dated just four days later, Mama continued the story of the odyssey that seemed to consume so many families at that time.

Papa had packed the Renault and attached a cart to its rear, piled high with whatever we could carry. We left the relative safety of the mountains, thought we would take our chances in the south In Mamette's big house, and then thought better of it—like other refugees doing their best to stay out of harm's way, and finally decided to travel west to the province of *La Sarthe* where Papa had been working, and where he had many relatives with whom we might join together.

Letter to Sister — June 2, 1940

La Sarthe

Our address has changed as you will notice. Italy was getting so threatening that we felt it was wise to move from the South. Saint Raphael is near a very large aviation base and our chalet in Samoens is almost on the Swiss-Italian frontier so that either residence would be evacuated if Italy came into the war. Paul was able to get some gas to bring the family to a safer area. He drove from Chantenay in la Sarthe to gather us up from the chalet.

We only stayed at the chalet twenty-four hours, just long enough to pack everything into a kind of box trailer that Paul had managed to find. We had to plan for an indeterminate stay with as many of our belongings as we could take with us. That meant the children's bedding and household necessities. We spread everything out on the floor and spent as much time choosing what to eliminate as packing what to take. It was like packing for a camping trip for a future, questionable as to time, place or duration.

Early the following morning we left the chalet, and drove steadily in that poor over-burdened car. The roads were full of cars from the northern and eastern borders of France, all full of baggage and children, often with mattresses on the roofs.

We are now staying with the family in Chantenay where the household at present numbers seventeen, with three more refugees expected from north of Paris. The ones already here are from Montbeliard, in Eastern France, the cradle of Mamette's family. It is south of Alsace near the German border.

We have rented a house in Poillé where we expect to stay until the end of the war, barring unexpected emergencies. Here we are very near Paul's work. We have a very small furnished house, with a garden... but no conveniences whatever... outhouse... no water except from the village pump... but it is safe so the rest doesn't count. The family members who are here tell stories of sudden evacuation of entire villages, of being bombarded by planes on the roads... stories of the inhumanities of men that have no excuse even in war time.

We feel safe here now. Refugees from Belgium stream past the house. I'm so glad we are together.

More news later. Love to all

We had left the chalet soon after Pierre was born, and instead of going west to *la Sarthe,* Papa thought we might be safer staying in the south, with Mamette and Grandpère. But within a few months, it was time to move on.

We landed in *Poillet,* in a small house facing the main thoroughfare. Streams of frightened refugees passed slowly by the house, each with a story more horrific than the last. There was no food to be had, they said. A brother was shot on the road. A grandfather had to be left behind when he couldn't keep up. A mother was distraught to madness when she lost her child in the crowd.

Journal — June 4, 1940

One of Paul's cousins is from the district north of Paris. They were told to evacuate on very short notice. The whole village left. They were on the roads three days and three nights going south very slowly... all the population of their little village, some on foot, some on bikes, some in wagons, and the lucky ones in cars. They had to stop often to stay together until they reached certain designated destinations.

The whole time they were on that road they were bombarded by waves of German planes.

Some left their dead on the road and the rest went on with their cars and wagons pitted with bullet holes.

Then the Germans were pushed back and they were recalled to their village only to be reordered out again a few days later.

André and his family had to leave their chickens, rabbits and the grandmother. They had hoped to go back to get the grandmother but the car broke down and there was no one left anywhere to repair it. They tried to find some conveyance to get back and eventually found an old car in Paris. They are now working their way back to get the grandmother before orders are given to send her elsewhere. If they don't reach her in time, she will be gone and it will take months to find where she has been sent.

All the refugees tell similar stories. They have to evacuate, sometimes in half an hour, so members of a family are very often separated. Although they are all directed to one 'departement', it is a long time before they can be traced. It would be like sending all the inhabitants of a dozen villages to Rhode Island... In the chaos of a moving population it is a wonder that anyone finds other family members.

Our house here in Poillé is on the main road south and we sorrow for the pitiful families that file past us in an endless stream... cars with mattresses on the roofs and branches above it all to camouflage the vehicle.

André said that the planes come in waves and shoot from the height of a two story building.

They swoop down, fire and when everyone runs to the ditches to hide, they leave and come back only when they see that everyone is in formation again. What sadism lies buried in a human being to be able to commit such massacres, even under orders?

The *Préfet*, the Mayor, directed us to evacuate. We could no longer stay, he said; it was too dangerous, he said; so we joined the river of refugees and moved on to *Barbazon*, in the *Haute Garonnes*, in the *Pyrenees*. Papa met his professor from his days of doing his *Grand Prix de Rome* thesis, and he joined our little caravan for a time.

My memories of that strange time are confused and ephemeral. I'm not sure where the stories leave off and how much is what I remember or did I see it all in a movie? I wasn't quite three when we finally landed in *St-Rafaël*.

Letter to sister June 14, 1940

June 14, 1940, Poillé
Dear family,

I write this as we pack to leave. The préfet phoned Paul this morning urging us to leave at once. We went to Marguerite's to discuss with all the family gathered there. There are now 23 family members mostly from Montbéliard. André, who had gone back for the grandmother, found her just as the convoy of the village was planning to leave for a safer 'département' in the interior.

André would never have found her if she had left with the village convoy because she would not have known where to reach him.

Today is my birthday. Paul somehow found a dainty pair of pink slippers for me. They look like a beacon of hope in the midst of all the packing spread all over the beds and floor.

We will go to Barbazon in the Haute-Garonne in the Pyrénées where a cousin, who is now in Algeria, has a house where we could all stay. We are lucky to have gas; Marguerite because she is a doctor, and Paul because he has special permits from the préfet.

I say so long now, dear family. These are tense times but our daily routines are a blessing in disguise to prevent us from brooding or having time to be bitter. I will write as soon as we reach a safer haven, you may be sure. We will take the back roads as I have no papers and also the planes will be less apt to find us on the meandering farm roads of the back country.

When I read these letters, I was struck by my mother's eternal optimism, and her enduring philosophy, and the quiet courage which she carried to the end of her life: when events and circumstances are beyond your control, the only sensible thing to do is to carry on as best you can, with a routine that will allow you to move forward, in spite of your circumstances.

Journal — June 25, 1940
Journal Entry

We are in Barbazon, Haute Garonne, where we are luxuriously lodged in Cousin Renée's enormous three bathroom house.

Our trip was more eventful than we bargained for. As we left Chantenay we found Marguerite's maid, Jeanne, standing in the middle of the street, waving us to stop, tears streaming down her face.

"Madame told me to go to my parents, but there is no way," she sobbed. "No cars, no buses, no trains and it is 100 miles."

Of course, we gathered her in. Our little Renault now had two mattresses on the roof, and inside, very much squeezed and tangled, were five adults, four children under six years of age, and a fifty liter tank of gasoline. Behind us rattled a box-like contraption covered with a tarpaulin into which we had stuffed all our worldly possessions and what food we could manage to salvage from our garden in Poillé. Hanging to the back of the trailer swung a pail in which a ten pound piece of butter swished merrily in cold water. The tires sagged disconsolately under the load in spite of the extra air pressed into them.

Paul and 'Le professeur' were regally ensconced in front with Miqué between them. I was in the back seat with Marthe, each of us with a child on our laps and another between us. Jeanne, being the smallest adult, was precariously installed on top of the tank of gas. Numerous legs and feet were tangled in the few remaining inches of the floor space. Since I had no papers, and would have been arrested if caught, we bounced very carefully over the back roads, expecting a blow-out at any minute.

The first day went very well. The sky was a cloudless blue. Even Pierre at nine months sensed that it would be inopportune to proclaim his pangs of hunger. We crossed the Loire at Saumur, glad to be among those who crossed before the bridge was blown up. We tried to find a vacancy in a hotel but soon realized that such luxury would be impossible.

Pierre had been without a bottle for seven hours when we finally stopped at a farm house and asked if they could let us stay for the night. Like Mary and Joseph, who could find no room at the inn, we were offered shelter in the stable which we gladly accepted.

The stable, like on most French farms, was part of the main building. It had a kind of vestibule entrance behind which the cows were stationed in neat clean stalls. We spread out our blankets in the vestibule and slept a dreamless sleep in spite of the cobblestones which nudged us in the ribs.

There is something serene and comforting about a farm. Even the word stable to indicate the shelter for farm animals carries with it a basic sense of security. Surely Mary and Joseph must have felt this. How fitting for the Prince of Peace to have been born in a stable, isolated from the trivia of the transient guests at the inn and to share instead the gentle presence of dumb animals under the guardian stars of the night.

There was an air of security about that farm which, I am sure, is typical of all the farms in the world. The rigid schedule of daily tasks, the seasonal ebb and flow of rain and sunshine, heat and cold move with the regularity of a heart beat with Mother Earth tending the pulse rate. In spite of our anxiety of the moment, we too were affected.

We spent the evening with the family. International news was discussed with a minimum of panic, but rather, whether the animals had been watered, the barn door closed or if the potatoes would need rationing before the next harvest... these were problems that were immediate and which could be handled... all the rest was beyond control and must be borne if necessary, but futile to be discussed at length. The daughters, two fresh and smiling teenagers, (three brothers were mobilized) sat at their parents' feet. Rags, and bottles of copper polish, and papers were spread between them as they took up their weekly chore to clean the copper pots and brass andirons because tomorrow was Sunday and the brass was always done on Saturday. It was also June 25, only days since the Germans occupied Paris.

As we went south, the next day we replenished supplies of whatever was being produced in the particular regions we passed through. I found shoes for the boys where leather goods seemed plentiful. We went through one sinister area where slate roofing was the only industry. The ground seemed to have no soil, just slate rising in dark slabs like tombstones. Even the few trees seemed gaunt and tired of living...

I asked Paul,"What can they eat around here? There don't seem to be any gardens."

"The land is not very fertile, that's true," he said. "The staple food of their diet is from chestnuts."

"Chestnuts!" I exclaimed. "Do they eat them raw?"

"No," he answered, "they are cooked and mashed. They taste something like sweet potatoes."

"They must be very nourishing. Is this where the chestnuts for 'marrons glacés' come from?"

"Yes, they are very sweet, more like candy. They are difficult to prepare. They must be boiled very slowly in a sugar syrup for hours. They crumble easily if not handled with great care."

There were not many cities as we tried to avoid them. We did stop a few moments at Périgueux, normally a bustling industrial town. It was mute and listless. In the enormous central square the sun beat down mercilessly on small clumps of gray people, just weary, waiting people...

Except for the continual scurrying of cars going south on the roads, the whole country seems to have come to a halt like an engine whirring aimlessly in neutral.

The radio intermittently ordered all cars to stop where they were. Police patrolled the roads to see that they did. In mid-afternoon of the second day we were stopped by a gendarme who asked where we were going.

"We are going to stay with relatives in a hamlet ten miles from here," Paul lied glibly.

Whether he believed the story is doubtful, but one look inside that car with four little faces of young humanity would have melted the heart of even a big Irish cop. He let us continue and told us to be careful. We reached Barbazon that evening.

Barbazon is in the foothills of the Pyrénées. Nature has endowed the country with rolling hills where sheep graze and small farms struggle to survive.

We are having trouble replenishing our supplies and the farmers seem reluctant to help in any way. The potatoes and butter we brought from Poillé have been a godsend but they are nearly gone. We are thinking of going directly on to Mamette's big house and garden in Saint Raphael. If we do, we will have to"borrow" the gasoline which Cousin Renée has in a big tank in her cellar. Even so, it will be difficult because the police are really clamping down on any people in cars.

Again, I am struck by the steadfast stoicism of people caught up in a mighty maelstrom. The awesome power of a devastating war touches every citizen, yet life goes on, however that can be managed. And I am struck by the courage of our parents as they did the best they could to keep safe and somehow move along with as much normalcy as could be managed.

Journal Entry

The fourth of July... Independence Day? What irony! We have been here in Saint Raphael for two days. Others of the family were already here. We are now sixteen to feed at every meal, counting Fernande, Mamette's caretaker. We have service (Fernande, Jeanne, and Marthe), more than we know what to do with, but Mamette manages to keep all of them busy, polishing every square inch of the house or sending them to different stores to find spare fish or sea food of some kind.

Our trip east from Barbazon was even more newsworthy than the one two weeks ago.

Two weeks... it seems six months. In one month the world has been turned upside down. Only the sky remains its everlasting blue, a mockery of our mood which is pretty black most of the time.

We broke into Cousin Renée's gas tank and shared its precious cargo for the cars. Even so, there was barely enough. Paul had one more" coupon d'essence" from Poillé but it was for June.

We tried to use it in June but could not find a station with any gas, but on July first we found one that let us have the five liters (one gallon) allotted by the coupon. We took it, paid for it, and fled before the poor girl gas attendant had time to see that it was no longer valid. I felt guilty but Paul said,

"Her station is doomed to close like all the others anyway." It gave us enough to get here with a dribble left over.

We all left Barbazon shortly after Marguerite and her family arrived from Chantenay. In spite of nature's display of lush vegetation, we were struck by the stand-still look of each area. Hour after hour under the blazing sun, the road cut through the endless vineyards of France's 'vin ordinaire'. It may not yet be the season for the harvest but the motionless expanse of vines with no one around seemed unnatural.

Farther on we passed through apricot orchards where the fruit had been gathered but since there was no way to distribute it, pyramid of apricots were stacked in every farmyard, and flies, hens and ducks were swarming happily over the unexpected bonus of rotting fruit. In another region near Salon, there seemed to be quantities of laundry soap, probably because of the factories using oil from Algeria (peanut oil). Marguerite bought twenty pounds. I bought some too which helped to neutralize the odor of the gasoline tank in the car.

We had trouble, as was to be expected, to find a place to stay overnight. Carcassonne was a logical spot but we arrived late at night and knew it would be futile to look for hotels. We stopped in the middle of the eerily lit main square, surrounded by buildings looming dark and unfriendly in the night. As I stepped out of the car with the baby in my arms, a woman was crossing the pavement carrying a milk pot that rattled with its own echo as she came closer. As I moved to speak to her she stopped and watched the procession of people getting out of the car, each one leading a small child or a senior citizen. I barely needed to mention our dilemma. She interrupted me and said,

"I couldn't think of your looking any further for lodging. The hotels are all full. I have plenty of room for all of you."

She did. She had an exquisite apartment, each high ceilinged room furnished with taste and elegance. The children were reduced to open-mouthed awe. When Sally-Anne was led to a bed with a monogrammed, hem-stitched fine linen sheet she touched it reverently and murmured,

"O Mama, comme c'est doux!" (How soft it is) and then she leaned over and smelled it.

Like all sheets in France these had been put away with a sachet of lavender. I felt grubby but that fragrance alone was the first step to total relaxation. We were all offered baths in innumerable bathrooms. I felt like an invited guest of Marie Antoinette.

Monsieur Bigot, who moved with the poise and assurance of King Louis himself, bowed graciously and kissed his hostess' hand as he thanked her, and left us for his own private room and bath. The boys, who had not often been called upon to display manners or tact, and certainly not without a parental nudge, sensed that here was a dramatic occasion. Five-year-old Jean came up to Madame, our hostess, and with his warm smile he looked her straight in the eye and said,

"Tu es très gentille, Madame." (You are very nice.)

I am sure she forgave him the familiar use of" tu". She seemed touched because she took his hand and patted his head which he did not seem to mind. Miqué, shy and speechless, shifted uneasily from one foot to the other but he did manage a," Merci beaucoup, bonne nuit, Madame."

Sally-Anne was too overcome with the soft smooth sheets, and just smiled. This was a memorable, refreshing experience to end a very long day.

The next day we reached Saint Raphael and Mamette installed us in the whole upstairs apartment where we will offer a minimum of disturbance to the rest of the family.

Grandpère and *Mamette* were preparing for a long occupation. They had built a room between two rooms, a sort of secret space, into which they moved all their prized antiques: furniture, paintings, tapestries, silver, china and crystal that was worth thousands and that they certainly would not give up easily to Germans or Italians. As they were busy with this exercise, we settled into their upstairs apartment.

When Mama spoke of those days, she took on a distant look, as if remembering was simply too difficult, as if events had taken such a twist that the whole world was suddenly mad and nothing could possibly make sense again.

She recalled that there seemed to be a seismic shift underway, as if France might be stirring from a complacent, easy sleep to find that the warm covers of peace and tranquility had been dropped to the floor and the nation was suddenly naked in its uncertainty. Even as we were moving east from the Pyrenees, we became part of the streams of frightened families, belongings helter-skelter with their children, in cars, donkey carts, trucks, whatever conveyance they might have, and always with branches over the roofs as camouflage, traveling mostly at night for safety, our headlights dimmed to blackout regulation.

It was as if a giant boot had landed on an anthill, sending the industrious, busy ants scurrying in every direction, confused in their efforts because they had to leave their queen behind. Who was in charge now, to direct an anxious population?

We passed rows of neat grape vines that were silent and neglected, quietly waiting for the harvest that would not come. Apricot orchards dropped their fruit for the flies and the birds and the wild animals which now had free range in the abandoned fields. There was no way to get a harvest to market. The talk in all the villages was "Who will be next? Where will we go?" And the women and old men and children were left with the constant and consuming effort to find enough food for their families.

When I think about this crazy journey of ours, I have to think we might have been just as safe in the mountains as by the sea, probably safer. But Mama was truly anxious. She told Papa about the men who had been lined up in the village and shot, because they supported the maquis, the underground. As an American, the same could happen to her, she feared. It seemed that this war was an unstoppable torrent which could not be diverted or dammed.

— **9** —

VICHY FRANCE

August 1, 1940 Saint Raphael (letter to sister)

Dear Barbie,

All the letters are coming by air now and it is much faster. Yesterday a letter came that was only two weeks old.

You are all very dear to offer to help us get to America. Before we left Barbazon we thought of it very seriously but red tape complications seem insurmountable. Not only for the papers involved, but mostly that there is no way to move around to get them.

On the map, Marseille may not seem far from Saint Raphael but without gas it might as well be on the moon. So we have girded ourselves with optimism, perhaps false, but superficially effective, and are preparing to settle down to a life of enforced idleness. Aside from lacking several things that we are learning to get along without like butter, gasoline and oil and diminished supplies of almost everything else, we have lots to be thankful for. Everyone is healthy, the sun shines every day, the beach offers endless diversion for the children and we are all together.

Paul is bursting at the seams in a ferment of frustrated energy and I am just plain bored with routines of child care, and unhappy about being a burden to relatives. We are thinking of building a small shelter on the beach until we can find Oncle Victor. He might lend us money to get a house for ourselves. He would lend the money towardcredit on money in America which would be reimbursed after the war. It is no longer allowed to export funds out of France so this would, in the end, be doing him a service.

I'll let you know if anything develops.

I remember the fragrance of the mimosa, so sweet in its promise of spring, the yellow puffball blossoms appearing suddenly as great, lavish bouquets in all the trees along the avenue. *Mamette* magically produced a treat of delicacies of Easter in a large wicker basket. There was a furry stuffed bear for me, and little boxes filled with the traditional *dragées,* the candy coated almonds in pastel shades of pink, blue, green and yellow. What did Mama think, I wondered later, as we children squealed with delight at the bounty that filled the wicker basket.

August 10, 1940, le Midi
Journal Entry

Our lives are completely isolated. The newspapers and radio are full of strange stories that no one believes. Reports from French, German, Italian and Swiss sources are all hysterical fantasies of how everything is normal. News from England is very effectively scrambled. While we were in Barbazon we were able to hear England and de Gaulle for almost two weeks, but the Germans have now successfully silenced them. Sunshine and the joyful innocence of children cannot offset the oppressive atmosphere of living in quarantine. We are isolated from the rest of the world which perhaps knows more about our future than we can learn.

If the transportation facilities could be re-established before winter, France might not really suffer... but there is no gasoline. There are a few trucks which work on bottled gas and there are all sorts of stories of marvelous inventions to replace gasoline but they are still stories in gossip form and the sight of a car is about as remarkable as it was thirty years ago when we would leap out the front door to watch it go speeding down the dusty street at twenty miles an hour. Paul wants to distill oil from the aromatic plants here or try turpentine. I only hope he tries it on some other motor than the engine of our car.

Things may look grim, but we are really comparatively well off. There are some places that we went through that are now full of refugees where there is no farming whatsoever. Regions which are considered safe for the refugees are more often areas of a single industry like the one making slate for roofs or the extensive winemaking regions. France, which in normal times, is almost completely autonomous, is now starving for lack of transportation. Gasoline must be imported. The network of canals and railroads no longer links vital centers of north and south. All the coal is in the northeast or in Germany and only a dribble passes to the southern zone.

I cannot help but wonder what the United States would do if gasoline were suddenly cut off completely. It would be so easy to blow up a few refineries and those enormous cylindrical tanks lying around so exposed to sudden attack or sabotage. The United States would have to survive on railroads and coal but here we have to grovel for coal from Germany or occupied France.

This was only the beginning of the long journey that would lead us back to the chalet. Papa, who seemed to be forever in search of work, left us with his parents, promising to return when he could. And he would write often. We would be safe, he assured Mama; and he would be safe also. France would eventually prevail against the Axis Powers. France could not be conquered. They had seen the *Chasseurs Alpins*, had they not? And Vichy was still unoccupied, was it not?

Papa's latest job hadn't lasted, as all effort was now focused on defending France. There could be no work unless it directly related to the war effort. Now he would have to figure out how he could support his family, and where we all might be able to live. We could no longer stay in his parents' small upstairs apartment. He would need to find someplace else. He found a small house nestled in an olive grove in *le Miradou*. But how could he possibly buy this? We had no money. His job with the refugee housing had evaporated before he could ever see any compensation. We couldn't live off his parents any longer. The idea of borrowing the money, to be paid back from Mama's ever bountiful "Fort Knox" in New Jersey once the war ended, could not be negotiated. What if Germany won the war?

Papa finally approached his father.

"*Enfin,* Paul, you need to take care of your family!" Grandpère was growing impatient and critical of Papa's inability to make a living. "I had such faith in you, Paul. With your intellect and your enormous talents, I really expected you to go far, to be very successful in your career. But you have done nothing with any of that. When are you going to show some sense of responsibility? And begin to really care for your family? for what you are doing?"

"*Papa, tu ne comprends pas!* You don't understand how difficult it is now. What can I do? There is no work. My talents are useless in this terrible war. Everything I try ends in a closed door or a dead end. I need your help. I know you have the wherewithal. I'm your son! Won't you lend me the money for this wonderful house I found for the family?" It was hard for him to beg. The two men had equal measures of pride.

"*Bah!* And how do you think you would ever pay it back? I'm very disappointed in you, Paul. I had expected great promise from you. You go traipsing all over the countryside with your head in the clouds—and you keep having more babies—while your wife…"

"Don't dare bring Liv into this discussion. This is between you and me. You can't seem to appreciate how impossible everything has become. Look around you! You have been careful and foresighted enough to squirrel away your treasures, knowing how bad things will get before anything even begins to get better. I'm doing the best I can, and as hard as I may work, it's not enough. It's never enough…" Paul sighed and sat heavily, defeated.

"But you—you have all these fancy ideas, all this theory—but does any of it bring bread to the table? Of course not—especially now! Who's going to fund some frivolous scheme when this whole country is in such desperate straits?"

"That's the point, Papa. These are impossible times. You have made your fortune. Please help me—help us, now. I assure you, this will not be in vain. You will be paid back. That is my solemn promise to you."

Finally, a deal was struck: *Grandpère* would buy the house as a future investment. But Papa would have to manage it. He would have to somehow figure out how he could feed his family. *Grandpère* would give him shelter, but the rest was up to Papa.

Through it all, Mama was his unquestioning fan, forever loyal, the idealistic optimist. She trusted him. Papa would take care of everything. Somehow, good fortune always seemed to follow him, even as everything he touched, and all the money he ever had, flowed through his fingers like sand. If Mama ever showed exasperation, it was with his absolute innocence with money. He had it; then he didn't. Now, miraculously, we would live in a pretty little house, with a garden and an orchard, even olive trees.

Papa poured his heart into "bringing bread to the table" as his father had scornfully said he was helpless to do. He spent his days tending a garden that grew more bountiful as the sun baked his back and the cultivated earth responded to his care with lush lettuces, beans, tomatoes, and every possible vegetable that could be brought to the table. He planted strawberries, coaxed the olive trees to produce a gallon of oil for each of the six trees. He squatted in the neat rows of plantings, like the peasant he was becoming—his strong pianist hands growing callused and worn as he worked.

When Mama told me these stories of the war years, when I was older, I marveled at my mother's ability to always come to Papa's defense in all circumstances. Even if she knew a different truth, she could somehow make him the hero. And in these trying days, no doubt he was.

Storm clouds of war continued to advance. Germany took Poland on September 1st, 1939. Denmark and Norway fell in April of 1940. And finally, in an overwhelming blitz, Germany entered France, Belgium, Luxembourg and the Netherlands in May of 1940. Paris was bombed in early June, and finally, German troops entered Paris through the *Arc de Triomphe* on June 14th, 1940. *La Drôle de Guerre* was over. Hitler would leave the south and southeast of France to the Italians. Though it was called unoccupied France, it was anything but that.

September, 1940 (letter to sister)

Your letter saying the American Consul in Marseille was worried about us made me proud of our government that cares about its citizens abroad. I wrote him immediately to thank him for his concern and to re-assure him that we are all right.

Paul writes articles that he offers for sale for a pittance. He seems to get some satisfaction just expressing himself and continues to feel sure that everything will come out fine someday. He lives by an unwavering philosophy that makes him immune to reverses. "Don't worry about what can't be helped", so he puts up with crises that continue to make me fret.

There is talk of removing the boundary between the two zones and having all the French ports occupied. It is still being negotiated. This would mean strict censorship or even canceling all mail from the U.S.

Potatoes are out of circulation now because the price dictated by the government is too low to admit a profit so the wholesalers refuse to sell them to the retailers. So rats will consume them free. Only the people with bicycles, who can reach a farm and pay the black-market prices, will get them so we are restricted to macaroni, one half pound per month per person. We live on what we have in stock and Paul's prodigious garden.

Love to all and I will write more later,

Life in *le Miradou,* or anywhere in Vichy France, was isolated from the rest of the world. A virtual fence had been erected, a curtain dropped. Without coal, without gasoline, life returned to simpler times, yet was infinitely more complicated by the scarcity of everything. We lived without an increasing list of basic necessities. Though we were a large family, and entitled to more on the ration cards, and though Mama could always go to the head of the interminable lines, because of her young children, she still was unable to get much of anything, since all the stores were quite empty. And even if she could have, there was very little money to spend.

One early morning, on her way to hopefully find shoes for Miqué, she came upon an unusually long line of women, waiting for the fish store to open. "But there is nothing to buy," she commented to one of the women, "Why is everyone in line?"

"The fishmonger is coming back with a good catch, so we're just waiting for him," she replied.

Mama went to the head of the line and patiently waited with the other women. The fisherman pushed his cart, laden with his fresh catch, and opened the door to his store.

"Do you have a newspaper, Madame, or a cloth to wrap your fish?"

"Oh, I'm sorry, Monsieur. I wasn't expecting to find such a treasure today. May I still buy one?"

"Of course, Madame." He handed her a large fish, which she held by the tail, and gingerly mounted her bicycle and headed back home.

Such a feast we had that night! Mama had become quite ingenious at turning tiny morsels into gourmet fare. Papa was a skilled and passionate gardener and was able to keep her supplied with fresh vegetables in all seasons. She could take a treasured cube of cheese, her homemade tomato paste, and the ever-present pasta, and turn it into a nourishing meal fit for her ravenous family.

But it was becoming increasingly difficult to find even the basics that we think of today as bare necessities. Since gasoline was on the forbidden list, cars were put on blocks, the wheels removed. Bicycles and hand drawn carts were the new transportation. Trains ran once a day and had a limited range. Anything and everything of value went to Germany and Italy first.

It was Jean who told me of this encounter with Mama. She was sitting on the stoop, a potato in her cupped hands. She was crying as she took a bite from the raw potato.

"Why are you crying, Mama?" he asked her. "Because I'm so hungry and this is our last potato and I just took a bite out of it, so now I have less to make a soup with for you." He remembered hugging her and saying, "*ça va*, Mama? It's okay…" and in his small, but grown-up six year old voice, he continued, "the soup will be very good, because everything you do is always very good."

And of course, she really started to cry as she hugged him tightly.

January 19, 1941 — Le Miradou, Golfe Juan (letter to sister)

Dear family,

I am writing very small, there is so much to say and paper is so precious. Good news at last... I received a letter from a bank in Cannes saying there was money there... You are amazing!

How did you do it? You can't imagine how relieved I am... The link with home still stands. Thank you so much, dear ones.

Rations have again been reduced. They may be adequate for an office worker but for a manual laborer, it could affect his health and efficiency. For us, a family of six, we can hope to get two very small meat meals a week, enough oil to keep the food from sticking to the pan, and vegetables. There is no margarine or other fat, enough spaghetti for a once a week meal, and no potatoes. I wash diapers without soap, but lots of hot water, scrubbing, and many cold rinses.

Sugar will be reduced again next month but because of Paul's fantastic garden, we are just fine. We always have fresh tomatoes and I make condensed tomato paste daily. This makes tasteless foods acceptable. We also have green beans and a kind of lima bean that is intended for animals. It is quite nutritious, but very indigestible.

Other items are getting very scarce, like paper, matches, and of course, no coffee. We found a peculiar mixture to replace coffee, made of grain, an uninteresting but satisfactory substitute. I thought we would have oil because of the olive trees but there are few olive trees in France. The oil for cooking as well as for soap manufacture came from the peanuts from Algeria which is now as inaccessible as the planet Mars.

I am trying to teach the children to read and have gained enormous respect for first grade teachers. Arithmetic seems to be a lot easier for them because it relates or, at least can be made to relate, to the world they know, but all those squiggles for letters must be impossible to distinguish one from the other.

I haven't talked English for three years and get homesick for that good ole' Yankee twang that everyone makes fun of. I sometimes read your letters aloud so the children know I'm not the only person in the world who talks English.

Paul's book, "Les Arts au Service de la France" is beginning to be heard of and the book

"La Nouvelle Europe" is still being examined by the editors. His articles for the paper still appear every Sunday in the big Savoyard newspaper. He is now the best authority on housing in France, having traveled all over making quantities of photos and sketches from every province. He wants to write a book on it, but because of all the necessary pictures it would cost too much to consider now.

The curtain had come down. When I read these letters to her sisters, I was struck by the effectiveness of cutting off access to the familiar comforts, and inevitably, inexorably denying the necessities. In war, the citizen is always the first victim. As the war machine ramps up to gobble more and more resources, there is gradually very little left. And yet, we had enough, and more than our neighbors. Papa could write, he could garden, and he could still travel if he really wanted to. Mama had enough, with careful determination and ingenuity to bring food to the table. And we children were oblivious of our surrounding hardship. We didn't have toys, but we had our imaginations and we had one another.

We had our home, and we were safe. We no longer feared the possible strafing as we wandered helplessly, our worldly possessions pile on, in and around our groaning car. Our car was useless now, on blocks until (or if…) the war ended. We were settling in for the duration, however long that might take. We adapted to our new routine.

March 1, 1941
Journal Entry

We are having more and more difficulty finding things we really cannot do without, like bicycle tires and light bulbs. In order to get one light bulb we have to return two old ones as there are not enough for a one to one replacement. I desperately need new diapers for the new baby due in July. The ones I have now have more holes than substance.

We are nevertheless learning to get along without things generally considered necessities.

Yesterday I brought home the monthly ration of potatoes and Sally-Anne asked what they were.

The last ones we saw were at our Christmas meal. These we are saving to plant. I tried to describe ice cream to the children and different kinds of cereals, crackers, jam and candy. Miqué remembered ice cream, perhaps from his bout with the tonsillitis when he was four, but none of them remembered ever eating candy or even knew what I was talking about.

We are thinking of going to the chalet... at least for the summer. We could get milk, eggs and cheese and perhaps chickens. Here we have fruit and vegetables but very little protein except the children's milk... one pint per child and pregnant mother. It is even hard to find seeds to plant a garden. All over France there are idle lands and idle hands... and it all is due to lack of transportation.

In this land of sunshine and lush vegetation it is hard to accept that man cannot find ways to live on the bounties of Nature. The almond and apricot trees are in bloom and soon there will be peaches and in late May the orange blossoms will send their perfume all over the hillside and will overwhelm the salty fragrance of the sea.

Our big fig tree spreads its welcome shade over the terrace where Pluck and the children play. Poor Pluck endures the tortures of hunger with the patience of his faithful canine disposition. He lies down near Pierre and lets himself be pummeled and rolled and sat on and then when I think I should go to rescue him from his miseries, I find him trying to slobber all over Pierre as though to thank him for all the punishment. He is so thin! All I can feed him are table scraps and the outside leaves of vegetables. We certainly have no trouble with garbage disposal. Even paper gets saved for wrapping or for the bathroom and, of course, there are no more cans to throw away.

June 1, 1941, Le Miradou, Golfe Juan
Journal Entry

Miracle of miracles! Paul came home from a short prospecting trip to the chalet. What a Christmas in June. He brought 7 eggs, cream, butter, lettuce and a big bag of potatoes. He arrived at about 9:30 in the evening and went immediately into the kitchen. "You stay here and don't move" he said to me.

In a few minutes I smelled the unfamiliar aroma of butter cooking with all the appropriate spitting noises to go with it, and soon he came back with a meal of two eggs cooked in cream, potatoes sautéed in butter and lettuce salad with a dressing of cream and lemon juice. If I live to be a hundred that will be remembered as the best meal I have ever eaten. I felt guilty for having made such a pig of myself but was consoled when Paul said, "You shouldn't feel guilty. You represent one third of the family all by yourself," and enclosed my bulky frame in his arms.

The baby is due in less than a month. It should be a small baby because I have gained only fourteen pounds.

June 14, 1941, Le Miradou, Golfe Juan
Journal Entry

Today was a very special day, not only because it was my birthday, but mostly because of the event we made of it. Paul had promised,"We'll gather the first potatoes on Mommy's birthday."

So we all trooped down to the potato patch, Paul leading the way and the children, all very excited for the big event, tagging along behind. We gathered enough for a festive meal. Paul cooked the meal of boiled potatoes, green beans and garlic with salad oil from our own olive trees.

We had five quarts of oil from our five olive trees, but though we had to give two quarts to the government, we still have three quarts for us. It is a great help. We have discovered that there is much less loss from olive oil when frying or sautéing. We are saving it for salad mostly, but we once had a ratatouille with eggplant, tomatoes, peppers and garlic that was worthy of a before-the-war restaurant.

Another big event of the day was the arrival of the Red Cross boat with a layette for the new baby... all so white and fresh... with real cotton diapers and little gowns. I am sure that I will be very alone in knowing what to do with all those wrapping blankets. The French dress their babies so differently. French babies are wrapped from armpit to ten inches below their curled-up legs in a heavy pure wool blanket. Its advantage is warmth at night because French houses are never as heated as at home and wool is also quite soak proof. I still have two from Pierre's layette. I will line a wool blanket with the American wrapping blanket to chafe less when he kicks.

June 1941: The air was still, dry and dusty; it was too hot to move quickly. Mama sat on the stoop and watched us play. "Miqué is always so bossy," she mused. "And he is only seven." Miqué had a game that he was directing, trying to entice Jean and I to play too. But I guess I must have just looked at him, as if he might be some kind of annoying bug. Mama always said I would be like that all my life, patiently observing others as if they might be specimens under a microscope—a little repugnant, but also somewhat fascinating. I wasn't quite four; the only girl in this band of brothers, I was most content to simply observe the boy antics briefly, and then go back to putting my precious bear in his bed and wrapping him in a bedraggled piece of cloth that had once been a diaper.

Mama blew some wispy strands of hair off her face. Her blue eyes squinted away from the bright sun, even though she was wearing her big, floppy straw hat. Nearly thirty-seven and with her fifth baby huge in her belly, she still looked much younger, more innocent. Her baby face, full mouth and little piquant nose gave her a look of near surprise and naiveté. She put her hand, so long fingered and delicate, to her belly. She felt that familiar ache in her groin and lower back now. Her baby had quieted, in preparation for the first and most difficult journey of its life. It was nearly time; but Papa was off on another of his frequent trips.

"Mamette can be counted on to oversee the household and Eva would have to take care of the children," she decided. A Hungarian widow with a little boy Miqué's age, Eva had landed on our doorstep as a refugee of the war and Mama had taken her in to help with the household. Tall, big-boned and plain, she adored Mama with a fierce and straightforward loyalty. She was strict with us, but we always knew that no matter what we might do, she would be quick to forgive, ready to love.

Mama wasn't certain the clinic would take her in on such short notice, but after her previous quick births, she knew she'd better be off. Surely she presented quite a sight, her big belly out in front, shoulders straight, head back in her characteristic aristocratic grace, as she pedaled her bicycle off to the clinic.

"Oh, Madame, I'm so sorry," the nurse apologized when she arrived, breathless, disheveled and obviously in labor. "Our maternity ward is fully occupied. We will have to put you in our other wing." She fluttered off ahead, her winged coif, starched and bright white, like a strange bird perched on her head, and her black robes flapping like the wings of a magpie.

My little sister was born that night. Mama cried at her sweetness, the unique smell of her newness, and the downy softness of her silky almost curly hair caressing her cheek. "How will we manage?" she thought, "It is already so hard. I'm afraid, and I feel so alone…"

She became aware of a deep moaning, a sound that seemed to come from the depths of a pain that she could only begin to imagine. The mournful sound filled the quiet night, soaring to the sky and echoing within the walls of the clinic. It went on, sometimes as soft as a murmur, then rising to a crescendo of a shriek that made her rigid with fear. She held her new baby close, trying to protect her from such raw emotion.

There was a crash, suddenly, and the unmistakable shattering sound of glass exploding into the night. Running steps in the corridor passed by her closed door and disappeared. There were many voices now, outside her window, and urgent calls for help. She was paralyzed with fear, cowering in her bed with her baby. The tumult eventually died down and calm night returned. She finally slept.

"I hope last night's commotion didn't frighten you too much, Madame," the morning nurse patted her shoulder and held her hand. "It was one of our regulars. She is quite crazy! She does this every once in a while, and throws herself out her window. She doesn't hurt herself because she always lands in the bushes. But she's the most extreme of our patients in the asylum." She picked up little Betty, cooing softly as she tenderly rearranged her blanket.

She smiled at Mama, and went on, "I guess you didn't know that we are also an insane asylum. May I change your baby's diaper? I think she has soiled it." She was as friendly as the morning sun streaming in the open window. "Somehow," Mama thought, "it will really be all right."

Papa returned that day, and indeed now everything would be just fine. No matter how dire the day might seem, when he entered the scene, he brought calm assurance with him. By sheer will of his authority, he could quiet the storm.

June 24 (Antibes Hospital)
Journal Entry

Paul came back the morning after the baby was born, expecting to take me home. He was astonished. He never ceases to be amazed by the miracle of motherhood and looked at the small mite of humanity with awe and a kind of reverence for the little child who had suddenly appeared to become a member of the living, breathing world.

It was all so natural and by far the easiest of them all. She was quite small - - only six pounds - - but that was to be expected.

Betty is lovely with enormous dark eyes already curious and wide with wonder. I never saw a calmer baby. When she is awake she lies open-eyed gazing at the mosquito netting above her and blinks at the sight of a stray fly that could dare disturb her ladyship's serenity.

Paul stayed all morning sitting beside the bed. We both remarked that my being in the hospital gave us both time to be alone together.

"Pretty high price to pay for a cozy conversation," I said.

"Maybe we could get away sometime for a picnic, just the two of us," he answered.

I didn't answer because I know that even if we planned it weeks ahead, something, some important business engagement would intervene. In the meantime if we can find time to walk in the countryside, even with the children we can enjoy talking and dreaming of the house we may someday build.

I suppose it will have to be dictated by where the work is. I can't imagine either of us settling in a city or even a tract housing suburban development... but then our international marriage is in defiance of anything either of us ever pictured.

The reality of war has perhaps brought us closer than we could have been if times had been normal. I was jolted out of my middle class world of comparative ease and Paul has been obliged to face realities of farming, and coping with shortages that have removed him from the world of artists and creative architects.

I hope he will join that world after the war because I am convinced that he sees further into the future than most. I suppose that is why so many, especially now during hard times, consider him impractical... a dreamer and even a crackpot... but I feel he will be vindicated if his ideas ever reach the market place. All he strives for after all, is to use, not destroy the bounty of nature.

"The sun and rain do not have to be our enemies," Paul says, "and even ice and snow and wind can be used to our advantage if we build from the understanding of them."

— 10 —

JOURNEY TO SAFETY

After Betty, my new sister, was born, the serious planning for the last big move began to evolve. Vichy France was no longer a safe place to stay. The myth of "Free France" was, after all, a myth. Totally a protectorate of Germany, ruled by Mussolini's Italy, the inevitable vise of occupation meant that life for the average French citizen became ever more dismal. By September of 1941, we were ready for the long trip. We took the train, then caravanned up the mountain, with everything we could carry, and five children ranging in age from Miqué, now seven, to little Betty, barely three months old.

September 10, 1941 (letter to sister)

Dear ones all,

As you see from the address, we are in the chalet. We came up here for food reasons mostly, and to give the children a little altitude to build up their red corpuscles.

What a trip!! We sent two trunks ahead, but still had seven pieces of baggage (one had two ducks in it), five children and parents. We had to change trains or buses five times. We left at 8 P.M. Sunday and reached the chalet at 8 P.M. Monday after a sleepless night in the train and a four and a half hour wait in Taninges only eight miles from Samoens . We tried to find a conveyance of some kind to move us from Taninges but there are only two trains a day and we had, of course, missed the morning one.

We have been here two weeks and have all gained weight and live in a luxury unknown and undreamed of: five quarts of milk a day, eggs and cheese. We can often get meat and butter with our ration tickets, never the case in the south. We even brought cases of fruit and green vegetables from the Miradou. We intend to stay as long as we can. The only handicap will be the children's school during the winter. The one room school house in Chantemerle has no teacher and even if a teacher is assigned, the children will have to learn to ski to get there. It is about a 20 minute walk down the mountain in normal weather.

Miqué is not the least bit interested in the possibility of school and Jean finds too many other things to examine even to be curious about it. Sally Anne will be home and can help with Betty. She already can feed and burp her. She speaks more perfectly than any of the others at her age (4 years) and if once corrected for an error will not repeat it. Pierre is starting to talk too.

He is the funniest of the bunch, always up to pranks, teases Sally Anne until she screams at him and then whispers gentle nothings in her ear five minutes later. He adores the baby and climbs up into the big armchair waiting for me to put her on his lap to "seel" (sleep), then he pats her face and laughs pleased-as-punch laugh until I take her away. For him the whole world in general is as satisfactory as a kitten with a bowl of milk, but if he has a tantrum he is worse than all the others together. He generally prefers putting on a scene at two a.m. And, of course, wakes up everyone.

Like a violent summer thunderstorm it is all over in five minutes, ending as suddenly as it starts, and he becomes angelic and goes to sleep as soon as he is sure to have sufficiently aroused everyone from slumber. He is good-looking but not like the others... platinum blond hair and very pink cheeks with a chubby build. For a two year old it is becoming but, of course, at forty it could be disastrous.

Betty may have wavy hair. She has a dimple when she smiles and Pierre tries to tickle her into showing it, but when it doesn't work he slaps, she cries, and I take away his game by rescuing the baby.

Memories are fleeting and ephemeral, usually vague glimpses of a past colored by conflicting emotions. I was four when we arrived at the chalet. I was very, very tired, stumbling over my feet as we all groped in the dark, finding uneasy footing on the path to the chalet. I clutched big brother Miqué's hand, his sure and determined steps giving me strength to go on. As in all our adventures, I felt like an errant leaf tossed by the random wind of events that I could not begin to understand.

This latest turn was not like the exciting anticipation of Christmas, but nor was it the paralyzing fear that had gripped me on our frantic journey as refugees to the south of France two years before.

It had been my first hazy memory, pieced together and rounded out by the stories Mama told of those earliest years. At that time, we children had no idea what was happening, or why we began to drive at night in the packed car. And the airplanes that buzzed so close to us with a rat-tat-tat of rapid fire. Why were we being shot at? Sometimes we had to stop our car because there were so many other cars, and people and carts blocking our way. The planes would keep coming and we hid in the ditches by the side of the road, cowering to be as small as we could be to avoid the bullets that whizzed by. Why were we being shot at?

When we had moved south, the *Chasseurs Alpins,* the elite corps of mountain men, guerilla soldiers, were steadily, determinedly moving in the opposite direction, to the northern border. We slept in hay barns, trying to move only at night, the headlights of the big Renault cautiously darkened. Ultimately, we were desperately trying to move out of the way of the war and to the relative safety of the south of France.

I vividly remember the night we were invited to stay in a large comfortable home. The bed I slept in had heavy sheets, soft, scented with lavender. Miqué was dumbstruck that anyone could live like this. Jean could only say softly, "*Merci beaucoups, Madame. Tu est trés gentile*", using the familiar form in addressing our gracious hostess. And I, of course, caressed the sheets and could only repeat, again and again, "*Comme c'est doux…*" It's so soft…

Though difficult, this move back to the chalet was less frightening than the surreal and unrelenting madness of our refugee journey of two years earlier. Parents, by their mood, can instill fear, or confidence or excitement in their children. And on this trip, as hard as it was, we knew we were going someplace where our parents might not be so frightened—especially Mama. Because of that, we children could accept the journey as a great new adventure, filled with wonderful possibilities.

Mama said we would be farmers, like our neighbors. We would have a cow for milk and maybe chickens, and sheep and cats to catch the mice. Papa would plant another marvelous garden and she would stop being so sad because we would all have enough to eat now. And we would be safe up high in the mountains. Mama was no longer fearful she would be turned in for not having proper papers. For her, it was more important that she would be able to feed her children.

November 1941
Journal Entry

We are bombarded with propaganda, but we don't believe any of it... no one does. Since the Blitz the whole of France has become very skeptical. Here even more so because by being so close to the borders of both Italy and Switzerland we can hear (with difficulty) both sides, which are so blatantly propaganda that no one believes either side.

We never listen to French news any more, but try to hear Switzerland which attempts to steer a middle course by sounding pro-allies one week and pro-occupied French the next week.

We know that we are pawns and helpless about our own fate. No one wants anything in particular except the end of the war which they hope will bring back some food and shoes and all the other necessities that have disappeared.

We were so lucky to have this farm to come to. It will mean a new way of life for all of us but we are not afraid. We look forward to living in this beautiful country of changing skies and contrasting seasons, among simple people whose life goals are to make ends meet in the only way they know, learned from skills handed down through generations of honest, hard-working peasants whose ways we are eager to understand and imitate. There is always some way to find a rainbow in a storm.

– 11 –

LIFE IN THE CHALET

The transition from the south of France, *le Midi,* to the chalet, high in the French Alps, was transformative. Leaving behind a pretty little house with its grove of olive trees, endless sunshine, the sea and its beaches, wasn't a difficult decision for my parents, given the ever-increasing challenges they faced. Would they stay here and face increasing hardship or pack up and make the trek to relative safety in the high mountains, tending their own farm?

As I read my mother's journal, I see the peace she finally seems to know, and the gratitude she can finally express as she sheds the worry and fear that have been so much a part of her being these last difficult years.

Late fall 1941
Journal Entry

During the late fall the sun was our loyal friend. The air was still and the sea of clouds lay below us, a luminescent quilt of billowing white. Each day we transported Betty, 4 months old, in her cradle to the terrace where she lay gazing at the cloudless blue sky. Household chores and children's play were the unvarying program of the day during this, our first year, as we tried to read the moods of nature.

We were to learn that in this mountainous country of breathtaking beauty, nature bestowed its rewards only through constant vigilance, hard, back-breaking work and ingenuity to meet each new problem. Weeks of sunshine could be followed by even longer periods of heavy fog, drenching rain, or blizzards that buried us behind a six foot wall of snow blocking any view of the horizon.

Late October in the high Alps is its most rewarding season.

Each evening, as soon as the sun falls behind the mountain peaks, a cold breeze rises from the valley bringing with it a rolling wave of heavy mist which soon envelops the whole mountain.

Sounds are muffled and seem to come from everywhere at once. We welcome the warm glow of our cozy home.

In the morning when the sun filters through the tree tops, it chases the fog down the mountain. Rolling billows swirl and frolic until they settle over the valley in a sea of clouds that lie below us, pulsing like the backs of an enormous flock of sheep. The air is calm, the sun hot, the temperature often rising to 100 degrees. The rays of the sun often color the clouds with an iridescent shimmer as they lie below us day after day. The pattern of late autumn weather is set for weeks.

Each day the children play outdoors. The boys go off in search of adventure to return only when pangs of hunger dictate that the dinner hour is near.

On one occasion Betty was installed in her cradle on the terrace while the younger children played outside under the kitchen window.

We were tempted to eat outdoors on these beautiful fall days but in France the big meal is eaten at noon with all the ceremony befitting the event. We compromised by having after dinner coffee on the terrace.

As we were seated at the table, Miqué, who was close to the window said, "Look, the eagle just flew by."

Since no one else had noticed, we continued eating. Eagles often circled the chalet.

"There he goes again," shouted Paul, suddenly jumping up, "He's after the baby."

We all ran out on the terrace, I grabbed a broom; everyone shouted. The eagle flapped a wing in distain, circled the field below us and flew away screaming his objections. Pierre, at two and a half, joined the excitement running up and down, and shrieking. The noise and commotion woke up the baby who joined the chorus, while we carried her cradle indoors.

Thereafter when Betty was on the terrace, her cradle was protected by chicken wire that Paul attached to the hood above her head. Pierre stood guard nearby, his sturdy little legs firmly planted as he waved his arms menacingly and echoed the eagle's screams.

We had already lost several hens to the eagle but it was only after the daring attack on the cradle that we learned that eagles had been known to carry off cats and even small new-born lambs.

He never again came close to the terrace, but continued to voice his disapproval of our defense tactics as he circled and soared in the blue sky above us.

December 10, 1941 (letter to sister)

Dearest Barbie,

News of the attack on Pearl Harbor and war with Japan has stunned us all. We listen to the radio like people in a dream… I should say nightmare. What will happen now? So much of our navy has been destroyed, there will be no way to stop them… except by air. I wonder how much real news we get. Even news of Pearl Harbor is sifted through to us as though it was no concern of the European continent… Just another horror story.

Still no news from you. I wonder if this letter will reach you. They will probably close all the frontiers and harbors now that America is in the war. I will send this right away before the ports are blockaded.

Don't worry about us. I'm so glad we are here in the chalet. We feel confident that it is safer for survival than being in the South where food is so scarce. Here we have shelter, adequate food, and we, hopefully, have enough wood… which after all are the fundamentals. We will have to learn to get along without things we thought were necessities, like shoes and store-bought clothes.

Paul says he might find a way to get the news to you through the diplomatic pouch but I think it's pretty doubtful. I am contacting the consulate to see if we can get money from my bank in America. We really don't need much, since there is nothing to buy anyway. If Philip could manage to get 150 dollars to us every one or two months, I think we could manage.

The biggest item in the budget is the train fare for Paul who must get around to find work somewhere. His chances for jobs are slim. Who would want to venture money in any architectural schemes during war time? He has been writing articles for a local newspaper. But even they feel the crunch, and are getting thinner and rarer as paper gets scarce.

We are fine... together and safe... I miss you already thinking of the bleak times when no letters will come from you.

Dearest love to all the family... until better times.

In the refugee crises of these last few years, the only item of vital importance for anyone to have, more critical than anything—has been a cellphone. Families have carried their children, slinging their backpack with anything they could carry...and a cellphone, their vital link to family or friends who could help them or stay in touch. In the dark days of World War II, before the internet, our most essential link to one another was the mail—which could be sporadic and infrequent as normal life was anything but normal.

As Papa tried to generate interest in his ideas, he was confronted with the hard reality of a world preoccupied with the more mundane aspects of simply staying safe. He could farm—and he did, becoming even more expert than his peasant neighbors who had farmed the same land for generations. He could write about his discoveries—and he did, though his ideas had little audience in time of war. He felt he had no choice but to continue to travel to whomever might listen to him, wherever he might find meaningful work.

I suspect he traveled as an excuse and an escape from his sense of failure as a man capable of caring for his family. What did he do on so many long trips that were so expensive to take by rail? What did he have to show for his efforts? He could come home to his wife and tell her of all the interesting people he had met and the important contacts he had made; and the ephemeral promise of future work always dangled before both...for after the war. Always after the war...

After the refugee housing fell through, he persisted anyway in his efforts to find architectural work. Wherever he went, he was well received and gradually became the leading authority on housing in France. He took quantities of photos and made sketches of all he observed. The plan was to write a definitive book on the subject—but who would finance such an effort in wartime?

In 1943, he was asked to begin a school for architects in Nice. His contacts assured him that this could be a viable enterprise and that he would have enough students to pay his travel and living expenses. It would be worth the effort, he thought, to leave the chalet and his family for a time while he got the school up and started. He managed to get six students willing and able to pay for that first year. He would be gone from the chalet—again, this time for the whole year. Mama was on her own, again.

I continue to be baffled by the relationship my parents maintained, especially during the war. They were apart much of the time, yet seemed to preserve a deep and abiding love that endured through all their trials. And as the family grew, the challenges multiplied with every additional mouth crying to be fed.

I wonder, sometimes, if Mama was a saint or a fool. How did they manage, I pondered, when the borders were closed and the mails stopped and she could no longer get funds from her "Fort Knox" in New Jersey? Did Papa ever earn enough from all his efforts?

I had discovered Mama's journal in the attic, in a box with mementos of her childhood: a beaded bag from the Flapper era, a lace shawl that she picked up somewhere, photographs of her with her sisters, even a family Bible, and at the bottom, a plain manila envelope of the type used to store things like old tax returns, or possibly receipts or bank statements. I was surprised that I had forgotten about the contents of this box—which Joe had labeled, in his characteristic bold print, "MAMA'S WRITINGS".

We've moved a few times and with every move there is always a box or two that never gets unpacked. This one was particularly mystifying for me because it contained stuff I didn't really know what to do with. I wanted to keep all these remnants of Mama's past, but I'd already sorted through the important memorabilia, I thought. This stuff defied categorization—or was it simply too obscure for me to revisit and understand? What was I to do with a beaded bag which was gradually disintegrating? Or a black lace shawl? Even the family Bible could stay in the box for now. But the photos—and the fat manila envelope cried out for further examination now.

Maybe I would finally discover answers to the perplexing mystery of my parents' life together. Perhaps I might even begin to appreciate them better, through a filter of maturity, and hopefully more wisdom.

After my shameful behavior in Houston, it took me years to come back to Mama, to make amends. And in the meantime, my two sisters filled the void for her. They speak of painful journal entries, Rona especially, in which Mama describes her confusion over what I had done. Rona wouldn't show me these journals of Mama. "It would hurt you too much," she said. And Betty has only shared the photos she has kept over the years. In these small ways, I am bereft.

I had always thought I would finally have the courage, someday, to really spend time with the contents of that manila envelope. I can use the excuse that life just got in the way and the whole box ended up in one attic after another, in all the moves Joe and I made over the years. The manila envelope would be there, at the bottom of the box, silently waiting for me to hear Mama's voice again through the words she wrote in her elegant, spidery handwriting.

And now, someday was here. Mama was gone, but some of her essence was locked in the contents of that envelope. What would I find that perhaps I didn't already know?

The journal was a diary of the war years, as Mama understood them. Reading her entries was like hearing the stories she had told us so many times of what those days were like for our family as well as most families that were caught in the maelstrom. There were some notes that were copies of letters she wrote to her sisters— perhaps sent, perhaps not. Though all those pages were neatly typewritten—not in her own hand, as I had expected, Mama came alive for me that afternoon, in a way I had not anticipated.

January 1942
Journal Entry -Father Christmas

We think of Christmas in our French Alpine chalet as very special because we have the very best ingredients to make it so... several small children, snow, a plentiful forest of fir trees nearby and, as international parents, we can choose the best of two Christmas traditions from our Franco-American forebears.

Christmas this year was meager but very happy. We had a Christmas tree from the communal forest and we made garlands from Paul's office supply of paper. Though we had nothing to put under the tree, we had a festive meal with a roast of venison that Monsieur Gué, our neighbor, had brought home from a hunt on the cliffs of the Criou.

After marinating it for a long time in a mixture of spices and wine, Paul prepared it in a pot surrounded by vegetables. For dessert we had crême de Mocha - - having saved sugar and all our ¼ pound of coffee rations for the event.

It reminded me of our first Christmas in the chalet before the war when the two elder boys were four and three and the baby, whose whole world was still a universe of wide-eyed wonder, was a fifteen month little girl.

We had come from Paris to spend Christmas in the mountains.

In our Alpine retreat away from the bustle of Paris we welcome the hush of the new fallen snow, the wind sighing in the tops of the fir trees and the whining scream of eagles circling above us. Each morning the sun rises above the mountain peaks sifting through the tracery of the upper branches like enormous Christmas stars giving radiance and warmth to the chalets sheltered under a blanket of snow. We are refreshed by the serenity and cleanness of winter in the mountains that hide any reminder of the noisy city we left behind.

The boys are delighted and tumble and roll in the snow banks. They invented sleds with dish pans and wash pot covers. Their new six year old neighbor Dédé came to visit on his barrel-stave skis the morning after our arrival, promising to give the boys skiing lessons, but within an hour he too joined the dishpan sled parade.

That evening when the children were in bed, we planned their Christmas. I made them sweaters, but the big prize was a package from America with a teddy bear for each boy and a doll for Sally Anne. I told the boys about Santa Claus and they knew all about Comet and Vixen and Donner and Blitzen and the sleigh bells as the reindeer soar over the roofs on Christmas Eve.

They also knew all about Saint Nicholas with his shepherd staff who comes to see all good little French children to fill their shoes with goodies. They accepted both stories and seemed not a bit confused.

The day before Christmas was a big day. Paul put on his skis and seal ski runners to climb the slope behind the chalet where we, as residents of the valley, are permitted to get our firewood...and our Christmas tree. It was to be decorated with tinsel and paper garlands that the children had prepared one snowy day.

The children took off their shoes early that day and together we cleaned and polished them to be ready for Saint Nicholas. We sent out invitations to all the neighbors' children who could reach our chalet on foot or on ski to come to a small party at three the following afternoon. Mountains of small tarts filled with jam that I made days before were waiting in hidden security. I also made a long red coat for Saint Nicholas trimmed with white cotton fur like Santa Claus.

A white cotton beard and a skating cap borrowed from Miqué, our oldest, completed his Father Christmas costume.

It was quite late that night when Santa Claus- Saint Nicholas... was ready to visit the children, bells jingling on the belt of his costume. I went to awaken the children.

"Miqué, Jean... do you hear the bells... He has come to see you."

They were wide-eyed with excitement as Santa Claus pushed open the door and went to each bed to speak to them.

"Have you been a good boy, Miqué?"

Miqué stared in awe. Santa Claus spoke to him in English with a strong French accent.

It bothered him not a bit. A shy "yes" was all he could answer as Santa Claus handed him his teddy bear.

"Hello Jean, I hear you have been a good boy too," said this French version of Santa Claus.

"Thank you, merci beaucoup monsieur," answered Jean whose manners even at three were above par. Santa

Claus asked them if they liked bears, but they were too astonished to do anything but stare and giggle and clutch their teddy bears.

Santa Claus put the little doll on Sally Anne's pillow but did not awaken her.

The next morning the boys could hardly wait too tell me about their nighttime visitor and to show me the bears he had brought.

Sally Anne was already snug under the table undressing her new doll. Her voice rose and fell intoning maternal tenderness as she sat totally oblivious to the hubbub around her.

That afternoon at 2:15 the crowd of children began arriving for the party. It was probably the first and only party they had ever been to.

We set up a long drawing board on two carpentry horses and at exactly three o'clock we opened the door to seventeen neatly scrubbed children. They took their places quietly, the boys very politely taking off their caps as they sat on benches around the table. The small mountains of jam tarts disappeared quickly. The oranges presented more of a problem. Many of them had never seen an orange and bit into the skin. The chewing gum which had come in a package from America was also a new adventure. Two little girls swallowed theirs and were heartbroken to discover that they could have chewed all afternoon.

As they left the party, each one said a shy, "merci beaucoup, Madame", and hurried home before dark.

We heard echoes of the Grillo's Christmas party for weeks afterwards.

This year of 1941 the war made it impossible to find any of the little goodies that make Christmas a special festivity for children all over the world.

This year there are five small children and not much to celebrate. Paul found skis for the boys and I made a blanket for Sally Anne's bear. Even the socks, mittens and sweaters I had knitted were an unexpected bonus.

I remember those sweaters. We each kept them for our own children, so many years later. I remember that Mama learned to cure and spin the wool from our shorn sheep. She would mix that with yarn from other, threadbare sweaters that she painstakingly restored, to use again. The front of the sweaters had a checkerboard pattern of squares of new wool blended with the colored yarns of the old sweaters. Now, among the family treasures that have disappeared, except in memory.

Journal Entry, 1942

Still no news from home. We feel very isolated. News is difficult to hear on our little radio that we smuggled in under a pile of diapers years ago. It cracks and spits, but the stress of age is further complicated by the jamming used to cover broadcasts we are not supposed to listen to.

What rumors we do get are probably distorted and manipulated to try to make us believe that we are fortunate to be under foreign domination. The Japanese crisis in Pearl Harbor was minimized as though it belonged to the history of a planet in outer space. But as an American I feel the humiliation of such an overwhelming disaster.

This may continue to be a journal if the mails are permanently blocked. Our isolation from the outside world makes us very aware of our good fortune to be here, where we are somewhat able to be masters of our own destiny.

Our days, though ruled by the routine of farming have a kind of honeymoon closeness. When Paul gets up and leaves me with a quick good morning kiss, it is to start the fire while I lie in bed a few more luxurious moments. All those familiar noises tell me when I must move to join him to start our day together. I listen as he lifts the iron rings and wait to hear them clank on the hearth under the stove. I hear the breaking of small twigs as he lays them carefully among the warm embers of last night's fire. Then the grate door opens and I know he is crouched on the floor looking for a faint glow to light this one piece of paper... I hear the rapid swish, swish as he waves it to fan the sleeping embers, followed by gentle blowing in exactly the right place to awaken the flame... patience... it still will not light. Will he have to use a match? We have so few. No... more gentle blowing alternating with the swishing of the paper. After what seems an interminable time I hear the crackle of a twig as the flame ignites it and the grate closes.

Paul lifts the rings again to place the driest piece of wood he can find. As he comes back to get dressed I can hear the fire now roaring briskly. In seven minutes the chalet will be as warm as if central heating were the commanding presence. He comes back to give me a proper wake-up kiss as I leave the warm covers.

We, like the peasants around us, have a long day ahead. We are learning to appreciate the dogged perseverance of our neighbors whose work never ends. They grumble about basic freedoms that have been taken away: portions of their livestock or crops they can no longer call their own. They don't realize how lucky we all are to be able to raise our own food.

For us, the year unfolds its seasons. Each day we learn the changes they bring to the lives of our neighbors whose model of living we are trying to understand and follow. Though we live under the storm clouds of war, our days of seasonal routine are brightened by the excitement of the alternating pattern of brilliant sunshine under a cobalt blue sky quickly changing to heavy black storm clouds that dump their burden in a downpour of rain, hail or snow. As the weather varies, so must our tasks in the peasant role which we have adopted. Like the farmers around us we watch the sky to find the rhythm of work to the mood of the weather.

In summer the hay must be mowed, stacked and brought into the hayloft when the weather promises a series of fine days. In the fall the plowing and planting of the winter wheat must be timed so that the earth is still warm enough to encourage it to sprout, but not drenched to rot it in the ground. Every day is a new adventure of learning as we examine the signs of nature to give us the barometric reading for the day.

The view from the window above the kitchen sink changes with the flow of the seasons. The chalet faces south, opposite the seven mountains from which the village of Samoens was named.

Sunlight is rare on the northern slopes and farms are relatively few. Virgin forest, rising in random clumps of dark green until it reaches the timberline, covers most of the mountain, interrupted by rocky crags where vegetation cannot cling. Only the summits catch fleeting glimpses of sunshine.

The approach of winter brings Nature's phenomenon of the high altitudes. From late October until mid-December the air is still. The sky is a deep brilliant blue, as a sea of clouds settles over the Alpine valleys. All civilization disappears under a heavy blanket of impenetrable fog so thick that descending into it is like stepping into billows of cold wet down. The sun beats down on the snow and fog which blend into a shining white floor from which the high mountain peaks thrust a sharp outline of rocky grandeur. The Pointe de Sales to the east locks the end of the valley with its perpendicular precipice rising against the background of the silvery dome of the distant Mont Blanc.

The only movement in that winter stillness is the lazy flight of eagles soaring and gliding in everlasting circles above the blanketed valley. Only the sound of their screaming breaks the hush of winter stillness, as the mountains rise like silent sentinels keeping watch above a hidden world.

We are soon buried in snow, almost six feet of it on the roof. We had to have some of it shoveled off because of the weight on the supporting beams. This has been a very cold winter.

Except for the temperature which hovers at zero Fahrenheit outdoors and around 43 indoors we live in comparative comfort. We have so little wood that we can light the fire only for cooking. We all wear ski pants and several sweaters. Pierre, the only Savoyard in the bunch, is always frozen.

I have to put him in bed with a bottle filled with hot water to keep him warm. Nothing fazes the others who all have cheeks as red as circus clowns, and run in and out no matter what the weather.

Even when we are in a deep fog they ski in front of the chalet. They go to school on skis now that we at last have a teacher.

But Papa was gone so much of the time. He left the family for weeks, sometimes months. When he was there, I could see by her entries that he was utterly committed to his family and in particular his patient wife. There was wholeness to their marriage that made all the privation and hardship of wartime almost insignificant as they faced the many sacrifices and hardships together, as an enduring team.

But the more I read, the more I realized that she was an observer and had subsumed her essence, in favor of her husband and her children. Her voice became an echo, no longer her own, as she wrote of what she understood her husband was going through for the sake of his family. When she wrote about any of us, it was to marvel at who we were becoming—interesting, amusing, bright and wonderful. Where was she? Who was she? Even as she struggled with the hardship of simply surviving, she seemed to be telling a story that was outside of herself.

> "Paul is still trying to reform everything he thinks needs it. He writes articles all over the place, and letters to all kinds of people. Such inexhaustible enthusiasm should be rewarded, but after all these years of effort, he still meets with discouragement. The things he writes always surprise people from so young a man. When he appears on the scene with his teen-age smile and youthful step, everyone is astonished. He always manages to make an excellent impression. Then a week or so later, all those influential people fade away and he has to start impressing the new batch that comes to replace them. He has so much to say! It all makes so much sense!"
>
> On another page, she commented, "Paul has more to be pessimistic about than I, but he never looks back and never dwells on the blackness of the present, but seems to be guided by the hope of a brilliant future. At present, he can find absolutely no work, and no hope of finding any so he is working in the garden. From dawn to dusk, he works steadily. He planted as much of everything he could find seed for: potatoes, dried beans, vegetables of every sort. He carries compost from one terrace to another. He even tried grafting a tomato onto a potato plant to try to deceive a possible thief. He is very, very thin now..."

And finally, I found her voice. Dated vaguely in the spring of 1943, she spoke with a shy intimacy and vulnerability that brought me to wish I could touch her hand, or hold her close in a way I never had been able to when she was still alive.

> "The days and nights are long while Paul is away. His life is so active, it makes me feel dull. He writes of the many people he is meeting and the projects he is planning. And I wonder how he can be happy to come home to the children and me, to a life of hard work and routine. What can I say, or do to interest a man whose dreams are all beyond the horizons of our mountains, in a world of fascinating people?
>
> His letters, so buoyant and full of hope for our future, seem to me to be impossible dreams. He knows his skills and has confidence in his talent but always underestimates the limitations that will inevitably restrict him, multiplied a hundred times by this war.

What should be my role to help him? I have great confidence in his ability. So how can I possibly put a damper on his enthusiasm—and crush his faith in me? What do I know of that world of professionals he moves among? Will his magnetism stimulate them to back him in his projects? What I see is that with every wall he tears down, he faces another even higher..."

And then, I found a letter folded carefully between two pages. It was from Papa, and it seemed to be a response to her despair.

"I'm coming home," he wrote. "We have had a good year in the school, but the students have gone into the Maquis, one by one to be a part of the Resistance. I have made many useful contacts but all the planned projects will have to wait. Life is at a standstill here: no more cement, wood or steel. No way to transport the snips of materials available. I have met with a man from the League of Nations. We are writing a brochure together about the cultivation of wheat...very interesting. I'll tell you all about it when I get home.

I am so anxious to get home. You sound discouraged, my sweet love. If you knew just once what you mean to me. You have such an influence in my life that I don't make a move without thinking to myself, 'what would Liv think of it? What advice would she give me?' Think how decisive was your counsel with just one letter some months ago. Come, come, my dearest, come back to the wonderful life our two international souls have woven with the very foam of angry seas and the dust of the northern winds, and think that it is only the beginning of a richer life, and more happiness to come when we are together again in our home."

I folded the flimsy yellowed paper along its timeworn creases and placed it carefully between the two journal pages. How those words must have resonated in her heart—in every fiber of her tired, anxious body.

I understood, finally, the power of their love—and the ineffable bond they shared together. Such a love is rare, I thought. Could I ever begin to understand it? I realized she was neither a saint, nor a fool in her life with Papa. They were two complementary souls who were only half if they couldn't be one whole—together.

– 12 –

THE CREATIVE CUISINE
OF NECESSITY

Spring and Summer 1942
Journal Entry

Though, of course, neither of us had ever worked on a farm before, we both enjoyed it. Paul liked to work outdoors and I took pleasure in anything we could do together. When he was working in the garden I did chores in the kitchen.

During the berry season we could climb the slopes together to sit under the bushes in the hot sun and pick blueberries or raspberries. His dexterity and speed always made me feel clumsy until I recognized that I was only normal and that his skill astonished everyone else too.

As summer approached we looked forward to being able to have feasts from the berries. The frequent spring rains followed by the short period of intense summer sunshine produced fruit that surpassed any that grew in lower and drier valleys.

Like housewives all over the world, the French put up garden vegetables and fruits and made jams and jellies. However, putting up preserves became impossible when mason jars and rubber were unavailable. Since there was no sugar to make jam or jellies, that too was out of the question.

It was because of these difficulties that Paul, in 1941, when we were still in the Midi, had written to the California Department of Agriculture to inquire about systems of preservation without refrigeration. The results were very rewarding.

In the Midi we had a fig tree whose branches towered above our little house in Golfe Juan.

It was because of the delicious figs from this tree that the information from California was so vital for us.

Figs that fell from those high branches invariably smashed, so we resorted to the method used in the area to bring them down. A ten to twelve foot bamboo pole slit four ways up to the first intersection was kept open by a pebble pushed into the opening. This gave just the amount of spring for the pole to grasp the fig and gently detach it from its stem. The unripe figs didn't yield to the pressure so that those we were able to gather were at the peak of maturity: soft, plum and very sweet.

Since our ration of sugar for our household of six, was limited to less than a pound per month, those figs were very precious and we decided to try to dry most of them.

According to the information from the California Agriculture Department, the preparation for drying differs with each fruit. Some, like plums or cherries, must be dipped in a solution of boiling water and caustic soda to soften the skins and open small "pores", so that air may penetrate more easily. Others, like figs, had to be fumigated with sulfur before being set out to dry in the sun.

Paul prepared a series of slatted trays on which he laid the figs. He made a depression in the ground into which he placed the bowl of sulfur. He put the trays over the bowl and covered them with an air-tight box. Cracks he sealed with mud. The enclosure had to be air-proof except for a small vent at one end to allow air to enter for the combustion of the sulfur. The fumes of the sulfur penetrated the fruit and destroyed bacteria to prevent mildew. The fruit remained in the fumes for several hours after which it was placed in the sun to dry. In the hot sun of the Midi, the figs dried in about a week or ten days. They had to be turned often and sheltered from insects by a screen.

We tried to make prunes out of plums but they refused to accept the fate of getting wrinkles. Instead, they shriveled around the pit, or rotted.

When we moved to the chalet in the fall of 1941, we had managed to find a whole case of delicious white grapes which we brought with us with the firm intention of keeping them as long as possible. Any slightly imperfect specimen went to the table for immediate consumption. Each perfect, undamaged bunch was dipped in a weak solution of water and paraffin. Thus any break, that we might not detect visually, was carefully sealed. Then with clothespins we hung them, well-spaced from each other on a cord stretched across the cellar.

We examined them often, being careful not to disturb them so that stem and grape would not separate. We were thus able to keep several bunches for over two months.

When the raspberry season arrived in the Alps we found no way to preserve them since we had no sugar to make jam or jelly. They were too fragile to preserve by the method we used with blueberries, the most successful venture of all. So naturally, we ate them as we picked them, a luscious fruit treat on the spot.

The blueberries of the Alps were large and delicious and when they were ripe, we hiked up the slopes to the blueberry patches with special scoops. In a few hours we returned with two ten gallon milk containers ¾ full of berries.

We adapted the method of preserving blueberries advised by the Agricultural Department to our own particular specifications.

Paul's mother had a big reserve of excellent wine which we consumed with amazing speed and pleasure. All the bottles and their corks were carefully put aside to await the blueberry season.

After washing and sorting out the unripe fruit, the remaining berries were set aside while we prepared the bottles. Into the neck of a bottle Paul placed a wick of sulfur and lit it. Sulfur fumes are a dark yellowish brown, and heavy, so that it was easy to watch them float, or rather sink throughout the bottle. When the bottle was completely full of sulfur fumes, I came with a funnel and the berries to pour into the narrow neck. As the berries passed through the funnel, the sulfur fumigated them. A second wick of sulfur was burned before sealing each bottle. To be sure that the corks were in tight, the corked bottles were dipped in melted paraffin. Thus preserved, the berries kept all winter long. Desserts of blueberries and cream were delicious and frequent. One bottle of blueberries, sweetened with a tablet of saccharin, was sufficient for the big events to make one delicious pie, using flour from our carefully rationed reserve of flour from before the war.

Spring sunshine and warmer days came at last. The winter had been long. As soon as the snow began to melt the children came home from school carrying their boots, jumping from one spot of dirt to the next one to avoid the lingering snow in the shaded areas. They were now wearing the only shoes available; the tops were made of some kind of pressed cardboard and had wooden soles. We had not been able to find nails to keep them from slipping and the snow piled up in great lumps on the wooden soles. As a result, the more daring of the children invented a game they called "ski-piote", by which they sailed down the mountainside as if on skates—or miniature skis.

The shoe tops folded at the back and made bleeding blisters on their heels. I said nothing when I saw them returning with their shoes hung around their necks but treated the blisters with a small bottle of glycerin that was our only medication during the war. Even three drops went a long way to soothe their sore feet. Somehow they never caught cold from walking home on ground still frozen solid.

Other problems began to catch up with us. The only soap we could find was a kind of cube of coagulated fine sand and even that was with tickets. Fortunately mountain water is very soft and the daily laundry of two dozen diapers and children's underwear was easy to handle. Sheets and shirts presented more of a problem which we circumvented by a long overnight soak in tepid water in the marble-slabbed tub. This was an ordeal undertaken only at two week intervals. Our neighbor, Madame Antonioz, was only too glad to take over this task until we discovered that her voluminous apron had become a catch-all for items she took a fancy to. When Paul's shirts began to disappear at an alarming rate we no longer called on our neighbor and the intervals between washing became even less frequent as the household chores were increased by this new burden.

Food shortages we could handle by drastically changing the menu. Until our potato crop was due, we would have to find some nourishing substitute: flour, rice, pasta, corn, meal, sugar, fats or carbohydrates of any kind were available only with tickets which allowed five slices of bread and two teaspoons of sugar (children only) per day. Butter, oil or margarine were too rare to consider as part of our diet.

Instead of using our very restricted bread rations for breakfast we made hot cereal, and thereby discovered the processes by which the big cereal companies prepare breakfast foods.

That first summer we were able to buy a few kilos of wheat from the farmers nearby. I did not feel we were depriving them because they preferred to sell it to us than to have it requisitioned by the occupying troops.

We found that wheat boiled several hours was edible and nourishing though not particularly tasty for the discerning palate...We tried grinding it in the coffee grinder, but though it was dry to the touch, the inside was soft and became a pulp which clogged in the coffee mill. This meant that the wheat would have to be thoroughly toasted before grinding it. The simplest way to do this was to spread the wheat on cookie sheets and place it under the Franklin stove. A few stirrings every three or four hours to see that the grains were toasting evenly and they soon became crisp enough to go through the coffee grinder. Cooked and served with milk from the dairy, it made a delicious whole wheat breakfast food.

Encouraged by this success, we tried one step further and soon came up with a delicious malt breakfast cereal. Malt is nothing more than sprouted grain which we produced by spreading wheat grains on a moist towel. Again the cookie sheets went under the stove. We were careful to keep the towel moist and after 3 or 4 days the wheat sprouted. When the sprouts were about 3/8 of an inch long we removed the towel and let the wheat get crisp enough to grind. This was the favorite breakfast cereal but since its preparation was longer we served it on special occasions only.

A third cereal was oatmeal which appeared on our table regularly, often in the soup for dinner. It was by far the easiest to prepare, the cheapest and the most nourishing. Oats bought at a horse feed store could be obtained without tickets and were identical to Quaker Oats except for the bran which had to be rinsed away. The oats had to be washed several times to let all the bran and chaff float to the top to be siphoned off. The cost per meal averaged about one cent a day for the whole household.

The breakfast beverage was more of a problem. We were allotted about five ounces of coffee beans a month, totally insufficient, of course, for morning coffee. There was also a synthetic breakfast beverage sold on the black market that tasted like Postum but was very expensive. Most farmers added their coffee rations to this synthetic beverage to make a semblance of coffee. We, however, thought we would try to imitate it ourselves. Postum is nothing other than roasted wheat with some molasses added. We had no molasses but perhaps roasted wheat grains alone would make a satisfactory imitation. To roast wheat requires a very strong heat so our system of toasting under the stove was insufficient.

However, among the family heirlooms was a coffee bean roaster which we put to use with our wheat. It consisted of a sheet iron pot in which four blades revolved perpendicularly to a spindle in the center. A handle in the sealed cover, screwed to the spindle inside, regulated the movement of the four blades. The fire had to be very hot, but not so hot as to char the exterior before the core of the grain was roasted. This meant that the grains of wheat had to be continually moving. We soon became quite adept and though our breakfast beverage did not taste like coffee we sometimes added chicory which was available without tickets to remind us of the taste of coffee.

What we were drinking was a kind of Postum which many people drink instead of Sanka. The Postum, dissolved in hot milk, did not require sugar and tasted a little like French café au lait.

Perhaps because hunger is the best appetizer, breakfast in the chalet was a very special meal.

As I read this meticulously detailed account of some of the ingenious methods devised by our parents in basic food preparation, I realized how much they partnered together in all their endeavors. In so many ways, they seemed undaunted by their circumstances, instead embracing each new problem as a fresh challenge to be conquered. And I marvel as I remember that they both came from a background of ease and comfort and never had to be bothered by issues such as lack of refrigerators or stoves or basic necessities.

Today, when I make jam, or bread, or soap, or put up my tomatoes in the summer, my parents are with me in the kitchen, guiding my steps. But it is so much easier for me. I can Google my question if I'm not sure of a recipe or a process. I have a large refrigerator and a freezer and of course, a stove and oven. I have all sorts of small appliances and devices that make my job a breeze. And if I need an ingredient, I can hop in the car and drive to the supermarket a couple of miles away.

Worse than living like pioneers, they had to cope with increasing shortages of anything and everything they needed. Everything they did had to be thoroughly thought through before they could begin to attempt it. And through trial and error, they often succeeded—and often failed.

We spent almost five years in the mountains—until the war in Europe was finally over and victory was declared on May 8th, 1945.

Of course, I had to Google the exact date, since that kind of thing is elusive for me. But I do remember in particular that it was a momentous day that had all the neighbors buzzing in happy excitement. All my brothers and I could understand was that Mama had said that when the war was over, we'd be able to have candy again—though we weren't quite sure what that meant—except it must be good.

"Can we go to the village, can we go to *Samoëns* and buy some candy now?" We couldn't contain ourselves and finally Mama relented and we trooped down together, my brothers and I, and gave the man the coins she had given each of us. I was very proud, because she gave me an extra *centime,* a penny, so that I could bring some candy back for Betty, who was still too small to go with us. The man gave us each a cone half filled with little sour balls. I carefully clutched the extra cone for Betty.

My memories of those years are often crystal clear, yet also fuzzed over by time.

We settled into the rhythm of peasant farm life in the mountains. There was a cow, though she was sickly and didn't give much milk, so that it eventually became my job to take the aluminum can on my back and walk down the mountain to the next farm. The warm milk, straight from the cow, was poured into my can and the farmer helped me strap it to my back. I could then climb back up to our chalet with both hands free.

We lived so high that the clouds often gathered below us; *La Mère de Nuage,* the "sea of clouds", the farmers called it.

Mama recalled a particularly harrowing experience. She described it in one of her journal entries of our time in the chalet.

The Chalet, Winter, 1943
Journal Entry

It was during this second year in the chalet that we learned of the treachery of the weather.

One crisp, clear day of February the sun rose bright and warm on the white blanket of winter snow. The sky was cloudless except for a small cloud hanging over Mont Blanc in the distance. Paul was home from Nice.

"I have to phone Geneva. If you could come with me we could do the errands together,"Paul told me.

We put on our skis to take advantage of the fine weather leaving Paulette with the smaller children and telling her to make sure that the boys set off for school in plenty of time for the nine A.M. opening.

The descent was rapid and uneventful, but on reaching the village we noticed the sky had begun to darken with heavy clouds. Paul went to the post office to phone as I hurried through the errands. We started the climb back up the mountain before 10 o'clock.

Snow had begun to fall. Paul led the way. I worried about the boys. Had they gone to school before the snow began to fall? How would they get home if it continued all day?

We were heavily laden with back packs and skis over our shoulders... no use putting on skis in this heavy snow.

Hoping to make the trip as quickly as possible we took the short cut, steep but much more direct. The snow continued to fall, now no longer in flakes but in heavy, wet splotches.

"I'm taking shorter strides so that you can step in my tracks. We'll go slowly but we'd better not stop," Paul warned me.

The snow was soon ten inches deep and still coming down making visibility close to zero.

"Where are we?" I shouted.

"Approaching Mathonex," he called back, but his voice sounded dim and distant, muffled by the thick gray veil floating around us.

We plodded on. As we gained altitude the snow was deeper and falling faster. At each step we sank to knee depth and the pace was very slow. After an interminable length of time, lifting each foot and placing it in the track ahead, Paul turned,

"We're about half way now. Are you all right?"

"I'm fine. Do you think Paulette sent the children to school?"

"Even if she did, they're all right. They would be glad to ski down in fresh snow."

"But how about coming back?"

"Don't worry. Renée will keep them at the school if this goes on all day."

I did not answer. We needed every breath to keep moving.

The day wore on. It seemed hours. Lift one foot, place it in the next foot print... over and over, each step accompanied by rhythmic panting, pulling ourselves up the steep slope.

"Where are we now?"

"I think we're just below Les Turches, but it's hard to tell. I'll stop at a chalet if we pass one and ask."

I again said nothing. Paul had an unfailing sense of direction. How could he even doubt where we were? The sky had long since disappeared and our horizon on all sides was limited to a few feet. Even Paul, four feet ahead of me was a gray blob in the lazy floating, veil of snow that seemed not to land anywhere. It just grew underfoot.

We came to a chalet.

"Stay here, don't move. I'll go in and find out where we are."

I leaned on my ski poles watching him move away, a dark shadow being swallowed by the falling snow.

In a minute his voice called out to me from the lighted doorway.

"Madame Corbet wants to offer us coffee. Do you want to come in?"

"I'd rather not, but thank her... Merci, Madame," I repeated as she appeared in the doorway.

"Merci encore, Madame," said Paul, and as the door closed we continued our climb.

"We are right on track," said Paul. "We'll soon be home... another half hour or more perhaps."

But it was almost two hours before we glimpsed the chalet. Paul was now almost hip deep at every step.

Paulette had hung a lantern outside to guide us through the early darkness. It was almost four o'clock... six hours for the trip we generally made in an hour and a half.

Paulette met us at the door.

"Are the children all right?" I asked not even waiting to greet her.

"Oui Madame, they're fine now.'"

Paul was talking to Miqué who was recounting the day's event.

"... so Paulette went to get André Antonioz to help." I heard him say.

"What happened? Where is Jean? Is he hurt?"

Paulette interrupted to reassure me and to tell us what had happened.

"I wanted to keep them home. The clouds were bad and it began to snow, they wanted to ski, so a little after nine I let them go and watched them as they went over the ridge down there."

She pointed to the spot we had named Les Deux Pierres, the landmark which marked the approach to the last hill before reaching the chalet.

She continued, "I went back inside and was cleaning up when Miqué came back about a half hour later..."

"What's the matter? Where's Jean?" I asked him.

"He's down there, stuck in a snow bank."

"What do you mean?"

"He really is stuck. He tried to jump the bank where the road is and he fell and the snow came down on top of him."

"Didn't you try to get him out?"

"Sure, but he's stuck. His skis are tangled and he's upside down."

This was the graphic description eight year old Miqué was telling Paulette about his seven year old brother trapped in a snow bank.

Paulette did not wait to hear more but ran to get help. André Antonioz went down and dug out the young skier. Except for having twisted his ankle and being wet and cold from being buried under a three foot avalanche, Jean was none the worse for his adventure. He and Miqué shared the glory we showered on them... Miqué for having come home to get help, and Jean for being brave while he waited... Paulette too came in for a very large share of praise. She had reacted quickly in an emergency.

That day was the first day of a steady two week snowfall. The snow fell silent and mysterious. It did not come down in large crystalline flakes, but filled the air like a gray veil, and floated like a palpable fog. There was no wind. Familiar landmarks disappeared as the white blanket rose to cover the land. Imperceptibly the horizon met the leaden sky and disappeared. We found ourselves enclosed by a high wall, buried within a cocoon of snow.

When at last the sun reappeared, it filtered through the snow bank outside our windows with a pale translucent light. Like Noah after the flood we ventured outdoors to discover that we had to negotiate an eight foot bank of snow before we could survey the scene around us. The brilliance of the white snow against the dark, almost purple sky was more dazzling than the sun. Our neighbors' familiar chalets were buried, rolling mounds in the stark expanse of whiteness. Only the tracery of smoke rising above the Gué chalet signaled that we were not alone.

We were to learn later that an early morning bonnet-like cloud on Mount Blanc is an unfailing signal for bad weather. In winter it is particularly dangerous because the snow it predicts can be a disastrous blizzard lasting two or three weeks.

We had fourteen sheep, a goat (sweet Bibine) who was the shepherd and leader of the sheep, a cow that didn't give much milk, and a very undersized pig which never really grew to be a hog. Papa sheared the sheep so that Mama could spin the wool and make sweaters for us. I remember sitting at her feet, as I learned to sew.

Mama became skilled and dexterous as her foot moved steadily on the foot pedal, the spinning wheel whirring, and her hand over hand movements flowing with ease as she wrapped the yarn into an increasingly large ball of wool.

For someone who had lived her life in easy privilege, never to be concerned about a roof over her head or a meal on the table, she adjusted to her current circumstances with strength and grace, and remarkable determination. She purchased her spinning wheel from one of the neighbors, and was taught the timeless art of taking raw wool from the sheep, to finally spin it into a fat ball of soft yarn. She washed the raw wool in the grainy, ashy soap that she learned to make. She carded it with the paddles her neighbor had also taught her to use. She spun the mounds of fluffy wool into even strands of yarn that became the large ball in her lap. She unraveled old sweaters and combined their threads with her own new yarn, to be knitted together. She created checkered patterns and designs in the fronts of the new sweaters she made.

Old and tattered sheets became shirts or pillow cases, or

diapers. She took a velvet curtain and made a dress for me to wear to a wedding in the village.

She learned to make *Sérac* something we all detested, even though she said it was nourishing and good for us. When she made cheese, this was the watery whey left from the curd, which she would mix together so that it was like thin gray cottage cheese, completely without taste.

When she could, she made jam, sweetening it with honey from our bees, since sugar was so scarce. All the cooking she did was done on the Franklin stove, which also served to heat the chalet.

One particularly memorable event was the time Papa's mother, our grandmother, Mamette, came up from Paris for a visit. It was already a challenge to feed all of us, but now, we would have our aristocratic grandmother for a guest. What to do? We had no meat, but many vegetables from Papa's bounteous garden.

The Chalet, and Civet de Lapin
Journal Entry

Paul's mother was coming from Paris where she had been living with her daughter since the death of her husband. Conditions in Paris as in all urban areas of France were desperate and often tragic. Marguerite, Paul's sister, had patients whose lives had been shattered. Mothers who had cracked under the strain were in asylums, their children in orphanages. Elderly parents, unable to face both hunger and a bitter Paris winter in unheated rooms had died or were too weak to care.

Paul's mother had lost 25 pounds, her health was poor and we were looking forward to helping her recuperate in the mountains.

When we returned to the chalet in the Fall of 1941 we were struck by the fresh greenness of the valleys. Nature had been bountiful, supplying alternating rain and sunshine. Life, though restricted, was much closer to normal than in the South where resignation left a pall of sorrow on a once joyful people. In the Alps there were animals. Each farm had cows, sheep and a pig. There were still horses and mules on the farms. Each peasant home still had a dog lying in the sun twitching his ears to flick off the tormenting flies. There were cats daintily stepping in and out of doorways or hovering, poised and silent over a mole hole in the fields.

Like our neighbors we too had a cat. Since she was a female cat, the nearby tomcats often came to pay her their respects. One of our neighbors, the Pacots, had an enormous black cat.

We had assumed that he came to visit us only because we had a female cat. He would come to the kitchen door, stretch a tentative paw across the threshold and glare at whoever was in the kitchen; at which point Paulette, our housekeeper, or one of the children would scream and pounce at him and he would vanish without a trace... momentarily. He was not easily discouraged and though patience is supposed to be a virtue we were to learn that patience in a gluttonous philandering tomcat rewards only the cat. Stealth and evil intention lurked in his whole makeup.

Our farm was giving us vegetables, potatoes and milk but we had a great difficulty finding protein. Cheese was minimal and with tickets only. Meat was available only by slaughtering a farm animal which we could not spare.

We had saved cream and made butter from it. The four precious tablespoons of butter were safely locked away in a kitchen cabinet awaiting Mamette's arrival. We planned to make a special dessert for Paul's mother but the black tomcat must have known there was a special dainty behind the locked door. He also knew that if he waited long enough someone would open that door and forget to close it. One day the inevitable happened and when Paulette returned from a short errand she came back to find the door ajar, a broken plate on the floor, and the black tail of a cat flashing through the door.

The children, who were our main source for local news, told us that all our neighbors too had been pillaged by the black thief and were out to get him. But it was Madame Pacot who was more than ready for action and it was not with too much surprise that we learned the villain had met his demise at the end of her broom stick with a thrashing that had been building up for months.

When Paul heard the news he said, "Burying that cat is too good for him. He should be enjoyed as the main course of Mamette's welcoming meal."

"Mamette would never eat a cat!" I exclaimed, incredulous.

"She will never know. I'll make a "Civet de Lapin." The bone structures of a rabbit and a cat are very similar."

Marie Pacot brought the animal that evening and Paul proceeded to prepare the festive meal.

He put it in a marinade of wine and spices, turning each piece for hours, until the meat had acquired a deep rosy glow.

When Mamette came through the door, she was greeted by the tempting aroma of Paul's "rabbit stew" gently simmering on the stove.

"What are you cooking?" she asked. "It smells delicious.'

She approached the stove and lifted the cover of the fragrant stew.

"A civet (meat stew)," she exclaimed. "I didn't know the farmers here raised rabbits."

"Some do," I remarked.

"This is rather a special animal," Paul commented.

"Yes," I went on, "he was even known to neighbors because he was so big and fat."

"Perhaps the owners gave him extra ratios, like the force-fed gees of Alsace," Mamette observed admiringly as she lifted a succulent morsel of meat with a fork and turned it in the bubbling stew juice.

"Well," I wouldn't say he had been 'gavé' (force-fed)," said Paul.

"No," I intervened. "Let's say rather that he just found a way to thrive better than average farm animals."

Mamette replaced the cover, still marveling at the size and plumpness of the big chunks of meat simmering in the pot.

The meal that evening was indeed festive, with hors d'oeuvres of radishes, beets and deviled eggs. The civet, served with mashed potatoes, was delicious and Mamette asked for the recipe.

Paul was eager to oblige, giving an accurate resumé of the spices and wines that had gone into the stew.

It was not until the following year that she learned she had eaten a "civet de chat." By that time it was too late to regret it.

This story has become one of the favorite folktales I tell again and again, of some of our adventures in the chalet, high in the Alps, where we stayed safe and happy during the war.

— 13 —

DREAMING DREAMS

In turn, Mama spoke often of life in America. We liked to sit near her, as we listened in rapt attention. We gathered near the pot-bellied stove, the source of heat as well as where the meals were made. The coals glowed through the grate, sending a wave of comfort and peace as well as warmth. In those times, as I struggled with the needle and thread, I was overcome with admiration for my mother. Mama was, in fact, the center of my world, the person I most wanted to emulate. Everything I knew, I felt that I was learning it from my mother. Now Mama was telling another story about America, and how different it was from everything we knew in our little world.

"Do you know," she began, "that in America, we buy bread in a store. The bread is soft, and it's sliced, and it comes in a bag! And you can buy everything in the same store. You buy milk, which comes in a glass bottle. You buy cereal—you don't even know what that is, do you? Cereal in America usually comes in a box, and it looks like flakes—like petals, sort of…"she was having difficulty describing simple things for which we had no easy frame of reference.

She tried to describe candy. She became more animated, her eyes sparkling, the ball of yarn forgotten as her birdlike hands flew in quick animation, as she talked of the wonders of America. Her middle-class America was more than another country. She made it the essence of yearning, the land of promise, and the place of plenty. And yet, as she spoke of these wondrous things, there never seemed to be the sense that she was unhappy where she was, high up in the mountains, with a pot-bellied stove to keep everyone warm.

As bedtime neared, we took turns standing on the dining table, arms outstretched, as she had each of us turn slowly while she wrapped a blanket tightly under our arms. In the meantime, if he wasn't on one of his frequent trips, Papa would have put a few smoldering coals in the long-handled copper brazier, closed the lid, and then passed it between the sheets of each of the beds, warming them in preparation. We stood in an obedient line, wrapped to our chests in our blankets, waiting for him to carry each of us to bed. We all slept together in what had once been the cheese cellar. The stone walls were always icy in winter and damp in summer. Mama came in then, and tucked each of us in. She took our pillows, each in turn, and fluffed them around our waiting faces, giving us "rabbit ears".

When my own children were small, they learned of the "rabbit ears". And now, my grandchildren have been comforted to sleep with the same loving gesture.

Winter could be cozy and snug in the chalet, while alpine snowstorms whirled outside.

Papa was often gone, on a perpetual quest to generate interest in his ideas, believing that if he could only get some funding, his projects would make us all rich. For a while, he tried to interest his *Savoyard* neighbors to band together and develop a saw mill to produce plywood from the bounty of trees all around them. Another idea was to grow strawberries out of season to sell to hotels in Switzerland. He made prototypes of wooden toys; he invented board games. And, he continued to write his articles. Even in the midst of a cataclysmic war which had paralyzed the entire country, he charged ahead with his idealistic optimism. Through it all, the family's shared excitement was palpable. Mama supported him in all his ventures, firmly believing that it was better to power on and at least try to make a difference, than to let the war become an excuse for doing nothing at all. He traveled from Paris to Switzerland and points in between, pushing his ideas where he could.

His trips were always "important", according to Mama. But when he returned, I sometimes saw a conflicting change come over her. She was always relieved, because now he would be there to help her with the overwhelming task of running the farm and the family. But she seemed to also visibly grow timid, as she checked any doubts she might have about the wisdom of his latest venture, yet always succumbing to his overpowering enthusiasm.

We were all shy in his presence, somehow losing a little confidence in our timid efforts to navigate his mercurial moods. He could begin in cheerful good humor, playing and teasing with us, but as if a cloud had suddenly passed in front of the sun, he could as easily descend into impatient anger that would send us cowering as if we had been disobedient dogs that needed a scolding. Through it all, we were always excited to show some new skill that had been learned, to demonstrate intelligence, strength of character, and especially—new artistic talent. Sometimes, he came back from his trips with a pad of paper, or colored pencils, nearly impossible to find art supplies. These he usually gave to me; I treasured them and hoarded them, fiercely guarding my gifts to keep my brothers from stealing them.

Mama tried not to show the fear that gripped her so often. As an American, she was especially vulnerable, even here in the relative safety of the mountains. She had to be careful and was terrified that one of her neighbors might expose her. She seldom ventured into *Samöens,* especially after three men were lined up in the square and killed by the SS, as an example, when it was discovered that the *Maquis,* the French underground, was doing sabotage in the area. She heard the stories of escaped prisoners bound for the labor camps in Germany, and the dire circumstances that would befall them if they were discovered.

And, one day, one such escaped prisoner made his way to the chalet. Would they hide him? In exchange he would do the heavy work of the farm.

Serge was young, handsome, and strong. He was a hard worker and forever cheerful. I especially remember his sunny grin and his beret, rakishly perched on his sunburned face. He loved to tease us, especially Pierre, who was so gullible and would do whatever Serge might ask of him, even to one day taking one of the cats by the tail, whirling it around and around, before shaking it against a tree "to get the fleas out". The cat ran off, dazed and astonished, while Serge laughed his hearty, good-natured chortle.

He was very protective of Mama, doing the work of two men, not allowing her to do anything strenuous. He was infinitely polite with her, treating her with the respect he might show to a queen. She was so different. She wasn't like French women. She was an American.

Papa seemed to have a breakthrough, finally. After the failed architectural school in Nice, he seriously began to rethink his limited options. After spinning his wheels making toys and inventing games, failed attempts to interest his neighbors in planting strawberries in winter, it seemed there was nothing left to do but accept his lot—and be a farmer—at least until the war might be over. There was no point in embarking on any kind of serious planning toward a future that was unsettled.

But Papa, ever the idealist, the dreamer, had an idea.

Sitting on the long bench on the terrace, with the afternoon sun warming the stone at his back, he looked out over the valley and the range of mountains on the other side. It was late spring so the meadow below was a verdant green that was almost iridescent in its pure brilliance. The evergreens were a dark green blanket reaching up toward the peaks, still covered with snow.

"Liv," he called out to her in eager excitement. "Come see! I have an idea! I have a plan that will make us rich beyond our wildest dreams!"

She joined him on the terrace, hesitant to hear his new scheme.

"When this war is over, we can do something really grand in this valley."

"When this war is over..." she interrupted. "What if the Germans win? I just wish we could go back to America."

"The Germans won't win. They're losing even now. The Allies are planning an invasion—to begin soon."

"How do you know that?" she interrupted again.

"It's what I've been hearing. But never mind that. Be assured—we will have a free France sooner than you think. But anyway, listen to my idea. Please—tell me it's not pie-in-the-sky. You always have more sense about things than I do."

"I'll listen, but I'll be honest with you, Paul."

"I know you will. And you're so sensible, so pragmatic; you'll surely let me know if this is viable."

"What's your plan? And how will you execute it?"

"I knew you'd ask the right questions. Look out over the valley—and beyond. What do you see?"

"The most beautiful spot in all the world. It is a magical valley, pristine in its perfect loveliness."

"Yes! Yes! But what else?" he asked eagerly.

She searched his face, trying to grasp his excitement. She waited for him to go on.

"This can be a premier tourist center—even better than Chamonix. Look at those hills. They are perfect ski runs, and the valley below is ideal for building resort housing. And in the summer, people will hike—just as you and I have done so many times as we've explored these marvelous hills and mountain trails."

She caught her breath, understanding his vision. "Oh, Paul! You're right! This whole area could be developed! All three valleys linked by ski and mountaineering activities. But, but how will you do this? Who can you talk to about such a grand plan? Who do you know who could fund it for you?"

"No matter. That's not important at this stage. I'll map the area. I'll take pictures and connect them together to create a panorama. People need to see before they will understand. And then, the right people will be there to execute the vision. I'll find the right people. You know I have a lot of contacts—from all the traveling I've been doing. Wasn't that the point? But I must hurry this through—before someone else can take this idea."

In particular, Mama recounted later, Papa wrote a letter to one of his old friends from his days at the *Beaux Arts*. This led to an introduction to a British Colonel, Peter Lindsay, who had long been fascinated by the ideal possibilities of developing a ski resort in the region.

In my memory, there is a word that is like a lilting melody that flows in and out of the past to be forever linked to my father. *Méribel*—such a lovely word—from the Roman *mira bellum*, beautiful view. This was the ski resort that Peter Lindsay had begun in the late thirties, when it became obvious that some of the Austrian slopes would no longer be available for regular tourists.

And this eventually became the site of the winter Olympics of 1992.

By the time he and Papa met, the project was well under way and he already had a young architect from Paris for the continuing development. But the Colonel was impressed with Papa's ideas and brought him into the mix.

They became good friends, I remember. When he first came to the chalet to meet Papa, I was fascinated by his funny accent and realized that French was not the only way to talk. Mama had tried to speak to us in English, but this was different. It didn't sound at all like the English Mama spoke.

"How come he talks so funny?" I asked her. "He doesn't sound at all like you and Papa."

"It's the same, dear, just a different accent. If you were in Paris, people would say you talk a little funny too. Different places have a different ways of speaking."

It turned out that Papa and Colonel Lindsay shared the same vision. Here at last was an avenue for funding the idea of interconnected ski resorts in the three valleys. War or no war, they would go ahead with the planning. Finally, Papa would realize his dream of a profitable venture within a framework of sensible architectural aesthetics. He convinced the Colonel that the resorts should be in the model of traditional mountain chalets.

Papa went to Switzerland to work with the Parisian architect and the interior group that had been put together. He only came back a few times over that whole year—and even then, for a really short visit. Mama was alone again, to run the farm, but was happy and relieved that he was finally making some money doing what he loved most— and Serge was there to do the heavy lifting of the work of the farm.

When Mama was in her deepest despair, when she was trying to puzzle through the nightmare that her life had become in Houston, she told me of an encounter with Serge. As she told her story, I finally began to understand why she had found it so necessary to put her painful memories in a box, not to ever be opened until so much later in her life. The cost was simply too high.

"Madame," Serge approached her shyly, that day long ago. He took off his beret and fumbled with it, not sure what to do, nor what to say next. "I need to talk to you about your husband," he began.

"Yes? What is it?" She was a little impatient because she was elbow deep in hot soapy water, washing the endless mound of diapers.

"Um…your husband, Monsieur, do you know what he does on his trips?"

"Of course. He's been working on the ski village in *Méribel*, with Colonel Lindsay and *M. Durupt*, and the rest of the team. It's very exciting and fascinating to hear what they're planning. Why do you ask?"

"Well…" he stammered, "he approached me before he left, and…um…"

"Yes?" Mama waited as Serge tried again to compose himself.

"I think maybe he does some other things…he may not be quite the man you think…"

"Oh, I think I know him quite well, Serge. We've been married almost fourteen years, you know." Mama was growing apprehensive at the tone of this conversation.

"But, Madame—he's always traveled a lot, hasn't he?"

"Yes, of course—in search of work, mostly. The war has made life quite complicated." Mama was growing irritated.

"Madame, I'm sorry to have bothered you. It's nothing, really."

"Well, Serge, it's just that I don't understand what you're trying to say."

"I know, I know. No matter. But I think I must tell you I will be leaving—as soon as might be practical for you, when Monsieur comes back."

"Really? This is kind of sudden, don't you think? What will I do without your help?"

"I'm sorry, Madame...I will stay as long as necessary." He left abruptly, as if unwilling to say more.

Serge eventually went down to the village and married Renée.

Mama later spoke to Papa of this strange conversation, thinking that perhaps he might be able to fill in details where Serge had been so cryptic. He just laughed, Mama recalled, and added,

"Maybe he has a bit of a crush on you, Liv, and didn't want to jeopardize his relationship with me, as his boss."

"That's utterly ridiculous! But what do you think he was really trying to say? Not the man I think you are? How silly! What could he have been alluding to? What did he mean?"

"I have no idea, Liv! But good riddance, then." He was clearly irritated.

Papa's frequent trips continued, as work on the ski resort intensified. Somewhere in the deep recesses of her mind, she wondered a little about this close partnership that her husband had with all these people on the project. Did he...? Did they...? But she could never fully frame the question.

In fact, when Papa came home from his latest trip with his "special people" at *Méribel*, she attempted to prove—to herself at least—that he loved her most of all. She didn't deliberately plan this last pregnancy, but she was grateful for the proof of it.

— 14 —

SAGA OF THE ALPS

The cherry tree outside my office window has almost finished its glorious display, covering the driveway, my car and the lush lawn of spring with its pink snowfall of fallen blooms. Now the rain is coming in a steady drizzle, so that I feel no need to venture out. A perfect day to finally study the contents of my mother's manila envelope, her journal of the years we spent in the Alps, in our chalet, being farmers like our neighbors—yet so different from our neighbors, who had inhabited the side of the mountains for generations, becoming a part of the soil they worked and the air they breathed.

I knew the stories. There were even some short movies, grainy black and white images that my father took with his 8mm movie camera. But I had never read the whole odyssey, as my mother had written it so long ago, and then transcribed it before she died.

I realized, as I read, that her journal had always been intended as a living legacy for her children and grandchildren and generations yet to come. This was no longer an oral history, but the true telling of words, marching across the page, one after the next, to bring life to a period that might otherwise be lost.

1942, A New Teacher
Journal Entry

This fall the little school at Chantemerle did not open because there was no teacher who would accept to stay in the primitive accommodations offered: no plumbing whatsoever, only a brook running to the village water trough, a little wood stove in the one room school house with all the benches drawn up close to it. In October a young man came, looked at the situation, turned around and went down the mountain again.

We were concerned about schooling for the boys. Paul realized the problem even better than I. Schools in France are very demanding, run by strict government standards which are the same whether the school is in the country or the city. If children cannot keep up each year, it is impossible to consider a higher education where the classes are even more rigorous.

Fortunately the crisis did not last long. Renée, the pretty school mistress who finally accepted the post, came in mid-December. She had a happy nature and was well-fitted for teaching in Chantemerle which means "the blackbird sings". Her voice rippled with the purity of a mountain brook. It was not long before the children brought home echoes of her teaching.

One day Renée came home with the children after school. I had gone up to the balcony to bring down the daily wash of diapers and when I returned, Paul was talking to her.

"I'm so glad you could come, Mademoiselle," I greeted her. "The children speak of you and seem to really enjoy school. I hope you'll like it well enough to stay."

Renée was very small. She looked like a little girl as she spoke with enthusiasm of her new job. Her eyes sparkled and the mop of curly brown hair bounced as she tossed her head, shifting her gaze from the children to us.

"The children are eager and well-behaved. I think they enjoy the singing best. For all of us, that's the fun part of school."

"The boys have mentioned how well you sing," said Paul. "Perhaps you could sing something after dinner. I would be happy to accompany you."

The children knew that any evening entertainment meant they would be in bed and they had their own opinions about such an arrangement.

"Why not now," said Miqué, always ready to take command of a situation. From my point of view, the singing session was not too successful, interrupted as it was by the children's bath and supper.

While I was preparing them for bed, Paul played as Renée stood by the piano and sang. Paul was enchanted by the simple untrained purity of her voice and found music that he felt she could learn.

A new world was opening for her. She looked at Paul, too moved to say more than a plain "Merci". Paul bowed graciously, and like a noble from a royal court, answered her.

"Non pas. De rien... Not at all. It is nothing, Mademoiselle, it is my pleasure to hear you sing."

Thereafter, Renée took special pains to help the children learn music. She taught them folk songs, ballads, scout tunes and rondos. Paul found song flutes for her which she used not only in her class but also to learn the more difficult music of Bach that Paul introduced to her.

Bibine
Journal Entry

In the summer of 1942 when Betty was about one year old she developed a digestive problem that I thought might be due to the milk — richer in summer than in winter when the cows were confined to the stable. I learned that the fat globules of goat milk, being smaller and thus naturally homogenized, made the milk more digestible. Goats, moreover, were biologically immune to tuberculosis which was a constant threat with cows in the Alps.

After making a few inquiries we were offered a goat which had just had twins. Twin kids are rather rare and this particular goat seemed to realize that she was special.

She was brought to us leading her little ones, who scampered happily around her. When she reached the chalet, she stopped and nibbled a bit of grass as if to inspect its qualifications. She looked us over much more cautiously than we, in our enthusiasm, examined her.

We led her to her new quarters which had formerly been a horse stable. I think when she realized that she would be alone with her family in this regal apartment, she accepted us into the bargain.

We named her Bibine. Sally Anne and Peter were ecstatic and followed her around pulling up grass to feed her by hand. Or they sat in the field holding her kids in their laps. Bibine tolerated their presence with a glance and a feeble bleat of disapproval, but she went on chewing and soon was quite unaware of them.

When the kids were old enough to be weaned and had mysteriously disappeared, to reappear on the dinner table, Bibine supplied us with milk enough for Betty, and enough left over to make a few varied but not too successful attempts at goat cheese.

Bibine may have missed her twins but she gave no sign of it, except to spend longer and longer hours away from home base.

But she was not just a goat. She was a character we learned to respect and like. She soon learned to expect the good morning greeting as I gave her a lick of salt and patted her head before milking her. She often showed her displeasure if I was late by "marking time" with her hind legs, making it clear that she was in a hurry to be off to her breakfast on the slopes behind the chalet.

She roamed the hills all day, but where she went no one really knew. At first I was worried and sent the boys out after her. Even the neighbors' children joined the posse but Bibine remained aloof and alone.

I gave up looking for her when I discovered I could call her home. I would climb the hill behind the house and imitate the "baa baa" of a goat, and she would come out of the woods scrambling over the rocks and down the steep embankment, to regain a dignified stride as she came near the stable to enter her palatial residence.

As summer came to a close the Alpine fog came down every evening, enveloping us with a thick impenetrable blanket; cold, dank, and mysterious. Being a mere human I worried about Bibine out there in that dense fog. I wondered how she could find her way home. I learned that she had instinctive guideposts that brought her back to her stable, when one evening I found her outside her door, eating a shirt off the clothes line that was near the stable. That was a very effective way to tell me that I should leave the door open for her.

Fall came and with it the first chill of approaching winter. Our farmer friends drifted in to ask how we were getting along with our goat. They were always ready with some friendly advice.

"You've a nice goat there, but she'll lose her milk if you don't put some sheep in with her," said Antonioz.

"Why do we need sheep?" I asked. Bibine was the most independent and self-sufficient animal I had ever met.

"Well," said Antonioz, "she'll freeze to death in there alone."

This was corroborated by other neighbors who assured me that they kept sheep with their cows to keep them warm.

We had had dealings with Monsieur Antonioz before, and our estimation was that he was crafty and dishonest when it proved worthwhile to his welfare but on the whole he knew a lot more about farming in the Alps than we would ever learn. So before the winter cold set in we bought a ewe, heavy with a lamb that she would have in spring.

We named her Douillette which, translated, means "Softy". Her name could refer equally to her fleece or her gentle eyes, or even to the polite bleat with which she let us know that it was mealtime. Douillette was very much a lady.

Douillette and Bibine were soon fast friends and in a few weeks were joined by another sheep, this one smaller than Douillette, and a grubby brown in color. Any name that would have been appropriate might have hurt her feelings so she never had a name.

Though they all left the chalet together, with Bibine leading the way, the difference in their menu preferences soon caused them to drift apart. Bibine headed for the forest where pine cones and needles and the tender leaves of the underbrush were her staple diet. The sheep grazed in the meadow nearby.

The two sheep seemed to sense that Bibine was a leader, born to the purple by being a goat, a sure-footed, independent loner. Bibine did not ask for their company but she accepted their presence.

It wasn't long before the Antonioz' sheep joined the little band, and then the Gué sheep and a little later another neighbor's sheep ambled over. Soon Bibine found herself grazing among a flock of thirty or forty sheep which accepted her leadership even when she took precipitous paths into low bushes.

Because of Bibine's shepherding ability, I often neglected to call her home. She seemed to manage on her own, accepting the responsibility of bringing home the sheep every evening.

One evening when the fog was particularly heavy, the difference between night and day was imperceptible, blended by the mist that shrouded the hills like an opaque blanket.

Looking into the stable I realized that Bibine and the sheep hadn't come home. I ran upstairs to Paul's office where he was busy at his drawing board.

"Bibine didn't come home," I cried. "The sheep are out on the hills in this fog."

Paul looked up, his eyes still blank, concentrating on his work.

"The sheep! They didn't come home," I repeated.

Once his mind is focused, Paul has a solution for everything. This time was no exception.

He came downstairs just as three of our neighbors were approaching the chalet.

"Do you know anything about the sheep?" asked Henri Simond, a rather distant neighbor. "Our sheep haven't come home. Is your goat here?"

"They may be down the alley of Les Allamands with your goat," said Gué accusingly.

The Allamands valley was more of a gorge, approached by a steep path of crumbly terrain covered with dense underbrush, an ideal grazing ground for a goat but not good for sheep whose fleece could get entangled in the thorns and twigs.

The men had already spent an hour looking for the sheep and were not in the best of moods.

I left them to get back to the children's' supper and bedtime but stopped to look in the stable on the way. To my surprise, Bibine was lying in a darkened corner, peacefully chewing. She looked up at me, got up and ambled over hoping for a handout.

"Where did you leave the sheep?" I shouted at her as though she could understand. "Where are they?"

She watched me a moment and turned, expressing in her slow deliberate gait all the indifference she had for sheep and humans alike, and plopped down in her corner, burped and continued chewing, haughty contempt in every movement of her head and jaw as she stared me down.

In the meantime Paul, surrounded by the now half dozen worried sheep owners, was saying that he would find the sheep. He held a ball of Doillette's newly spun fleece in one hand and in the other his pendulum which he often had used to find a lost key or mislaid paper. The ball of fleece was to identify what the pendulum was to search for. The pendulum would swing in the direction he was to search. The peasants were familiar with the pendulum process but the system in common practice was the more familiar divining rod.

The men looked in vain, stumbling around in the dense fog and darkness, but soon realized that it was impossible to continue the search that night and returned to their homes, grumbling about "that Grillo goat".

The following morning the men returned to the chalet hoping that Paul or Bibine might lead them to the lost flock.

The sun had already been up two hours and had burned away the fog which had retreated to hover above the valley like a dense billowy blanket. This was the famous "mer de nuages", the sea of clouds, a familiar sight during the months of October and November in the higher Alps.

Paul, with his pendulum swinging and Bibine tagging along on a rope, led the group to the Criou mountain, where the night before the pendulum had seemed to indicate the location of the sheep. The Criou was the mountain on the other side of the deep gorge that formed the valley of the Allamands.

As the men approached the rim of the steep slope opposite the Criou, they could hear the bleating sheep somewhere deep in the gorge below them. Had the sheep followed Bibine into such rugged, crumbly terrain? Peering over the edge they were able to glimpse an open area below... a small patch of meadow. Perhaps the sheep had followed the goat to this bonanza and then had not been willing to leave when Bibine left for home.

Since the goat had been able to lead the sheep to this spot there must be a path or trail she had traced to get them there. Spreading out along the ridge the men searched. Only heavy brush and low bushes traced the rim of the slope. Suddenly Henri Simond shouted that perhaps he had found something. What he had discovered was not even an identifiable trail, but when Paul led Bibine to it, she seemed to recognize the area and started pulling on the nearby bushes. After a persuasive push, Henri got her started down, munching steadily as she made her way into the canyon.

She was about half way down when one of the sheep spotted her, and with a bleat of welcome Douillette came up the trail to greet her. The other sheep quickly followed and within an hour the sheep were again on the hillside, grazing in the sunlit meadows.

The first snow of the season fell a few days later and the animals were confined to their winter quarters. Henri Simond must have forgiven Bibine for her errant ways because he came over to ask if we would sell her, but by this time Bibine was a member of our household and remained with us until we bought a cow.

The Sick Cow
Journal Entry

Les Marllys, the hamlet in the French Alps where our chalet was situated, consisted of three families, the Antonioz, our own, and the Gués. The Antonioz and their three grown sons lived on a knoll to the east of us and the Gués and their three young children had a chalet a half mile to the west of us.

There were no other inhabited chalets higher than Les Marllys. Monsieur Antonioz was a constant source of advice which mingled common sense, superstition and greed in about equal measure. There is no doubt that Monsieur Antonioz knew more than we did about farming in the Alps. When it was to his advantage he was glad to share it. When the most remote opportunity turned up, Antonioz was not one to ignore what was to him a bargain. From our point of view it was more often a wily scheme to cheat us.

One of these occurred when we sold our first cow, Lorraine, to the market. Though he sold us milk after Lorraine had left us, he also knew we were looking for a replacement.

One day he came over to see us. He sat down on the three-legged chair in the kitchen and settled down for a morning's chat. A five or ten minute preamble about the weather was a prelude to something important.

"Fall is coming early this year. We'll have snow before December." He grumbled about the war which had taken his two older sons to the front, he was "too old to do all the work, and nowadays what you have isn't yours anyway with the government taking it all.

"Can't even make my own bread. They won't let me keep my own flour..." He finally came to the reason he had come in the first place.

"I have a cow you can have cheap. She's not very well right now but I'll give you some medicine and she'll be fine in a few days."

The price was intriguing and a half hour later he came back with a miserable specimen that he said was a slightly sick cow. She was thin, approaching the skin-and-bone stage; she hung her head as if it was too heavy to lift and her legs wobbled like rubber hoses.

Paul, however was anxious to try a new panacea which he had heard about from a "friend" who called himself Dr. B... and traveled all over France like a barefoot pilgrim to advertise the value of magnesium for any frailty, animal or human. Though I was unconvinced of its potency, I knew that I would end by joining the crusade for magnesium, especially since the next day the cow seemed sicker than ever on Monsieur Antonioz' medicine.

The next day Paul left for Nice, giving me instructions and a bottle of magnesium pills. Since the bottle contained 20 pills and the cow was supposed to get ten a day, I hurried to the village to get some more magnesium, leaving Paulette in charge of the children.

Since there was only one drugstore in Samoens and they had only ten pills, the next morning at dawn I was off again to get more pills in Annemasse where there were three drugstores. Down the mountain, one hour, train to Annemasse, one hour and a half, search for pills, one hour, wait for return train, three hours, return train, one and one half hours and climb back to the chalet arriving at nightfall.

I went immediately to see my patient. She was gaunt, her eyes looked wild, and she wobbled from side to side. The cow was dying... I was sure. This was another of Monsieur Antonioz' schemes.

By this time, I was mad enough to face Monsieur Antonioz myself and I was ready to stomp over there to see him when he appeared at the door.

"Bonsoir, Madame. "Ca va mieux la vache?" (Is the cow better?)

"You know very well she's no better. You sold us a cow that will never get well. I want you to take her back and give us back our money."

"Mais non, Madame, maybe that medicine you gave her was too strong. I tell you what I'll do."

He then went on to tell me that I was to give her an enema with a special tool that I could "borrow anywhere"... and that this medicine would produce a miraculous cure. I didn't believe him but he added, "And if it doesn't, I'll take her back and give you half your money back."

What could I do? Even half the money was better than to lose it all and have to find a way to get rid of a sick or maybe even a dead cow. I accepted and the following morning I borrowed the gadget I could "find anywhere" from the fourth farmer I contacted.

Serge, our farm hand, refused to have anything whatever to do with Antonioz' cow.

When I came back to tell Paulette that we had serious business to undertake on the cow, and explained that I would do everything if she would just hold the tail up, Paulette was almost hysterical with terror.

"I can't... I'm scared of cows. Please, no Madame... I can't!"

I told her she could stand on a chair far enough away from any stray emissions from the cow, and that I would deliver the tail to her when she was already on the chair... and anyway...the cow was too weak to make much of a fuss.

She finally agreed and we set up arrangements.

The cow proved to be not as weak as we thought, but Paulette held on bravely while I danced back and forth trying to deliver the medicine at the proper angle. J u s t when I thought my maneuvers were successful, the cow jumped to one side and the gadget broke, leaving me holding the handle and the cow, in a mad fury, trying to get rid of the rest of it.

Paulette jumped off the chair and ran into the house and I picked up the pieces and the chair.

The next morning Monsieur Antonioz was again in our kitchen.

"Well," I said, "You can take back your cow."

He grumbled and tried to tell me that we had poisoned his cow with that new-fangled medicine, that she would have recovered; that she was young and small, just what I should have...but I would hear none of it.

In the end he took back the cow. All that day we heard no more from Monsieur Antonioz.

What had he done with the cow? Had he really found a miraculous cure? With my anger waning, my conscience returned. Maybe it was our fault... maybe I should have waited longer.

The next morning as Paulette and I were cleaning up, the children came running in to tell me.

"Monsieur Antonioz is taking our cow to market. He cured her, Maman; she's really fat!"

I let Monsieur Antonioz get a half hour head start and prepared to follow him to the village to find out what he was up to. When I reached the market place, there was the cow waiting for the butcher to appraise her.

After doing my errands, I returned to the market place. The cow was still there, standing in a puddle of her own making, but now as scrawny as she had been when I returned her to Monsieur Antonioz. Monsieur had filled her with as much salt water as she would hold so as to raise the sale price based on weight.

We bought no meat or sausages for several weeks nor did we ever buy another cow from Monsieur Antonioz.

We were still without a cow and didn't know where to turn, when a few days later Dubois, a fine young conscientious peasant, came to offer me a young cow which, he said, gave only eight quarts of milk, but was an easy milker. He offered to let us keep her for a small fee until he could take her back again as he had no room for her at the time. This was Bazaine, our second cow.

Bazaine, unlike her predecessor, was so small that we put the sheep in the stable with her to keep her warm. Unlike her namesake, the notorious French turncoat, General Bazaine, our four-footed friend was faithful in her dairy duty. Bazaine was indeed an easy milker as I learned quite quickly.

She seemed to know and like us and when she heard me coming she would moo, stomp her hoof and I would rattle the pail in answer, and as I opened the door her rear end lurched sideways in welcome as I patted her on the rump and called her name. She stayed with us until we had to give her back to her owners when we left Les Marllys, on our way to America.

From Fleece to Yarn
Journal Entry

It is said of the hog that everything is useful except his squeal. Sheep are even more useful, from their abundant fleece, to the milk they give. They just aren't very smart.

In the Alps, during the farmer's busy summer season, his sheep are out of his way, high on the rocky slopes of the mountain peaks. Sheep can graze on very poor pasture and though, perhaps even because they're not so smart, they tend to band together and prefer to graze facing the upward slope so that the shepherd and his dog are able to control several flocks from a whole village, often several hundred sheep.

We were to learn and appreciate the value of our sheep which soon became a flock of fourteen. They supplied meat for the table as well as sweaters socks, mittens, and even a quilt or two for our whole family.

In late fall after the hay is in and before the threat of winter storms and snow, the sheep are brought down from their high pastures. They must be fleeced immediately before their wool can become soiled and matted in the confined winter quarters. Though sheep are shorn twice a year, the spring wool is of greatly inferior quality.

The shearing of the sheep was an arduous task in our remote valley, as it was still done by hand. No forty five seconds per sheep like the Australian rancher with his electric clippers, but closer to forty-five minutes of tedious hand clipping.

One by one the sheep were brought in from an impromptu enclosure and laid on the kitchen table with fore and hind legs held by thongs. In this helpless position the sheep lay docile and silent.

I had expected the floor to look like a barber shop with a scattered mass of wool all over the floor.

Not at all, the fleece peeled off in a continuous rolling billow of soft fluff like a three inch thick pillow.

Though hand clippers are apt to nick the sheep's tender skin, no cut heals more quickly than that of a newly shorn sheep. Lanolin, the sheep's natural oil, seeps through to the surface and prevents any cut from bleeding.

Once released of its thongs and off the table, the sheep, now pink and much thinner ambled off looking slightly embarrassed to be so naked.

The wool of fourteen sheep almost filled my kitchen. This soft mound now had to be soaked in cool water and rinsed six or seven times until not a trace of soil remained. At the end of the day the billowy hill had become a sodden mass and my arms ached from the cold of pure mountain water.

The next day the weather cooperated with a windless, warm, sunny day and the fleece was set out to dry on clean white sheets spread out on the chalet balconies. It had to be constantly watched, or as it dried, it would blow off the balcony and roll gently down the mountain in happy puff ball bounces. When it was completely dry it was piled into sheets tied by the corners where it remained until I could find time to card and spin it.

Wool set aside for spinning should be of similar color, quality and length. Douillette, our first ewe, had ideal fleece. It was strong but soft and quite long. Having been washed only in cold water, it had also retained its lanolin which rendered it more water repellent, excellent for the sweaters, socks and mittens destined for its use.

Before spinning it, the wool must be combed and fluffed by a process called carding. A card is a board about eight by six inches, on which has been stretched padded leather, into which short, bent, headless nails have been driven about one half inch apart. The spinster holds a card in each hand. Any stray dirt or twig will fall off during this process and the wool will be soft and even enough to be placed on the spindle of the spinning wheel.

I had a spinning wheel but Madame Dunoyen was the only person in the valley who could teach me to spin. She was the grandmother of the young neighbor who had helped us with the haying in the summer. She lived about three miles away on the same slope as our chalet. One day, leaving the children in Paulette's capable hands, I went to visit her. She greeted me graciously and asked me into her immaculate, simple home.

"Spinning," she told me, "is not hard. It is just a knack of keeping a steady coordinated rhythm of the foot pedaling the wheel and the hand feeding the wool from the spindle."

It took me a few minutes to catch on. It is like patting your head and rubbing your stomach at the same time in a very even, unbroken rhythm. If the foot goes too fast, the yarn is tight and hard. If the rhythm is jumpy and uneven it makes lumps on the yarn, and if the pedaling is too slow, the yarn will break. It takes several hours of spinning to learn how to keep a steady, automatic rhythm.

After one strand of yarn is spun and rolled in a ball, a second and third are spun. Then the three balls, placed in separate baskets, feed the wheel to be spun together. Spinning is very long. It is longer to spin enough yarn for a sweater than to knit it.

Wool too coarse, or of mottled coloring is either discarded or used for making mattresses and quilts. A mattress made of freshly carded wool is one of the joys of former generations. A "Matelassier" or mattress maker of Paris, used to come to the door in early morning, take out a mattress, rip it open, card and fluff the wool, place it in new ticking fastened to a frame the size of the bed and then with a needle eight to ten inches long, sew it together. And at five or six in the evening the new mattress would be on the bed again.

A home-made mattress of freshly combed fleece is firm but resilient. It is a luxury like the down quilt which can be enjoyed only by a farmer's family or a millionaire.

Except for their bleat, sheep are like hogs in their utility, but it takes about fourteen sheep to be as productive as one hog.

Bringing Down the Hay and the Wood
Journal Entry

It is often thought that farmers' chores in winter are greatly reduced because there is no planting, mowing or harvesting... In the Alps a farmer's work is never done.

Alpine farmers depend on hay to feed their animals all year long. In order to have enough of it, they must mow the whole mountain in summer. Hay from the upper slopes is stored in barns, or "miches" scattered over the hillsides and it remains there until mid-winter. Since there are no roads on these higher slopes, the farmers must wait for snow and use sleds to get the hay down to the cattle in the valleys.

These sleds are amazing contraptions of ingenuity and require enormous skill. They are made from three different kinds of wood... each serving a unique purpose. The sled must be light, since it is often carried on the men's shoulders as they climb to the hay barns. It must be strong for it will carry enormous bales of hay which must be carefully balanced on the sled during the descent to the valley, and finally, it must be flexible to withstand the twists and turns the farmer will give it to guide it over the trackless slopes.

Since one loaded sled could feed a cow for about ten to fifteen days and farmers often had more than a dozen cows plus sheep and goats, they were obliged to make many trips to the upper slope barns every time the weather was clear.

Going after the hay in winter was a new venture for Serge so he was to be accompanied by André Antonioz and Henri Simond, both skilled in this operation.

Since Antonioz shared our hay in exchange for mowing and storing it in the hayloft, André carried the long serrated curved knife or saw which would serve to slice the hay in equal portions.

Henri and Serge each carried a sled or pulled it behind him.

All proceeded as planned. Once in the barn, André used the long knife to slice the hay, next the men criss-crossed ropes on which they piled the hay to be transferred to the waiting sleds.

When they were loaded, each man took his stand in front of the sled, guiding it by holding the upturned runners and leaning against the high bale of hay to help maneuver its direction with his body. They also wore long spurs on the heels of their boots to dig into the snow to break the speed should the sled accelerate too fast. The sled is cumbersome to steer, and any sudden jerk will tip it over. Henri Simond was in back with a rope to help brake the sled Serge was guiding, but when Serge tried to maneuver a curve, it overturned. It took all three men to set it straight.

The felling of the trees is not done until late October when all the harvesting of the wheat and potatoes is finished and the sheep have been fleeced.

Each year, every resident is allotted a certain number of trees in the communal forest, which he may cut for the use of his household. We used more wood than the average peasant partly because we were unaccustomed to being as frugal as they, and partly because Paul's office above the stable and Serge's quarters also had stoves.

In late October or early November, just before the first snows, the men go up the forested slope to fell the trees and saw the branches into one meter lengths. The wood is left in the forest until the snow falls when it can be carried down the mountains on sleds, the same ingeniously built sleds which are used for the hay.

This is a very dangerous maneuver. The center of gravity of a sled, heavily laden with wood, is very low. A man guiding it has only the power of his feet, strengthened by spurs digging into the snow, to break the speed of the descent. His whole body is vulnerable. The sled, as it gains speed, may throw him and run right over him.

Serge had been warned of this possibility, but young and impetuous as he was, he was convinced that strength was the main factor to be considered. He and André prepared the wood and in early December went up with sleds to bring it down. Serge's sled, piled high with wood was on almost level ground. The runners had stuck in the frozen snow. In order to release it, Serge set it on a course too steep to maneuver. When suddenly the sled came loose and started downhill, it threatened to run over him.

He tried desperately to brake against the growing momentum. When he realized his efforts would be of no avail, he threw himself to the ground and let the sled hurtle over him. He was dragged several yards, his jacket and shirt torn off his back, but the sled flew past him and smashed into a tree below. By miraculous chance he was not seriously hurt. Thereafter Serge listened carefully and followed the instructions of the peasants who were well aware of the dangers to be faced on these treacherous slopes.

After a week of nursing a bruised and bleeding back, Serge was ready to try again. He and André shared the job of bringing down and cutting both the Antonioz wood and ours. Using an electric saw, they cut the wood into one foot lengths until Serge had time to chop it into split logs for fuel. Then it was placed on the wood balconies to dry in the blazing winter sun of the high altitudes.

We braced ourselves for winter's worst storms.

A Pig Is Not Always a Hog
Journal Entry

As the war dragged on, shortages became more acute. Lack of gasoline and coal affected transportation, and trains which had run hourly now ran only daily. Cars were rare and the few trucks ran on synthetic fuel of various ingenious compositions. Clothes of any sort were available only with tickets, one item to a family at six month intervals. Even with the proper coupon it was often impossible to buy the item requested or if it were available it would be of synthetic rayon and lasted about six weeks.

We had become accustomed to food shortages in the Midi. In Savoie our farm was beginning to produce, and food was less of a problem. Shortages of household supplies were now affecting us. Soap, safety pins, children's underwear, and cotton diapers were my biggest problem.

They had been out of circulation for more than a year.

Paul could find very little paper and no thumb tacks, nails, paper clips or glue or even paint for his art supplies. If the children had been familiar with toys, candy, ice cream, cake, breakfast foods, French fries, hot dogs and hamburgers, they too would probably have complained.

But they were too young to know. They were only familiar with wartime shortages. They wore ski suits until they were gray and threadbare, and shoes with uppers made of pressed paper and wooden soles.

I found that I was spending more and more time at the sewing machine making diapers out of damask table cloths, blouses and shirts from sheets. Sally Anne acquired a lovely bathrobe made from a blue, pure wool blanket that had a hole in it. Betty too had a portion of it, as a wrapping blanket.

Paul, in the meantime, had been busy in the garden. By the end of the summer of 1942, due to his efforts, we had a great variety of vegetables. Lettuce and enormous beets, tender and sweet, supplied daily salads. Carrots, onions, and a bountiful crop of potatoes appeared on the table, whole and boiled at noon, mashed in the soup for supper.

Meat was rare but when summer tasks were finished and left him time for his favorite pastime, Monsieur Gué bounded off for the mountain slopes. He sometimes returned with a chamois or mountain goat, which he sold to neighbors who would be forced to listen to his heroic adventures chasing the elusive animal. Venison which Monsieur Gué so loudly acclaimed was, in our opinion, pretty tough and had a very gamey taste but in a marinade of wine and spices, it became delicious.

Cabbage was the one vegetable from the garden that was overabundant. When it appeared more often than it was welcome we thought of getting a pig.

This was recommended to us by our neighbor Antonioz one eventful summer day when I found his goats nibbling contentedly in the cabbage patch below the terrace.

Futile screams of "Get out," "scram", and various epithets in English and French had no effect. The goats lifted their heads and continued chewing on another succulent leaf of cabbage.

The children joined me and we started throwing stones. My aim for throwing anything was notoriously bad, but just as I threw a good sized rock, one of the smaller goats sauntered over to receive it directly on its thigh... and slumped to the ground with a thud.

We were forced to deal with the anger of Monsieur Antonioz.

"No one plants cabbages without a fence," he accused us.

"You shouldn't let your goats wander on other people's property."

"Why did you plant cabbages? You don't seem to be eating them."

"We eat them," I answered feebly but we bought his goat.

Not long after the goat episode, we bought a pig which, we decided would help us eat the cabbage... and we could plan to have a Christmas ham.

Twice a week Serge built a fire under the copper tank and made the soup for the pig. In spite of its very small dimensions the pig ate everything offered as long as it was cooked: potatoes too small to be pared, vegetable peelings, carrot and beet tops, as well as all leftovers from our rather bland boiled dinners. We began to dream of "killing the hog at Christmas", and of celebrating with a ham, and mostly of cooking with bacon which would very much improve the taste of our diet.

Weeks went by; the piglet became a pig, but was still very far from being a hog. In fact, he seemed to be growing only in length and soon resembled a kind of high-slung dachshund.

Monsieur Antonioz, who as usual was our final authority on animal husbandry, came over to appraise the situation.

"What's the matter with our pig? Shouldn't he start to get fat soon?" asked Paul.

Antonioz went to look at him. The pig was lying down on the far side of the stall. Even with a poke in his ribs, he wouldn't get up.

"Do you give him milk? He won't get fat unless you give him milk."

Bazaine gave sufficient milk for our household of five children and four adults plus a couple of cats, but we didn't have a lot of milk to spare. However, ham and bacon still loomed high in our horizon of dreams. So we shared our milk supply with the pig.

Paul left again for his school in Nice and when he came back a few weeks later, he was shocked by the appearance of the pig.

"What's the matter with him? If he's going to be ready by Christmas, he's got a long way to go."

The pig walked over to the corner of his stall and began nodding his head back and forth.

" He does that all the time," I said. "Do you suppose he has something in his ears?"

Antonioz came over later that day and gave his verdict.

"He is sick. Don't know what he's got, looks like worms. Don't let him die. You wouldn't be able to eat him... all that poison going through him."

"How sick is he?"

"I'd say he's pretty sick."

"Maybe we should call the vet."

"Not worth spending money on a vet," said Antonioz. "Maybe he has worms. I've got a worm medicine that might help."

He sauntered off and soon returned with medicine which, dissolved in milk, the pig seemed to relish.

"That ought to clean him out anyway." As he left he called back. "Don't let him die natural."

We stood in the stall watching the pig. He had moved farther into the corner and now when he nodded, his head banged the corner. He finally slumped to the floor with a combination of pig noises, a kind of hiccup and a belch.

"I'll stay here to watch him a while." I said.

I stayed near the door watching the alarming behavior of the pig. Head banging continued but just when it seemed time to call Antonioz he turned around in his bed of straw, lay down and fell asleep. At around midnight Paul arrived to take his turn to watch. The pig had again reached the head banging state.

"He'll stop in a minute and fall asleep," I said.

"Standing up?"

"No, he wobbles a little, then falls down and goes to sleep."

"It's late, Liv. Let's go to bed."

We watched a while longer and finally left the pig sleeping and snorting.

The following morning Antonioz came at seven to find us both in the pig stall. The pig was lying down. He looked less uncomfortable and eyed us suspiciously from his corner.

"Do you think he's going to die soon?" asked Paul. "Maybe he should be slaughtered now. Maybe you should have done it last night."

"No use then; had to wait 'til the medicine cleaned him out. Did he puke?"

Paul seemed startled by the word, but he answered quickly... "Oh, yes. Yes, he certainly did."

The autopsy indeed proved that he had had worms. Somehow the idea of eating that elongated wienie did not appeal to me but Paul assured me that once it was salted down and smoked when the weather was cooler, everything would be fine.

Paul went to get the "pétrin" from the hayloft. This was a kind of cradle that had formerly been used to knead the bread dough. He put the pig in it with a lot of salt. Every time I looked at that pig lying in the bed of salt, it seemed to get smaller and paler and even more unappetizing.

The weather stayed warm and sunny but the pig had to be smoked. Paul was to leave again for Nice so we tried to hurry the process. Serge and Paul combed the hillside for branches of juniper which burned with lots of smoke.

They suspended the pig on hooks extending from a bar inside the five foot wide wooden chimney. All day long juniper branches burned on the flagstone hearth in the kitchen. The fragrance of juniper smoke filled the house. I was beginning to think that maybe after all even a lean ham could be improved by the process of smoking.

Paul left as soon as the ham was smoked. It was now a dark reddish brown even black in spots where smoke, too hot, perhaps, had toasted it. I had never seen such small hams but they were ours and we were proud.

When Paul returned from Nice in December, he was accompanied by two men. He introduced them as members of the famous society of French gourmets. They were looking forward to a good square meal which they could not experience in Nice. The mention of ham made them eloquent with politely restrained excitement. Paul took over the whole culinary process for preparing the festive dinner. I thought the ham had a peculiar odor only weakly concealed by the smoking process. Paul said nothing. I noticed, however, that wine and plenty of spices were being added to the "'pièce de résistance". The meat was surrounded by a "garniture" of mushrooms, gathered that morning, accompanied by mashed potatoes and glazed carrots. A salad of tomatoes from Golfe Juan completed the main course. For dessert we made a luxurious whipped cream concoction flavored with the grated lemon peel and sweetened with saccharin. A delicious bottle of Mamette's Beaujolais completed the sumptuous feast.

Dinner proceeded with animated conversation. The men proclaimed the meal delicious and "the ham", said one of our guests, "has a most distinctive flavor." Though he asked for the recipe I was convinced that no one could reproduce the "most distinctive flavor" of that ham.

"I'm coming home. We have had a good year in the school but the students one by one have gone into the Maquis (underground resistance) to help. I have made many useful contacts but all the projects planned will have to wait. Life is at a standstill here; no more cement, wood or steel. No way to transport the snips of material available. I have met with a man from the League of Nations. We are together writing a brochure about the cultivation of wheat... very interesting. I will tell you when I come home.

I am so anxious to get home. You sound discouraged, my sweet love. If you knew just once what you mean to me. You have such an influence on my life that I don't make a move without thinking to myself, 'What would she think of it? What advice would she tell me?' Think how decisive was your influence just with one letter months ago. Come, come my dearest, come back to the wonderful life our two international souls have weaved with the very foam of angry seas and the dust of the northern winds, and think that it is only the beginning of a richer life and more happiness to come when we are together again in our home.

I send this in a gust of wind before you even have time to think of it, and don't worry, we, I am sure, will make heaps of money, but money won't ever count as an all powerful god. I just have to look through my fingers when I keep my hands before my eyes to see all the bright lovely landscape and joy of living through the cracks which let drip the money as fast as it comes in. Is it not so, my sweet love... tender kisses from your warm soft lips."

Such confidence overwhelmed me! His happy spirit conveyed in the poetry of his still awkward English, made me long to hold him close, to tell him once again, "I believe in you. You cannot lose, because you have the will to win, but deep in myself my reasoning did not believe my heart.

Again, and again, as her words speak from a long-ago time of hardship and struggle, I marvel at her silent courage, her ability to rise to any challenge, to always continue to do what must be done. The story of the sick cow that was left in her charge while her husband blithely left the scene; the pig that she was helpless to rescue which he miraculously turned into a feast for his friends... how could she not be bitter and resentful—and discouraged, in the face of his impossible optimism?

So many decades later, I am angry for her because she never confronted his terrible neglect as he chased his dreams and curried favor with his "important contact" and special friends. Surely, he worked hard and was diligent in his efforts, but how could he leave her to deal with such problems alone? I imagine her cleaning the muck out of the stalls of these sick beasts, of trying to give a cow an enema, or deal with a pig that had worms.

I have to conclude that they were both naïve and unwilling to challenge circumstances they could do nothing about. Better to power on, moving forward one step at a time. What good would it do to shake a fist at this never-ending war that robbed them both of the dreams they had shared?

In these last words, I understood her profound discouragement, even as he tried, so valiantly in all his letters, to dispel it and show her a silver lining to the bleak cloud that seemed to envelop them both like a fog.

1943 Strawberries and the Pharaoh's Wheat
Journal Entry

Paul came back to the chalet to find other outlets for his talents and energy.

He was asked to build a memorial for seven citizens of a border town between France and Switzerland. They had been shot down by the SS as a "lesson" for rebellious behavior. While there, Paul made a trip to Swiss farms located at the same altitude as our hamlet, Les Marllys, and learned of the very lucrative production of strawberries being undertaken there.

The fruit from each farm was handled in the same way as the milk, being brought to a central location from which it was distributed to markets in Geneva. Since strawberries ripened much later at a mile-high altitude, the fruit commanded a higher price in the market than during the main season.

Paul was eager to launch a similar enterprise in our valley. He came home, planted strawberries across the whole bank of the terrace in front of the chalet and was soon off again to round up twenty-eight farmers and twelve mayors from different hamlets along the whole river valley to escort them for a personal view of the Swiss mile-high farms. The complications involved, in order to persuade the farmers to go to Switzerland, to urge authorities from both France and Switzerland to approve his worthy efforts, to coax the farmers, once they had accepted to go, to do the necessary paperwork of obtaining permits and passports, and finally to find funds to finance the whole affair, would have discouraged any other zealous enthusiast...

Not Paul... he worked tirelessly. It took him several weeks, but in the meantime the strawberries were ripening to their peak of glory and when, at last, the farmers and their city-farmer leader came back from their trip, enthusiasm for Paul and strawberries knew no bounds. They drank to his health and he to theirs with inexhaustible fervor, until at last, when he staggered home at around four in the morning he explained nothing, but simply apologized and said, "I'll tell you later," and went to bed.

The farmer's enthusiasm lasted as long as their hangovers. But Paul, convinced of the merit of the project, said, "Wait till they see our strawberries. I'll show them how easy it is to grow them. I'll ask Vilmorin (a nursery) to get me some good plants for the project next year."

The Pharaoh's Wheat

One of Paul's enthusiastic dreams was to improve the lot of the Savoyard peasant. Even the family's wealth was less important. A mountaineer's life is a constant struggle. Farming on steep Alpine slopes precludes the use of tractors so the farmer must use a horse and plow for his fields. He also must deal with long snow-bound winters which leave him a very short growing season. But perhaps the biggest handicap to progress is the unyielding inflexibility of the peasants to accept change. Any method not practiced by their great grandfathers is regarded with suspicion.

Because of his exuberant acceptance of the trial-and-error method of attacking any problem, Paul inspired only dubious credibility in the sober-minded peasant. But he was not easily discouraged. He was convinced that even if the plow and horse had to remain, the quality and quantity of wheat from a given acre could be improved.

During the war, hunger was everyone's main preoccupation. Food supplies by ticket rations provided only near starvation diets, and often even with tickets, energy foods like potatoes and pasta, or oil and margarine were unavailable. People raised vegetables but tomatoes and string beans do not allay a ravenous appetite.

While Paul was teaching a small group of student architects in the Midi, he made the acquaintance of a man who had served as interpreter in the League of Nations. Because of the wide horizon of contacts, Monsieur S... had learned about a few ears of wheat that had been excavated from an Egyptian tomb. These five ears were shriveled and dried, but nevertheless, interested men had carefully restored them to near normal size and planted them. Though they were not given much hope for survival, three grains from five ears sprouted. These precious three grains were planted by expert nurserymen and the following year fifty grains survived.

The wheat was different from any modern wheat, with small grains closely encased, difficult to harvest by modern methods. The third year the fifty treasured grains were cross-pollinated with more successful modern variety of wheat and the hybrid was fairly successful.

Paul was able to obtain two grains of this remarkable harvest. He planted them with great care in the garden of the Miradou in the south of France, where we had lived before moving to the chalet.

Monsieur S... and Paul had also made a study of wheat cultivated around the world and through the ages, and thus learned the ancient method practiced by the Egyptians in 3000 B.C.

When he came home to the chalet in the Spring of 1943 he brought with him an ear from the two grains he had planted and showed me a picture of an ancient frieze from an Egyptian Db.

"Look at this," he said, "the Egyptians planted wheat in rows. See how they are cutting the wheat? They are using sickles to cut off the top of the stalks."

"How does that prove they planted in rows?" I objected.

"They are walking beside the wheat, not tramping on wheat already cut."

On further investigation he had discovered that not only did they plant in rows far enough apart to walk between them, but that each row was carefully cultivated. Soil tilled from between the rows was hoed against each plant to encourage the growth of shoots from new roots. A single grain of wheat cultivated in this fashion in his garden in the south of France had produced over forty ears of wheat from so many stalks, all grown from a single grain.

Though I knew nothing about wheat culture I had seen the miles of wheat in our own Western ranches gently swaying like a rippling golden sheet. This was an entirely new concept.

"If a single grain produces that much wheat, why hasn't it been done before?" I asked,

"Or rather why isn't it possible to grow wheat like that now?"

"It could be done, of course, but the labor required would make it uneconomical. There are no machines or combines that could till the plants every week or two or two rows at a time."

"It would have to be an elevated platform on legs that could till the soil up around the plants," I suggested.

"Perhaps someday such a machine could be designed but for now, during war time this method could save about 95% of the grain that the farmer must put aside for planting his next crop. Since he also has to give a big portion to the occupying troops, he will need more wheat per acre to fill his family needs. Even if it requires more hand labor, it could be worthwhile for him during hardship periods."

"Do you think the farmers would accept such an alternative? It would mean a lot of manual labor during the season that they are the most hard pressed for time."

"They wouldn't even believe it and certainly wouldn't try until they saw results," answered Paul.

"I'm going to try it here in the chalet with some wheat I'll borrow for seed."

Eager to prove his theory, the next day Paul asked our neighbor Antonioz for ten kilos of wheat.

"You going to plant wheat? You won't have enough room for potatoes if you plant all that wheat," said our agricultural advisor, Antonioz.

"Okay, just give me five kilos and I'll show you that I'll have more wheat than you with ten kilos," answered Paul.

"How are you going to do that?"

Paul told him the Egyptian method but Antonioz only half-listened, and with a sidewise grin of skepticism, he left the house shaking his head in doubt as though the 3000 year old Pharaoh and Paul both belonged in the same asylum of crackpots.

Paul sowed a quarter of an acre of Antonioz' wheat in the conventional method but saved a small handful of wheat to plant four rows, three feet apart, with each grain separated by five inches.

In a few days the wheat sprouted. When it was about four inches tall he did his first tilling job, piling up fresh soil around each plant. All through the summer at weekly intervals the process continued.

There was one little plant which received our almost daily inspection. The water of the drainpipe from the kitchen sink flowed underground in front of the chalet until it reached the road where it joined the drainage provided for the road. Somehow a stray grain of wheat had taken root at the exit of the pipe. We discovered it by following the line of lush green meadow that tracked the pipe-line from the sink. Each time the sink was emptied, debris from table scraps accompanied the water down the drainpipe. That plant flourished like a tenderly loved houseplant. By midsummer it had over 20 stalks rising bravely by the road-side. When it was time to mow the hay we put up stakes to shelter it from the blade of the scythe.

By September we began to get impatient for threshing time. Paul's wheat was magnificent, taller than the wheat sown "à la volée" like the miller's wheat in Millet's painting. The heads were long and full, and rose from sturdy stems that could withstand rain and heavy wind. Serge, our handyman, reaped all the wheat with a scythe and piled it in two separate areas in the hayloft. The wheat planted in rows was placed in a corner, an insignificant pile in comparison with the quarter acre sown by the traditional method.

At last, in October, the thresher arrived and with it a team of strong young farmers who would take turns at the heavy wheel which had to be rotated by hand one man on each side of the wheel.

Threshing is done at night after the day's work is over. The brisk cold air of autumn was chilly, but the big barn door was open on the moonlit night. High on a rafter swung a lantern lighting the glistening bodies of the men, stripped to the waist as they turned the enormous wheel.

I had put the children to bed and was working in the kitchen listening to the dull riffle of wheat as it fell from the thresher in the hayloft above our living quarters. This continued for several minutes, then a pause... a shuffling of feet above my head. Were they getting ready for Paul's wheat?

Suddenly, I could hear the men exclaim, and the sound of the wheat grinding through the thresher was now a loud, rapid rat-a-tat-tat. I dashed up the outside staircase to the hayloft. They were all so engrossed watching the lush, fat grains tumble from the thresher they didn't even hear me.

I went around the thresher to Paul. He put his arm on my shoulder and grinned.

"You did it!" I said. "You're going to have as much wheat from that handful of seed as from the big plot."

"The drainpipe plant had 38 ears. I put it over in the corner with the rest of the Pharaoh's wheat."

"Perhaps it will give a pound of wheat all by itself," I said.

"Well, maybe not that much, but I took a picture of it. We can develop it when they all leave."

The next day Antonioz came over to ask Paul. "Where did you get that wheat? I'd like to plant some of it next year."

"But it's your wheat! Do you remember the five kilos you gave me this spring? This is from a handful of that seed."

"Give me ten kilos. I'll plant it in part of last year's potato patch," said Antonioz.

"You won't need one-tenth that much if you plant it in rows, "answered Paul, "but I'll give you back your five kilos."

Antonioz slouched out with his five kilos still convinced that his great grandfather knew best how to plant wheat.

Paul shared another five kilos with two of the young farmers who had helped with the thresher.

They left the chalet together, eagerly planning where and how they would plant their special gift of lush grain produced by the "new" method introduced by the Egyptians 3000 years before.

1943 Our Friends, The Bees
Journal Entry

In the Spring of 1943, after spending two rigorous Alpine winters in the chalet, we were given two bee hives. Though neither of us knew anything about bees, we were anxious to learn. The hives were two dome-shaped upturned baskets made of woven straw. We placed them on a shelf outside a window facing due south. As soon as the spring sun warmed their home, the bees streamed out from the small opening at the base of the hives to search for the first blossoms of spring. We watched fascinated, as each bee returned with her back legs bulging with two brilliant green bumps. This, we learned, was the first pollen taken from the fir tree cones in the nearby forest.

As the season advanced, the color of the pollen changed with the new flowers. Dandelion pollen was a brilliant yellow-orange. Later they came in with pink pollen in their back leg pollen baskets. Perhaps this was from the early pink primroses; they never came in with two colors at once. Bees' habits are very tidy. They will never mix pollen.

By midsummer the traffic of bees flying in and out in a steady stream resembled a freeway rush hour. The hives were noisy with the hum of their activity.

From research done on bees through an article in the National Geographic, and a book on beekeeping, we found out about modern methods and invested in two

Langstroth hives and a smoker. A smoker is a kind of can with an elongated spout. In the bottom of the "can" there is a smoldering fire. The smoke from the fire released through the spout will calm the bees and prevent them from stinging.

The modern hive is a topless and bottomless box which contains ten frames of foundation wax. The frames are suspended vertically and spaced a little less than an inch apart so that the bees can move freely between them. It is on this wax that the bees build their comb. As soon as the cells are built, the queen, starting from the middle of the frame, will lay her eggs, moving around the comb in a spiral. A good queen may lay as many as 1000 to 3000 eggs a day. Unfertilized eggs produce drones, or male bees, which are useless except when a new queen is being produced.

When the new queen hatches she will go on her nuptial flight, chased by the drones which follow her, each one hoping to be the lucky one to impregnate the queen for her lifetime of about three years. When the young queen returns to the hive she will meet the old queen in a fight to the death. This is the only time that queens will use their stingers... the duel between the queens is watched by the workers who remove the body of the slain queen. The drones are then banished from the hive. The workers prevent them from access to the honey comb, by fighting them off at the entrance.

The worker bees number about 3000 to 4000 in a strong healthy hive. Their duties vary with their age. For the first 12 to 14 days they care for the larvae, delivering to the brood chambers the protein-rich pollen brought to the hive by the older workers. When they are from 14 to 18 days old, their wax-producing glands develop, and they turn to the duty of building brood cells in which the queen will deposit her eggs. The workers' last duty within the hive is as guard at the entrance where they will prevent intrusion of bees from another hive or drones no longer needed. The guards also serve as air conditioners when the temperature soars. The rapid whir of their wings serves to ventilate the hive and evaporate the excess moisture from nectar brought in from the fields.

Bees can make honey from many flowers, but commercial honey is produced from a fragrant clover which grows over six feet tall and blooms with abundant yellow flowers. Since beekeeper often plant this mélilot (may-lee-lo) clover, Paul ordered seeds and planted a small plot in front of our hives. The bees responded gratefully to this close supply of nectar and we were soon faced with the urgency of handling a swarm from an overcrowded hive.

All the reading about capturing a swarm of bees did not help in the real emergency. One beautiful warm sunny day we noticed that bees were leaving one of the hives in an excited flurry of activity. In a dense cloud they flew over the mélilot onto the lower branches of a tree. With the smoker and a frame from an empty hive we tried to entice them to move to new quarters...

Suddenly, off they flew and settled in the meadow just below the chalet. I ran to follow them and sat down nearby trying to find the queen in the midst of a cluster of bees. Gradually they shifted location and though I could hear their contented buzzing, I could see very few bees.

Paul came closer carrying their new hive.

"Look, there they are in the grass. But they seem listless, as though wondering what to do," I said as he came near.

"Did you find the queen?" he asked.

"No, but they shift around so much. It's hard to tell."

"There is quite a cluster of bees on your back."

"There is!" I was surprised. "Maybe they are the ones making the loud hum that I hear."

"There are more and more bees, and they are in a real cluster. Maybe the queen is in the middle."

"I'd feel honored if she chose my back to land on. Can you see her?"

He looked closely. "I could use the smoker but I'm afraid they'd take off and we'd never catch them."

"Maybe you could use the smoker to direct them to a frame. Maybe the queen is in there even if you can't see her." I suggested.

He used the smoker and as the bees scattered he burst out, "There she is!"

With a gentle puff from the smoker he maneuvered them into their new home.

This was our first swarm of many. Over the years we increased our bee population to four thriving colonies, each one of which had at least one super, or supplementary honey comb. In the winter we covered them from winds and snow, but always the little front door remained open. As soon as the sun shone they scurried out, carrying all the waste and grime that had soiled their tidy home. The snow was spotted with their debris.

Bees live on their stored honey during the winter. They huddle in a close ball in the center of the hive whirring their wings to keep warm. There are no drones in winter. They are starved out, or killed and pushed out if they don't take the hint.

One year, in early August, we noticed that one hive was producing drones in abundance. This meant that the hive was dying. Either the queen had died or was no longer laying and the workers were trying to produce a new queen, or the hive had lost its young queen in her nuptial flight.

We had to find a new queen before the drones ate up all the reserves of honey. Our bees were black European bees but we had heard that the yellow Italian bees were more productive because the queen was a prodigious egg layer.

A beekeeper in Albertville, a day's bicycle trip away, had Italian queens. Pau decided to make the trip. When he returned from his 75 mile journey, he had the precious queen. Her long slender yellow body was lying between two 2 ½ inch wire mesh squares. A bevy of adoring workers was caressing her, and feeding her from the walls of the small container which were entirely made of sugar. It was imperative to get the queen into the new hive before all the sugar walls were consumed. A new queen is in danger of being killed as an intruder, unless she can remain sheltered four or five days, until the workers in the hive accept her scent.

We watched anxiously, hoping that she would be graciously received, but it was too late.

The queen did not survive, either because of the cooler climate or because she was killed by the workers who smothered her by clustering in a tight ball around her.

Our failure with the Italian queen taught us that experience is wiser than experiment, and during the following years our European bees kept us supplied with a delicious and abundant supply of Alpine honey.

Fall 1943 Douillette Is Led Astray
Journal Entry

Living among farmers whose lives depend almost entirely on their own efforts and ingenuity taught us to respect and understand the precarious balance of their lives. A sick hog, or a cow too old to be useful were contingencies they could prepare for. But war, even in this remote area, changed their lives. Occupation troops were stationed in the village and the farmers were obliged to furnish a large portion of the food and supplies for them. Soldiers could appear on the threshold of a peasant home and take away a horse, or a sheep, or divert 50 pounds of grain before it could be milled.

We had heard of neighbors who had lost a cow or a sheep. Antonioz claimed that they didn't leave enough potatoes for his pig. Dunoyer lost two dairy cows. Gué had managed to keep a sheep they had come for, only by replacing it with a deer he had shot while hunting. Even the druggist had been tapped and had turned over to the authorities four fine linen sheets that had been in his family for years. These were stories of our neighbors whose lives of hard work were never easy. The natural tendencies of self-preservation, even in normal times, tended to separate families into closed centers of self-sufficiency. War, which had brought to the valley the occupation troops, made them even more insular and suspicious. Morality everywhere was at a low ebb.

We too were to be caught in this web, and were able to appreciate the tragedy of loss when two solders came to examine our sheep, which by this time had increased to a flock of fourteen. Paul and I were both absent at the time but when we returned from the village, we found Serge in a state of more than usual bad temper.

He greeted us with, "The soldiers came. They took our best ewe."

"You mean Douillette?" I cried.

"Yes, they took Douillette and she would have had a lamb in the spring."

Douillette's wool was by far the best of all our flock, and now she was to be slaughtered for a stew for occupation troops.

"Did they buy her, or just take her?'

"They paid, if you can call this payment!" and Serge laid on the table the few francs the soldiers had left.

"Where did they take her?" Do you know?" asked Paul.

"I think they took her to their camp in the Vallée des Allamands."

Serge, I think, was even more incensed than Paul, and after dinner he and Paul had a conference. I was not to learn the results of their conversation until after the incident was over, though I could guess they were about to take action. If I had known what they were brewing, it would have been difficult for me to answer questions if the soldiers had come back to ask about a lost sheep.

Serge, though he was often difficult to get along with because of his quick temper, was not one to retreat before a battle. It was hard to imagine Serge meekly leading the best ewe of the flock out of the stable to hand her over to the occupation authorities without at least imagining some way to retaliate, but he also knew that he was an escaped prisoner of one of the slave camps and any inquiry into his papers could have been disastrous.

By checking with the neighbors, he found that the occupying authorities kept the requisitioned supplies in a camp in the Vallée des Allamands. He also learned that there was a warehouse where the guards were posted and slept. The animals, however, were kept in an enclosure in back of the warehouse. This, he was told, was surrounded only by a wire fence.

During the night, when Paul got up and left, I was careful to ask no questions.

"Do be careful, dear.'

"Don't worry," he kissed me. "Wish you could come too."

"Don't tell me where you're going. I don't want to have any accurate information."

"I hope to be back for breakfast, but if I'm not I've set out some twigs for you to start the fire. I hope it lights easily. There may be one or two matches in the drawer. Otherwise, try the flint lighter. It might work, but I doubt it."

"I'll get up early so the embers will still be quite warm," I answered.

He kissed me again and I lay down to think of the many things that could go wrong.

A lost sheep was better than hours of questioning ending with imprisonment or worse. The method of eliciting information in our valley was to make the prisoner sit on a hot stove until he gave the answers or information they needed.

This was to be a dangerous exploit and we all knew it.

As I lay in bed listening, I heard Paul and Serge talking. Serge answering Paul's well-controlled voice with happy chuckles. I heard a sheep bleating. I heard the stable door close and then their voices joined the muffled silence of the night as their footsteps retreated and the bleating of the sheep dwindled to a distant echo in the night.

The following morning, no one came to ask me questions. The embers were still warm and I lit the fire without trouble. The children had breakfast and went out to play, unaware that a drama might be taking place.

It was not until mid-morning that Paul and Serge reappeared like two delighted youngsters back from a trip of playing hooky. They had Douillette on a rope leash. She looked none the worse for her long pilgrimage to Les Allamands and immediately went over to the daisies on the terrace to finish her delayed breakfast.

It was really quite simple, they assured me. They had picked the scroungiest sheep from our herd, put her on a leash and by moonlight had traced their way over the hill and down to the troop encampment in the valley. Serge found Douillette among about twenty other sheep in the enclosure, and jumped over the fence to get her. Paul handed him the runt they had brought from our stable and Serge lifted Douillette over the fence to Paul who reattached the leash. They were all three back to the chalet in time for a late breakfast.

The occupying soldiers had counted their captive sheep and had retired for the night. The next morning the count was again accurate. In this case, counting sheep was an excellent opiate.

Chocolate Delight
Journal Entry

Paul always kept in close touch with any contacts he made so it was without too much surprise that we had the visit of Monsieur Junot, the Swiss friend who had helped Paul clear the way for the trip to Switzerland with the 28 farmers. He appeared at our door one beautiful crisp fall day in 1943.

Paul introduced me; and like everyone from everywhere during those difficult times of war shortages, he asked how we were getting along.

"We are very fortunate to be on a farm where we can produce sufficient food. This year, due to your help in introducing our farmers to your enterprise, we have had strawberries this summer."

"Don't you have apples or pears and even plums? They should grow well here." he asked.

Paul answered, "Unfortunately the farms at this altitude have been abandoned and what orchards remain are now wild."

"Yes," I continued. "The children make trips to abandoned farms and shake the trees for the plums. They are pretty sour, but children are tough, and adventure is part of the fun." The boys were still playing outdoors, but Sally Anne was stretched out under the piano drawing a picture with one of Paul's soft pencils. Betty was close beside her playing with Bear.

"Where are your boys? I was told you had several boys and girls."

"They will be home soon." I answered. "They went fishing."

"Fishing? Where do they fish"

"In the mountain brook about a mile from here. They lie on the bank and watch for trout."

"Don't they have a rod?"

"No, they can catch them by hand."

At that moment the boys came into the room.

Monsieur Junot looked at them, bedraggled and muddy, and seemed amused at such boyish lack of concern for dirt.

Paul introduced them.

"Did you have any luck fishing?"

"No," answered Jean, but "Miqué nearly caught a big one."

"I'll try again tomorrow," Miqué said.

"How do you do it, boys?" asked our guest.

"Well we just watch for them." Miqué answered. "The fish always hide under a rock so all you can see is the tip of the tail, but if he moves I just grab with both hands and throw him on the bank before he slips back into the water."

"Have you ever caught one?"

"Yes, once," said Miqué.

"It was a big one," added Jean.

"It was a good-sized fish," I said. "We ate it for dinner."

"That is really remarkable. I would certainly like to watch that." He fumbled in his pocket and pulled out a bag. "Would you all like to share a chocolate bar?"

The boys looked at each other, awed, and the children under the piano were on their feet in a hurry.

Pierre and Betty had never seen any candy and Miqué, Jean and Sally Anne remembered only little Easter candies Mamette had given them years before.

They all gathered around as Monsieur Junot broke off bits of candy for each child.

They went off to a corner to enjoy this unbelievable stroke of good fortune.

Paul went to get a bottle of wine as I asked our guest to sit down.

When Paul returned with glasses and wine we tried to engage Monsieur Junot in conversation. Paul asked him about the strawberry enterprise.

"How many farmers contribute to this cooperative venture?" I asked.

Monsieur Junot didn't answer; he was still watching the children - - each one slowly licking the precious morsel of chocolate candy with murmurs of appreciation.

"Don't you have candy here?" he asked.

"No," I answered, "they didn't even know what it was until they tasted what you brought."

"I'm so sorry. I could have brought a bar for each one of them."

"What you did bring will last a long time. You will be remembered as the man who gave them their first piece of candy," I said.

Paul asked him if any mail was sent from Switzerland to the U.S.

"My wife has not heard from her family in over two years. Do you know of any way she could get a letter sent to the U.S.?"

"I think I could find a way to send it through the American Embassy by diplomatic pouch."

While Paul prepared dinner for everyone, I wrote a long letter home.

Monsieur Junot left in the late afternoon with my letter which he sent through the embassy as promised.

It was the only news they had until after the war.

Letter Sent Through A Swiss Friend — November 1943

Dearest Family,

It doesn't seem possible that this letter may ever reach you, but I am going to take the chance, sending it by a Swiss friend through the American Embassy in Geneva.

I think of you all so much and long for news of you. The war seems eternal; every day we all grow older just waiting for the world to come to its sense, or to an end. We are all well.

The children are rosy-cheeked and growing much too fast. The war doesn't touch them except for shoe lessness and lack of toys.

Here in the chalet we have all the necessities of life: a cow, pig, bees, a goat, and several sheep - - one with her little lamb that was born on the mountain pasture. The children play like farmers' children, the boys carving themselves threshing machines (very rudimentary) and Sally

Anne and Pierre play at taking care of the cow, each taking turns to be the cow. Betty is learning to walk. We have a man to take care of the wood and animals and a girl from Golfe Juan to help in the house.

I spend all my time racking my brains to keep clothes fit to wear without using new material. The problem becomes more and more impossible... I have made pillow cases from table cloths, diapers from sheets, handkerchiefs from old shirts, dresses from drapes, bags from old aprons, skirts from old pants, but there is a limit. I have found no way to replace cotton socks, and can't find warm material to make pajamas.

Fortunately, we have 14 sheep which have given us wool to put new feet in all our old socks and warm sweaters for Miqué and Jean. I have learned to spin on the family spinning wheel that Mamette gave us. Other sweaters are being ripped up and re-dyed and re-knitted, sometimes spinning old wool with new wool from our sheep to strengthen it.

Our greatest worry is being separated. Paul was Professor in Nice last year and all his work was in the South. He earned some money, fortunately, because everything costs about ten times as much as it did before the war, and most things money can't buy anyway. We have even had long spells without the bare necessities like salt, vinegar and matches and money change. People give you little pieces of paper saying, "This is worth two francs" because they haven't the change in coins.

The worst has been the shoes! We were all barefooted this summer and got so used to it that shoes were a burden when we finally had to put them on because of the cold. Paul managed to get a pair in exchange for a portrait he made for a Swiss friend. (Fortunately, his customer had some to give him. He gave him his own shoes.) For Jean and Miqué I finally managed to change their old pairs for larger ones, but old. No one has ordinary low shoes except me with all the ones you sent me before the ports were closed. I have a permit for one pair but it is no good as there are no shoes in the stores anywhere. I looked in three towns. I have made house slippers from my old felt hats for the children but they aren't strong or big enough for Paul.

We are so much better off than most people that we really have nothing to complain of.

Even the weather has been perfect and gave us a potato crop that was unusual. We have forgotten the taste of most things that we take for granted ordinarily: bananas, candy, dates, raisins, lemons, coffee, corn meal and corn starch, rice, pasta, and even eggs because hens don't lay in winter. We have learned to eat with relish things we never would consider before and feel lucky if we can find calf's head, heart, kidneys. When he is old enough, we will slaughter the little ram born in the summer.

For breakfast we eat boiled wheat. It takes two hours to get soft, but it is certainly nourishing. It is against the rules to make flour so we eat the wheat "au naturel". We make our coffee from our own wheat which I roast every three weeks.

Paul suffers from lack of paper and pencils. There are no more envelopes or writing paper.

He made a deal with a newspaper man for raw newspaper to write on. Our plumbing is all haywire because there is no more T.P. Old magazines, saved over the years are now being flushed down the toilet.

There is nothing I can think of that is not missing except what comes with food tickets and there is very little of that. We have to take turns eating because we haven't enough cups or soup plates for the whole family to eat together. Everything made of rubber or steel is completely extinct. String is made of paper; wool of rayon; cotton of cellulose; cleansers of powdered dirt; brooms of branches or straw; buttons of wood. Shoes are the greatest article of ingenuity. There is no more leather so soles are made of wood, tops of raffia, pieces of belting, or even fur. The best shoes are those made from old tires. They make excellent soles for summer shoes.

We can't even find nails to put in the wooden soles of the children s boots to keep them from slipping in the snow (made of pressed cardboard). One pound of nails is worth two pounds of butter. Six packages of tobacco (men are allowed three a month) are worth a permit for a shirt but generally useless as shirts are impossible to find and if you do find one it is of a slithery rayon.

Jean and Miqué are wearing the ski suits that Mrs. Warburg sent before the blockade. I never met her but I bless her every day. The pants are very threadbare and as I have no more material to patch them I darn them with wool dyed to match. The jackets have all been turned inside out but they will soon be as gray as the other side.

I talk so much of you and of America. They are all very anxious to go to camp someday.

They don't talk English any more, although Miqué and Jean understand what I say. Pierre can say, "Wanna kiss you Mommy. I'll be sweet now." He understands a little but always answers in French. I am sure they would learn quickly if they heard it spoken around them.

I am afraid that this very precious paper is being very badly used. I feel I have said very little and very poorly said it. I long for news of you. Will you try to write to me by writing to the same address this letter is sent from? I wonder about news of new arrivals... Did Barbie have her baby? Marguerite had a baby girl in July 1942... Marianne. We have had no pictures of her as nothing but inter zone postcards can cross the frontier zone. Our Betty is a big girl now, pretty straight haired like all the others.

Not a week passes but I dream of someone from home. I am so anxious for the children to have the pleasure of knowing and loving you all. Miqué is very interested in his cousins and can't get over Peter being taller than he is. They want to see his tunnel, train and toys. They have had no toys for two years. They make and carve their own... guns, pipes, hammers, swords, bows and arrows, whips and tools of all kinds. They are sometimes quite ingenious because they have so little to work with, not even a nail to help them. They use handmade pegs that they make holes for with corkscrews. Miqué has the patience of an angel and is very, very particular. Jean goes where his imagination and his supplies lead him. He starts with the idea for a derrick and ends up with a dagger or a bus. Sally Anne is learning to sew. All five are left-handed except Pierre. He adores Sally Anne and follows her like a little dog. Fortunately he is very obedient. They all are really. I guess because I let them yell and scream and settle their own battles. Miqué is assistant in command... unfortunately, he lays it on like a Prussian General sometimes.

No more paper. Write to me. Try to squeeze in as much news as possible about everybody.

I love you all so much. Did you get a cable I sent in October?

I can imagine the enormous relief her sisters must have felt when they finally received news after two long years of opaque silence. Like a flood, the words poured out from a pent-up frustration as my mother tried to describe a life she knew would be utterly foreign to her sisters, relatively safe on the other side of the world.

When Joe describes his childhood to me, when he lived with

his mother in Carmel, playing at the beach, untouched by the deprivation of no shoes, no toys, no candy, I marvel at the difference of our shared history. We were two children of roughly the same age, living as if on different planets, rather than continents apart. He could be barefooted, if he wanted, or wear comfortable shoes if he had to. He could beg his mother to buy him a candy bar, and though she might say no, she could have if he'd really wanted one. A neighbor gave him a model sailing ship to put in his window— which fell out and broke on a strong gust of wind because he was a little careless. He could be a plane-spotter and feel important and useful in his seven-year-old life. His father was serving in the South Pacific, in New Caledonia, frustrated that he couldn't be part of the action. My parents became peasant farmers—because the had to, if they were to survive a war that touched every citizen in small and inconsequential ways, as well as like-changing, or life-ending catastrophe.

1944 The Meribel Project
Journal Entry

I was glad, of course, that Paul had a job that fitted all his varied interests. All the work he had done studying Alpine architecture would at last bear fruit in the new ski resort where he planned to use the structural principle established by the common sense of generations of native inhabitants.

He was eager to get started but I tried to fight back the self-pity that kept surfacing. I would have to deal with Serge who would resent taking suggestions, much less orders from a woman. Paul would be moving in circles of brilliant, witty people. How could my life of farm routine and children compete to hold his interest? There would be no more cozy evenings for the two of us with him at the piano and me knitting or sewing near the stove. No more magic evenings as he told me of the stars and pointed them out with the telescope, our voices hushed in the intimacy of being alone together in the starlit night.

When Paul was home he worked in his office above the stable, but his frequent trips downstairs brought him among us so that there was a feeling of belonging and closeness within the household. Serge knew where to find him if he had a question. When Paul came down, he inspected what was cooking and often prepared a concoction to surprise us, but mostly he came to include me in whatever he was doing.

"I've brought down the plan. I've made a few changes. Can I show it to you?"

There is not much in housework that can't be put off for a half hour, so we would discuss the latest ideas or changes he had considered. Sometimes I would go up to call him for dinner and stay, listening to him organize his thinking. Sharing his ideas out loud seemed to clarify his thoughts. I was a sounding board that echoed his thinking sometimes interjecting a question or suggestion that initiated new changes or directions or helped crystallize a hazy organization. When he returned to his work again, his mind had been recharged with new energy and a clearer perspective of the goal he sought.

When he came down for supper, that signaled the end of his working day. He added imaginative touches to the evening meal, while Paulette and I bathed and fed the children.

The bath routine was organized with almost military precision. Each child undressed and came in turn to be hoisted to the kitchen sink where I scrubbed and dressed them for bed. This consisted not only of pajamas but a wrap-around blanket from armpits to feet.

In the meantime Paulette heated their sheets with the copper warming pan, filled with embers, and came back to piggy-back each child to bed. Their room, a former cheese cellar, was so cold and damp that when the door was opened billows of mist rolled around the ceiling and dripped moisture down the walls over their heads. In winter they wore skating caps to bed, but never, in the five years we lived in the chalet, did anyone contract a prolonged sniffle or cold.

Often while this routine was going on and after they were in bed, Paul played the piano and the children soon became acquainted with Bach, Beethoven, Mozart and Chopin, and were able to request special preferences by humming the first notes. Chopin's Raindrop prelude was one of their favorites.

Children interpret music into visual images or stories that move with the tempo or pitch. One evening Paul told them briefly of the story of the Elf King who tried to reach home riding through the stormy night with his little son wrapped in his cloak. The music is dramatic and as Paul played, the children lay very quiet, listening.

"You can hear the storm," said Sally Anne in a hushed voice.

Pierre could not resist imitating the moaning wind.

"Just listen, Pierre," I was afraid that Paul would stop playing if they disturbed him with comments.

As the music rose to a loud crescendo, so also the storm intensified. The wind howled to the rhythm of the hoof beats in the black night. At last, as exhaustion overtook the rider, and the tempo relaxed and stopped, there was a pause.

Then Jean in a small voice said, "What happened, Daddy? Did they get home safely?"

Perhaps Paul realized the impact the music had evoked on the children because he started playing a happier tune and did not answer.

"Did the little boy die, Mommy?" Almost a sob, this came from Betty's bed.

"It was cold and home was too far away," I answered moving to her bed to comfort her.

But children do not shrink from dramatic tragedy. The Ride of the Elf King became their favorite bedtime music.

Cozy between their heated sheets, their movements confined by the wrap-around blankets, they never tossed off their covers, but fell sound asleep within five minutes. We all learned that altitude is the best soporific ever created. The sudden quiet of the evenings was our well-earned reward after a day of the squabbles and play of noisy children.

It was at times like this that I remembered the comfort of the "rabbit ears", as Mama fluffed our pillows around our ears to snuggle us more completely in our beds, as we fell asleep to the song of the piano. All six of us, children who long ago have become parents, grandparents, even great-grandparents, have a deep appreciation for classical piano music, and our various iPhones have extensive playlists of Bach, Beethoven, et al.

Some winter evenings, after supper and before bedtime, Papa would pull out the game he invented, that he had hoped to market. The war made any such effort quite impossible, but we all loved "The Treasure Game" so when he placed the board on the table, with its meticulously crafted pirate ships, we gathered around in eager anticipation. I remember those lovely pieces, made of corks that he carved to look like tall ships, with brightly colored sails and little pirate flags. The object was to avoid or vanquish all the dangers of the seven seas and finally find safety on the treasure island at the center of the board. I remember that no one ever made it before it was time for bed, but we loved the game nonetheless—maybe because we were all gathered together.

Winter 1944
Journal Entry

This web of our interwoven lives was dramatically disrupted by Paul's new job in a glittering world of international business men and artists. I foresaw problems with Serge, difficulties of discipline with the children who were often unruly until I came up with the magic formula, "I'll talk it over with Daddy."

That final authority was soon to be withdrawn. Even when Paul was home, his influence was due more to awe than a fear of punishment, but it was none the less real for the children. He was the presence in the background, always ready to help with hot mustard chest plasters and haircuts or to give encouragement to a budding artist who had a problem with a cow or a cat.

But all minor squabbles, or cuts or bruises or new ideas for games or listening to children's problems and enthusiasm... these were my department. Paul was the rearguard on whom we all depended and tried hard to please.

My anxiety and dismay about his leaving were complicated by the fact that Paulette and Paul Vésey had decided to get married and Paulette was ready to return to the Midi to prepare for the wedding. Paul hoped to come home often but was unable to make promises.

When at last he left for what would be an extended period, we all gathered on the terrace to see him off. Paul gave his final commands.

"Serge, be sure to light the fire at seven... be sure there is enough wood in the bin for each day. You can borrow an electric saw for the new wood. André has one," and then to me,

"That fruit the children gathered last week…it will have to be cooked soon."

He was talking about the small mountain of pears and apples in the side yard, fruit that the children had gathered from trees deserted by their former owners.

"It will take several hours to cook," he went on. "Serge, you can make a fire under the copper tank. You'll have to keep plenty of wood on hand."

"The fruit will have to be pared and cored first," I commented curtly.

"Oh no, just core them. You can do that pretty quickly."

I wondered when I would find time to core a few hundred pounds of fruit. I must have shown my resentment… to be left with this burden.

"I'll core them," I answered sullenly and picked up his mountain sack to put on his back.

Why was it he so often left when there was a big problem to be solved like the sick cow I had been obliged to deal with, and the myriad other crises I had dealt with alone while he was off someplace important… and now a mountain of fruit to make apple butter with dubious results.

He kissed all the children, who clambered all over him and left. We all waved as he disappeared over the slope of the Deux Pierres.

That evening the house was silent and lonely. Paul Vésey came up to get Paulette. Serge too left for Chantemerle to see Renée. He would try to repair the quarrel that still smoldered. I felt very alone, sitting near the fire spinning. The hum of the wheel echoed the sigh of longing in my heart. I dreaded going to bed and stayed up until the embers were almost cool. It suddenly occurred to me, "I must bank the fire." The last duty of Paul's before we went to bed was a poignant reminder of this absence.

As I opened the door of the grate to see if there were enough embers, Serge came in through the kitchen.

"You are back so soon, Serge?" I said more to express surprise than as a question.

"Yes," he answered, and then, "Can I do that for you?"

"Thank you, I'd appreciate it." This unusual gesture of courtesy from Serge who was more often sullen, surprised me.

He fixed the fire, and rose to leave, "I'll be back in the morning to start the fire, Madame. You should go to bed now."

I followed his suggestion and lay there thinking how different men were; Serge, blunt, honest and stubborn.

167

Paul never raised his voice in anger though I knew he was impatient with my clumsy ways in comparison with his own easy skills. I was always conscious of wondering whether he would approve. What could I do to the soup to make it different? He wants me to say I like his plan. Should I try to convince him that those doors are badly placed and upset the logical balance of the room? I must be wrong. He's the architect. Why does he come to me for advice but still make me feel that all he wants is approval.

Nothing concerning the children, however, ever gave me any doubts. They saw him all day if he worked in the fields or the garden, as well as at the noon meal when they all competed to get his attention to tell about their very important small lives.

He always listened with amused detachment, as an artist would look at a painting. He observed the tilt of Sally Anne's lovely face or listened to Betty's enthusiastic prattle as she looked up at him, her little hand on his knee to establish contact. What the boys said always seemed to interest him, as they told of their adventures with their neighbor friends.

I wondered when Paul could come home again. I stretched out in the empty bed. The sheets were cold... How many new people had he met and impressed with his easy charm and that penetrating gaze from his intelligent eyes? Maybe he was still having a lively discussion with a lot of witty people. How different our lives were. I marveled at the ease Paul seemed to feel moving from our world among peasants to this new environment of businessmen.

Letter from Paul

My dearest love,

This letter, which was supposed to reach you last week, was delayed because I was too late for the postman.

I am thinking of you day and night. I think this separation is the greatest épreuve (trial) we ever went through and it all means so much patience

I see more clearly in the near future and will see even more clearly in a week. We made the estimate. Rosseau agreed on making, without guarantee, the prefabricated prototype which is really quite an astounding bit of ingenuity. It shows, he is convinced, that it must be a success.

Peter is happy about it and is trying to find money to finance it. I wish you could see it, really ingenious in its simplicity, the prefabricated heating and fireplace unit. I worked it out with Scoffier who says it should be economical.

These mountains are beautiful, higher but more open than in Samoens. I hope to find time to do some painting but we are too busy now. Charlotte P... is working with us. She is quite a well-known decorator. I am learning a lot from her.

I tell you again, my dearest love, Saturday will be a sad day, but I will try to be with you in the woods and will try to spend the day in a big hike across the fields, thinking that your arm is in mine and your kissable, happy little face close to mine.

I love you so, your

Paul

Return from Switzerland — A Forecast

Paul couldn't contain his enthusiasm. When he came home finally, he was nearly bursting with all his news, anxious to show me the results of his successes in Switzerland.

"How long will the Méribel project last?"

"It's impossible to see that far ahead. Several years perhaps. They are very enthusiastic about my work and plan to build a whole center, even shops, perhaps even a training school for skiers."

"Does it mean we would live there someday?" I asked.

He didn't answer the question directly. "Someday I hope to be on my own, not working for someone else. Peter is a good friend, a fine man, but some of his associates have tunnel vision, if they have any at all."

By this I knew he meant that his ideas for grandiose plans were being countered by people who handled a tight budget. Paul had no use for bureaucratic minds, and had no concept of working within financial constraints.

"Does Peter believe in your program?"

"Yes, but he is a day-to-day planner. Such a magnificent area needs a man with a long term vision."

"And lots of capital," I added.

"He'll get the money. Not even hard-headed businessmen can ignore the possibilities of these slopes. I wish you could see them."

Knowing such a possibility was out of the question, I was silent.

He got up to shift the wood in the stove and added another piece. He had tried to share his thoughts and visions with me and every comment I had ventured to make, pulled in his kite-string of unquenchable energy and optimism. How could I make him understand that much of what I said was because I couldn't really judge this new project from a smattering of one-sided reports from him? Even his own assessment couldn't be objective, much less impartial. Paul felt that success or failure of a program lay 90% in the excellence of the overall design which he understood well and for which he trusted his own ability. I too believed in his competence. But behind every project lie organization, financial backing, the ability and interpersonal relationships of those in charge. He hoped and sensed that the management trusted him, but I was not sure that he had complete confidence in them.

"How does the interior decorator get along with the business end of the association?" I asked.

"Charlotte?... Fine," he answered. "She's been in this kind of thing before."

"Is she confident of its success?"

Again he didn't answer yes or no. "She tries to encourage Peter and has offered him valuable contacts to help him find money."

"And you? What pitfalls do you see? Or possible stumbling blocks?"

He hesitated. "Well... everyone is willing to work hard but shortages of everything block progress. No decent tools; what material we order comes late or not at all, or is not what we asked for. Construction is stalled and workmen can't be paid or they threaten to quit. We can't even get enough nails, and when and if they do come, they are too big, too small, or not enough to finish what has been started. It is not easy. I spend more time unraveling all the hitches, mistakes, delays and shortages than doing my own work."

His most cherished dream, however, was to see Samoens become a ski resort. He had already made a photograph of a panoramic view of the northern slope on which he had traced possible ski lifts and downhill runs. When Paul had said earlier he wanted to be on his own, what he had in mind was the planning and execution of a ski resort in Samoens. Méribel was a necessary stepping stone to the fulfillment of that dream. He was patiently gathering data and support for the ambition of a life time... a goal which could only become definitive after the war.

The night was cold and crisp. Millions of stars shimmered above us and a veil of windswept clouds floated across the sky. I shivered; Paul put his arm around me and we went inside.

"I often feel like Solveig on her mountain. I wait and wonder about you and your busy active life." I paused. "We are each of us alone in very separate lives." I could feel his arm tighten around my shoulder. "No matter how much you tell me of your work and the people around you, it is a different world."

He didn't answer. How could he? We both knew that for the present, perhaps for a long time we would have to be separated. Paul was uncomfortable with complaints. He was always ready and willing to do his best, to exhaust all possible solutions, but when he had done his utmost and still couldn't change the outcome, he accepted the inevitable with good will. He expected the same of me.

"With each visit home," I went on, "I sense that we are further apart. Even the children are learning an independence which includes less of your presence and attention."

"I know, I miss them too, but I think this project is opening the path for our future. I'm becoming an expert on ski resort design. Someday I hope to develop the valley in the same way. That would bring money and security for the family. But right now, it means separation and it's hard on all of us. We have to be patient."

"You're right, of course. I'm glad for you, but somehow..." I stopped not knowing how to go on.

"But what?"

"Well," I said at last, "I'm certainly not unhappy. It's not that... It's just that I feel inadequate, incomplete somehow."

He held me close. "I wish you could hear how I talk about you. Everyone wonders how you can handle what you do, and still come up smiling."

His tenderness took the wind out of my sails. How could I let him down? What could I say when he was proud of what he thought was a strong self-reliant wife? I felt weak, defeated and too close to tears to say much.

"I'm not smiling now," I said, choking back a sob. He kissed away the tears. The last thing I wanted to do was to make him feel guilty for what we both knew had no solution.

"Paul," I said at last, "someday I'd like to do something other than housekeeping and family, but right now, that's what I do best... and at least we can do that together. What would you think of having another baby? We once decided that six could constitute the big family we both wanted."

"Do you think we should have one now? Maybe we should wait until after the war."

"Who knows when that would be? I might be too old to try by that time. Even while the war is on, the children and I are safe up here. We have shelter and food, and living in this remote area we have no suburban hassle of keeping up with the Joneses. You have a job that seems not only to promise security but it is the kind of work you enjoy."

"If this job brings lots of money," he answered, "and I think it will, maybe we can go to America after the war. At least you could go with the children until I could make a decent home for us all."

I smiled. "Who knows, Paul? When you get to be famous for ski resorts you might build one in America?"

He got up to fix the fire. We were both dreaming, and I suppose we were trying to replace the grim reality of the separation we would have to face, with a fantasy we half believed could really happen.

What we both needed and could not have was a return to the normal intimacy of our everyday lives. The web of the separate routines of farm life when he was home, had woven a bond of unspoken closeness between us. Words were often unnecessary. When what is said is part of living, even an ordinary sentence like, "Let's have flan for dessert," carries a meaning of intimacy more than the words themselves. Often no words at all can strengthen that bond. Even the gestures of a familiar routine become a picture etched in memory.

I watched him as he lifted the rings from the fire. With a precise and elegant flip of the wrist he laid the ring under the stove. His every movement was unconscious but with an economy of motion that combined speed and grace. As he crouched before the grate, his heels never touched the floor and his knees bounced with a young springiness that was uniquely his. He banked the fire and filled the warming pan with embers. The moon was rising outside our window as we found each other between the heated sheets.

His touch, so familiar, so warm and loving had a special tenderness. He must have sensed the unspoken loneliness I felt while he was in his gilded world of money and international contacts.

He held me close with all the love he could not express in words, and a passion that exploded in the echo of my own

burning need for him. Together we were happy dreamers in
a world of our own making... He left early the next morning.

The intimacy of this entry in Mama's journal was raw and
poignant. As if she knew of the trials to come and the heartbreak she
would experience, this would be far more difficult than anything
they had experienced together during all the long years of the war.

At least, the challenges of the war years could be attributed to
outside forces, beyond their control, circumstances that required
that they pull together as a team. This was different. They were
drifting apart, as Papa's world excluded her more and more.

October 1945 — A Visitor
Journal Entry

Again, I was without help, this time with five children and
expecting the new baby in two months.

Paul came home with his friend and associate
Christophe, whom he had known and liked for many years.

Christophe's dry wit and sensitive understanding of
how to be helpful and when to stay out of the way made
him more than a guest. He was a friend to embrace with a
warm and happy welcome.

It was fleecing time and he was eager to see how it
was done. Serge brought in the first sheep and laid it on
the table. Paul tied the front legs together while I held the
back legs until Serge could tie them. Christophe watching,
stepped in to take over as he said, "Let me do that, he might
kick the baby."

I was touched by his courtesy. Farmers' wives are
expected to be tough and strong but that little remark
reminded me that I was feminine and could accept special
attention because of pregnancy.

That evening Paul showed the documentary he had
made of the "Saga of the Alps". As he was preparing the
film, Christophe and I waited in the darkened room and
talked of Méribel. I asked him,

"Has the end of the war made much different for you?
Do supplies come more regularly?"

"What comes arrives faster," he answered, "but so far,
the orders are still very incomplete."

"Do you have room yet to lodge many tourists? From Paul's letters it sounds as though you had a full house all the time."

He smiled. "You should come see us some time, Liv. You could do with a little fun."

"Maybe someday. Not right now," I said patting my front bulge. "I'd love to see Paul uproariously tipsy. He works too hard at preserving his dignity."

Christophe didn't answer, but sat silent, his face averted.

"What is he like?" I went on. "Those parties must be very gay with so many bright and witty people."

After a long pause he spoke. "Paul is not the saint you imagine him to be, Liv."

I felt a sudden tremor sliver through my body. What did he mean? It never occurred to me to distrust Paul.

"Oh, I'm sure Paul is as wild and boisterous as anyone after the drinks have been around," I answered, but I wasn't sure what message he was trying to tell me. Christophe would never be disloyal to his friend, but I think he hoped I would be less naïve.

I was reminded of the strange conversation I had with Serge and Paul's scoffing response to it.

Paul was ready to show the film and I was glad for the interruption. I wasn't sure I wanted to pursue this conversation any further...

Christophe was small with an Einstein mop of hair above his intelligent face. His gaze was direct, with a listener's intensity. He was always ready to break into an appreciative grin. His laughter did not explode but spread into a wide smile that encompassed his whole face.

If Paul ever had doubts about a project he could be sure of an honest opinion from Christophe, though Paul often fretted about what he called Christophe's plodding imagination that was often unwilling to accept Paul's innovative ideas.

I was glad to have him visit. He enjoyed our life, the children and the change from the hotel atmosphere of Méribel. He never said much but he made everyone feel special. He laughed at the children's jokes and came up with a quip that made them think they were clever. He was careful to notice Pierre who was often alone left in the middle between the two older boys and the girls.

Paul and Christophe left for Paris the next day, for more meetings, more important contacts that I knew nothing about.

When Paul left he promised to be back in mid-December
to stay until the baby came.
Fine, I thought, with some resentment…

Again, I am mystified as I read these entries. It is a slow turning of the screw as if Mama is beginning to wake from a long and dreamy sleep of innocence. As full as her days were with the work of the farm and the constant care of her children, her mind must have been free to ponder first the words from Serge, and then, as if a validation of something going on, to have Christophe make his cryptic comments. Was Papa beguiled by his apparent success, or was it real, finally? And again, how could she fit into this unfolding world of his? She must have felt a little ambivalent about this new baby: on the one hand, she loved nothing more than the newness of a baby, so trusting and helpless in her nurturing arms; and, after all, it had been her idea to have another baby. On the other hand, this was one more child that would take all her attention and disconnect her even more from her husband's exciting life.

– 15 –

THE LONGEST JOURNEY

December 1945 – Rainbows in the Storm
Journal Entry

Fall weather had set in. Each morning the night time fog rolled down the mountain to reveal the brilliant, almost purple, sky of high altitudes, shining above us. Serge came each morning, did his chores, chopped wood and filled the bin. The children's day of school and homework was as routine as mine was, of cleaning and preparing meals.

Every year before the snow fell, it was hard to realize that it could come suddenly and completely change our way of life. That year winter came early. Clouds black and ominous rolled in and filled the sky. The wind howled down the canyons and whipped across the fields and forests.

The thermometer dropped several degrees in an hour. Sheets of rain and wet snow ripped across the landscape seeming to land nowhere though the ground became glossy with wetness. In a few hours the violence of the wind abated, but the rain which had now become heavy wet snow fell steadily.

That night the temperature dropped and the pipes froze though I had left the faucet running. I kept the children home. It had snowed all night and was still snowing. We had enough wood but no water. The bathroom was a skating rink. Condensation on the tiles had frozen solid...and where were the pipes that had to be defrosted? In the bathroom, of course.

I would wait for Serge, I decided... but Serge didn't come. Should I feed the animals and milk Bazaine? I could hear her complaining in her ladylike way. "Where's my breakfast? Where is everybody?" came her plaintive mooing from the stable beyond the bathroom door.

I climbed to the hayloft and shoved the hay through to her manger. That should keep her busy until Serge comes, I thought. But being without water was crucial. I could hear the water dripping from the brook above the rock garden in back of the house. It was only about thirty feet from the bathroom door.

If I could slide across the bathroom safely I could certainly make it to the brook and get at least a large potful of water to start the chores. During pregnancy it never occurred to me that my sense of balance could be other than normal. I found the biggest pot I could carry and inched across the icy tiles to the door which opened to the outside.

It was still snowing, a wet clinging snow, as I discovered as I stepped into it with my wooden-soled shoes. They slid with every step. But carefully and slowly I made it to the brook and filled my pot.

On my way back I slipped and to keep my balance, my arm jerked out and the water spilled.

The second try was successful and somehow I made it to the house holding the pot with both arms and was enormously relieved when Serge finally came.

He milked Bazaine and defrosted the pipes. From then on he stayed in the chalet until the two sisters came as they had promised in early November.

The weather cleared but the snow would remain for the winter. I showed the sisters the routine of the house, warned the children to behave, and went to Serge's old room to 'take a nap', and slept four hours. Having the work handled by these two capable young girls gave me the vacation I needed.

In the beginning of December we had another blizzard. It snowed steadily for days until there was a wall of snow blocking the view from the windows. It was like being in the trough of a wave during a storm at sea. The snow bank rose above the windows, darkly translucent, sending a mysterious gray light from the sky into the house.

By the time Paul came home the girls had totally spoiled me. I had gained three pounds. They watched me nervously and sent me to bed every time I tried to help. Though nothing was said, we were all worried that the baby would come during a storm and that the doctor would not be able to make it to the chalet.

The weather finally cleared, the sun appeared, and soon the snow was smooth and packed. Paul arrived a few days earlier than expected and we celebrated, by inviting Renée and Serge for dinner.

The evening was festive. The relief of having Paul home kindled an excitement that could not be laid entirely to the many bottles of wine we consumed.

Soon after supper I complained of a backache which soon shifted to the front and by nine o'clock Serge was leaping down the mountain to get the doctor. While we waited, Paul sat with me in the guest room cabin, replenishing the fire and the hot water and counting the minutes between pains. In one hand he held the old encyclopedia. It was turned to the chapter on delivering a baby.

Around midnight Serge returned with the doctor who gave me another two hours to wait.

When the final moments came, Paul administered the chloroform while the doctor was busy bringing our six pound baby, Rona, into the world. I could understand Paul's bewilderment when she came, but not the doctor's. I watched the two of them standing over me as though wondering what to do with her, still slippery and upside down in the doctor's hands. Finally I sat up and told them, "Over there, give her a bath, Paul," and I pointed to the water he had prepared.

The girls stayed until I was ready to take up my place in the house. I had hoped they would stay, but when Rona was seven days old they left saying the "work was too hard" and that they were homesick for the more active life of the village.

But Paul was there. Whatever he did, and he did anything and everything, he did competently and fast. Life again fell into the familiar pattern of interwoven work routines with Paul, Serge and I sharing the load.

Paul didn't like to be away from home in spring. Now that the war was over and he again had use of the car, he decided that if he could bring home two of his draftsmen he could work at home. Thus his trips to Méribel were shorter and less frequent and he was home for the spring plowing and planting.

Rona was a sickly baby. I was so worried that when Paul had to go to Paris on business, I sent Rona with him so that his sister, a pediatrician, could diagnose the problem. She determined that Rona couldn't digest the rich milk of the Alps. Though I took off the cream and diluted the milk, and tried other formulas, Rona still didn't gain weight and cried almost continually.

Housework and worry about the baby consumed my days and thoughts. Though I was glad that Paul was upstairs and couldn't hear her crying, I missed the former days when we were closer and shared our worries. Paul, of course, was concerned about the baby, but he lived in a different world in his office. I felt that though we lived under the same roof our lives were drifting apart. I no longer felt welcome to pore over his drawing board with him.

He was very busy; though he knew Rona was not well he thought I was exaggerating the problem. "Lots of babies are colicky. She'll grow out of it," he said.

But she didn't. Sally Anne tried to help by rocking the baby in an effort to help her sleep. I was homesick. Now that the war was over the possibility of a trip began to seem at least a reasonable goal. Maybe in America I could at least be near a doctor who could relieve my anxiety.

Even before the war ended we had discussed the possibility of a trip to the United States.

Now seemed to be as good a time as any. There was no question of Paul's going. He was involved not only in his Méribel job, but with the possibility of an art exhibit in Paris, with the book he was now able to seriously consider publishing, as well as the strawberry project that he had not relinquished.

We talked it over. "Of course I can't go now. But it would be a good time for you," he told me. "I could see about remodeling the chalet to fit our needs while you are in the U.S." It all seemed to make sense. There were many reasons for trying to make the journey.

My family was eager to help. An exchange of letters from both sides of the Atlantic to Washington, and to the American Embassy in France, crisscrossed the ocean for several months.

In late March, the U.S. Government offered to repatriate our family on the Santa Paula sailing in June, 1946.

And so it was that I returned home with our six children.

This was the first time in six years that the family had left the chalet. The two youngest had never been to the village, had never even seen a store, a road or even a village market. Though we knew this long separation would be difficult for us both, we accepted it with high hopes for the brilliant future that seemed to lie ahead. It was, however, with mixed feelings of joy and anxiety that we faced this test of our marriage.

Our descent from the chalet to the village was done in the old Renault. The children were noisy and boisterous with excitement. At last they would be going to America, the fabled land they had heard so much about.

"Will we be on the boat tomorrow?"

"Not tomorrow, Pierre," said Paul. "We have to take the train all the way across France."

"How long will that take?" asked Sally Anne.

"Two whole days," I answered, "but we will stop first to see Tante Marguerite in Paris."

"Will we sleep on the train?"

I looked at Paul. "I hope so, but you may have to try to sleep sitting up. We will probably have one complete compartment but they are planned for eight seated people."

"Will there be toys on the boat?" This from Pierre again.

"Perhaps," answered Paul, "but everyone will talk English like Mommy."

"But I can't talk English. Won't they talk French at all?"

"Don't worry, Sally Anne. The American sailors will love to hear you talk French. You can teach them... and some of the passengers will speak French. They are going to the U.S. just like you for the first time to live there with their American husbands."

"You will taste American food that you have never had," Paul told them.

"What kind of food?" asked Jean.

"Well, ice cream, candy, cake and fruit like grapefruit, watermelon and oranges."

"We had oranges in the Miradou," said Miqué.

"Yes, that's true, but Betty and Pierre don't remember."

"Yes, I do," said Betty.

"You couldn't, you were too little."

"I'm not little; I'm 4 1/2."

Sally Anne put her arm around Betty. "They're just teasing. Don't pay any attention. Did you put Bear in the car?"

"Do I have to, Mommy? Can't I hold Bear?"

I reassured her and we prepared to pile into the Renault, Betty clutching Bear. Sally Anne held the baby while Paul and I assembled the bags and Jean went back for the packed lunch.

"Sally Anne, you will carry the baby and sit between Mommy and me."

She climbed into the front seat and I handed her six month old Rona who seemed to like the idea and gave her sister a big smile. I squeezed in beside her with Betty on my lap.

"We forgot the cat!" I suddenly remembered.

She was peacefully sleeping under the stove. It seemed a shame to disturb her. "You could take her to Chantemerle when you come back in two weeks," I suggested. "The cat door is open and she can take care of the chalet while you are gone."

"I'd rather take her now. I'm not sure when I'll be able to get back. Pierre, you can hold the cat until we reach Chantemerle."

Betty shouted, "Let me, let me. I'll hold her."

"You have Bear," said Sally Anne. "It's too crowded up here now."

Paul settled the matter and put the cat on Pierre's lap. Betty puckered up ready for tears but Paul told her, "The cat might scratch the baby. She's safer in the back."

"No, she won't. I'll be careful."

"No, Betty, the cat goes in back," said her father firmly.

"You know that Bear wouldn't want anyone else on your lap," I tried to console her.

"Yes, he would." The tears were coming faster.

Sally Anne leaned over and pretended to listen to Bear.

"Bear says you don't love him. He wants you to hold him tight."

The tears stopped but the sobs continued as Betty hugged Bear and kissed him on the head.

"Hold on to the cat, Pierre, she's going to get out."

This was from Jean tightly squeezed in the middle of the back seat with the lunch on his lap.

"Pierre," said his father, "I gave you the cat to hold, now hold her. We'll be in Chantemerle in five minutes." Paul climbed into the car and we drove off.

Paul drove carefully as we bumped crazily on the unpaved road. Just as we reached the village of Chantemerle the cat jumped out of the window and sped across the road behind the nearest house.

"There goes the cat," shouted all three boys from the back seat.

Paul stopped the car suddenly, preparing to run after the cat.

"Don't bother, Paul. She'll find her way by herself." The whole episode struck me as hilariously funny and we were all laughing as we coasted to Madame Vésey's doorway.

She was talking to neighbors and waved to wish us "bon voyage".

"Thank you, Madame. We brought back the cat but she jumped out of the car just as we were arriving."

"That's all right, Madame," she answered. "No need to worry. She'll come when she gets hungry."

As we were talking, the cat came down the path with the deliberate gait of a feline whose ego had been vindicated. She crossed the threshold without a glance at anyone, and disappeared into the house.

"Well," said Paul. "That solves the cat problem."

We continued our way without further incident. When we reached Samoens, Betty burst into a voluble display of enthusiasm.

"What a big road! It is so wide and smooth!" She leaned over to touch the asphalt pavement. When she looked down the street where a group of six or seven people were talking, she came closer to me, surprised and a little anxious, "Quelle foule! What a crowd," she cried. "Where did they all come from?"

The boys stood around shifting from one foot to the other trying to look bored. At ten and eleven they knew all about the wonders of the village metropolis. It was new to Pierre but he said nothing except to stay close to me. Sally Anne held Betty's hand as Paul went to see about the baggage and the tickets.

The train trip to Paris was long, but the children stood for hours, pressed against the windows until the night blanketed the wonders of the passing landscape.

Their comments were witness to the total novelty of the adventure. They especially enjoyed the hustle and bustle at the stations along the way.

"What are those empty platforms on wheels for?"

"They are used to take the baggage off the train," answered Paul.

"Where's the baggage?"

"It's in a special car at the front of the train."

"Can we go see it?"

"That man is selling something. Can we get some? What is it?"

"Look! They're handing up pillows through the window? Can I take one?"

Paul brought back some pillows for the long night.

"Could you use these for the baby?" he asked and put them on the seat beside me. I laid the baby down for the night and went to join the family in the corridor.

The children were fascinated by the noise, the steam, and the chugging sound of the wheels that grated on the tracks each time we left a station. They imitated the hissing spit of steam and the clatter of the bell as the conductor swung aboard the train with his lantern.

Miqué and Jean even admitted that Pierre did a very plausible imitation of the clanking bell and accompanied him with proper hissing noises and chugs.

After the girls were introduced to the washroom, they used every excuse to go back. They washed the baby's bottle and marveled at the way the faucet stopped if they let go.

Pierre at six, with two older brothers who ignored him, and three sisters who had their own little girl world, was often alone and had to find his own amusement. Sociable by nature, he found company among adults who welcomed his cheerful disposition. It was not long before he wandered off to find someone to talk to in the next compartment. When he returned he was anxious to relay the information about our neighbors.

"They have a girl my age in Dijon. They're going to see her and bring her home. They have a cat in a basket in there. Why didn't we take our cat with us, Mommy?"

I smiled, "Our cat doesn't like to travel, Pierre; she even jumped out the car window, remember?"

"Maybe we could get a cat in America." he continued.

"We'll see. Aunt Betty has a dog. Maybe you will be invited to her house. You would like playing with a dog."

We had planned to have my sisters take the children until I could find a place for all of us.

What I had heard about my sister's dog did not seem too promising, but perhaps his name, Snappy, only meant young and frisky.

"His name is Snappy, Pierre. He's small and white and his fur covers him completely, even his face. You can't tell which end to grab until he suddenly jumps away."

"Even his eyes?"

"Yes, even his eyes, but he certainly sees everything through that veil of fur. He loves to chase cats."

Pierre laughed as I told him of Snappy and his antics. In a little while he left again to tell his new friends about the dog with too much fur on both ends.

As night fell we all came back to the compartment to eat the packed lunch which was to be our dinner. Sleeping was less of a problem than we had dared hope for, since we were able to have two complete compartments when the couple next door left the train at Dijon.

Paul and I stayed in the corridor while the children fell asleep. Watching the night fly by as we stood side by side, made me feel like Alice falling down the rabbit hole. Until then, time had been filled with preparations and routine duties. There had been no time to think or really plan. Suddenly I realized there would be no one beside me to soothe my fears, no one to make the insurmountable obstacles seem like ant hills. Over the years I had learned to accept Paul's way of brushing aside doubts and expecting a semblance of Utopia around the next corner.

We had coped during wartime with shortages by learning to limit our needs to what our farm produced. Only Paul's traveling expenses required money. Now I was to be alone in the United States with six young children where food, clothing, shelter, everything had to be paid for. I had planned to use money from my father's inheritance but knew that 300 dollars a month was as far as it would stretch for the year we expected to be there.

Paul, even on a salary would not be able to help much. Money, it seemed, always disappeared faster than it came in. As I stood there beside him, my thoughts raced in near panic as we sped through the darkness.

How could I afford camp for the boys? And clothes? We were all threadbare... a car was out of the question... perhaps a bicycle... How could I handle grocery shopping? To pay for it and to carry it home? We were to live during the summer in an almost rent free house my sister had found for us. But in September the landlord and her family would be returning to their home. I would have to find a place to live. It would have to be near a school.

This was not the first time I had thought of all this, but until then it had all worried me piecemeal. Now the enormity of the problems gathered momentum as the moment of separation from the stability of our life on the farm drew closer. I turned to look at Paul. His handsome profile was serene. His thoughts somewhere out there in the night. I touched his elbow. He turned and put his arm on my shoulder.

"The night is clear. There must be a moon," he said.

I paused, struggling to match his mood. "There are so many stars!" I answered. "Will we see the same stars in America?"

"They will be the same stars, but they will come up at a different time."

I turned to face him, he was smiling. Why and how did he always make me feel that I was fretting uselessly? Once again he had brushed aside the insurmountable obstacles that floated away like the whistle of the train fading in the distance.

Paul's sister met us in Paris and took us to her home outside the city for a much needed rest.

She examined all the children and expressed her professional, as well as loving, approval. Even the baby, who at six months, was underweight and pale, now seemed eager and alert, as though sensing the big adventure that lay ahead.

The next day we took the boat train to Le Havre.

The four hour trip seemed much longer than the twelve hour journey two days before. The little farms of Normandy were green and lush. As we raced through the countryside, war damage seemed minimal until we were a few miles from the coast.

Outside Le Havre, a kind of temporary station had been set up where the train stopped.

"Everybody out here," ordered the conductor. "You will be taken by bus to the boat."

"Why?" I asked.

"There is still too much damage. The railroad and the station are gone and have not yet been rebuilt," he answered.

The trip on the bus was a four or five mile bumpy ride through war rubble. Enormous slabs of destroyed bunkers towered on each side of an unpaved road. Mountains of concrete had been bulldozed aside to leave just enough room for the bus to pass through. Twisted rolls of barbed wire stuck out in the cracks between the piled up rubble.

"Where are we?" asked Miqué. A good question I thought. This indeed was the no man's land of war destruction.

"Where's the water?" said Sally Anne. "I thought we were going on a boat."

When at last we reached the dock, the boat was moored alongside a long and almost empty pier. Where was the life of shipyard cranes, of freight being loaded, of men shouting orders or scurrying to obey them? Even the passengers seemed disconcerted, as though they were being asked to board a phantom ship.

This was a scene of France, struggling to renew its peacetime rhythm. But Paul, always ready to see the drama of a situation called to us, "I'm going to take a picture. Stand over there."

We did as we were bidden, but it was not until the picture was developed that I realized that he had posed his family under the ship's name, SANTA PAULA, with the star-spangled banner floating above it.

We had reached another turning point in our lives.

Seeing him standing alone on the wide empty pier bravely waving goodbye, a pang of conscience overwhelmed me. How could I leave him? Taking with me all the little family that had become the anchor and guidepost of his life?

Together we had found strength in overcoming the hardships of war. Would our marriage now survive the test of a long separation?

I sat back in my chair, the weight of my mother's war journal resting on my lap. I turned the last page over and laid my hand on the worn paper, now soft and yellowing with the passage of years left in a dusty manila envelope.

It was raining again, the grey sky matching my melancholy, the rain, like tears unshed and trapped in time over all these many years. I have thought of my mother so often, in so many small ways, as I cook, as I make a bed, as I sew, as my hands move into auto-pilot doing all she taught me to do. But can I ever come to that place of courage and grace that became, finally, her lasting legacy? And my father? Lost to me in the dusk of time, I can only mourn that I only knew his vital life force as a child, and as I have experienced it through dusty memories, long since overshadowed by my own life.

Like a movie clip, a singularly vivid picture emerged full-blown.

This was the time I had the lunch of asparagus in vinaigrette with Papa, in Paris. We were all staying with his sister in the suburbs, before going to *Le Havre*.

"Come, Sally Anne. You and I are going to have a little adventure, just the two of us." He took me by the hand and we walked to the train station, not far away. For the first time, I was alone with my Papa. He was paying attention to only me. Mama wasn't there; my brothers weren't either. Not even Betty, though she was nearly five and could have come with us too, I thought. I tried to stand a bit taller, a bit more grown-up, so that he would be proud to take me wherever it was he had in mind.

When we got off the train at the *Gare St. Lazare*, the noise and confusion were overwhelming. I held his hand tightly as we moved through the surging crowd all around us. The trains huffed noisily and conductors called out the departures and arrivals. This was not like the peace of the mountains.

We got to the café, and sat at one of the tables outside. Streams of cars went by slowly, their gasoline fumes finally prompting Papa to take me inside. We sat at a table by the window, its stiff white tablecloth grazing my knees as I sat.

"Sally Anne," he began. "You're getting quite grown up, I see. You'll be nine this year, *n'est-ce pa*? I expect you to be a big help to Mama. She will need you, now that you have a little baby sister."

"Why can't you come with us, Papa? Will you be coming soon?"

"Probably not for a while. But we can write to each other. I would love to get some letters from you—and some drawings too. You're beginning to be quite a good little artist."

"But Papa, it's not the same—writing letters, I mean. You've never been so far away from us. I feel as if we might never see you again."

"Nonsense. I just have some business to do here, and with *Méribel,* which will take a bit of time. It will help me make enough money that maybe we never have to think about that again. Don't you think that's a smart thing to do?"

"I guess. And I promise to take good care of Rona—and Betty too, of course. But the boys will keep teasing us. I can't stand them!"

"Don't be silly, Sally Anne. They're your brothers. I know they'll look after you and defend you from anything and everything. That's what brothers do. Now let's have a lovely lunch, just you and me. I want to have a really sweet memory of you to carry around with me while you are so far away."

But I think it is I who has carried the memory buried in my heart even until now.

PART II
AMERICA

– 16 –

THE LETTERS

Perhaps our paths are ordained in the cosmos. Perhaps Rona was the outcome of a star-crossed encounter in the heavens. Of the six, Rona looks the most like our father. The rest of us have Mama's soft face, with rounded cheeks, and full-lipped mouth. Rona has Papa's stormy, smoldering dark eyes, fierce in barely contained passion. Her hair, black and almost curly, is an unruly hedge on her head.

She was the baby and was adored; her antics were a constant source of amusement. Her face could easily contort into wild expressions that mirrored her mood. As the baby caboose, she had everyone's attention. Of course, I made it my paramount duty to be the big sister in charge: her protector, her care giver, her teacher and counselor. If Paul or John, or Peter tried to tease Rona, they would have to answer to my anger. If she fell and skinned her knee, I was there to kiss the hurt away. I happily volunteered to be the surrogate mother in Mama's harried and complicated life. I determined early on that Betty could take care of herself, but Rona would always need a watchful eye to protect her from her own willfulness.

Rona was different from the very beginning. Six months old when we came to America, she had no personal memory of France, or the chalet, or the war and what that meant to the rest of us. And yet, it was Rona who eventually became the French teacher. Of all the siblings, she had a personal fascination for a life and a world that had never been part of her own memories.

Even Betty, who had her fifth birthday on the boat, proudly seated at the captain's table, eating a jiggly Jell-O cake that was like nothing she had ever known, could still have the profound memory of being awakened early one morning to go up on the deck of the *Santa Paula* with the rest of us as Mama pointed out the Statue of Liberty in New York Harbor.

"Do you know, children?" she asked, her voice catching with the pride of the moment, "On every trip I made back—for you Micqué, and Jean, and Sally Anne, my proudest moment was always this one—as we came into the harbor, with Lady Liberty and her arm hoisted high to light the way to these proud shores…"

"And from now on," she continued, "Micqué, your new name will be Paul; and Jean, you are now John; and Pierre, you are Peter. You girls already have American names, but now we will all be Americans. But you will never forget that you are French too.

The long war was finally over. Mama was never so proud to be an American as she was the day she knew that her country and its allies had prevailed, finally, over the juggernaut that had been Hitler's war machine.

She needed to go home. She needed to put France and the war years behind her. She never wanted to see another ration card. She was looking forward to buying a loaf of bread, soft and already sliced, sanitized in its bag, as she had described it to us.

Finally, in June 1946, Mama and the six of us boarded a converted cruise ship that became a converted troop ship that once again could cross the ocean in safety. Papa stayed behind, waving to us from the shore.

We were the only American civilians in a sea of perhaps a thousand returning American soldiers, many returning with their new French brides. But we were the only children and were therefore singularly special. We sat at the Captain's table for meals; soldiers plied us with candy and were mesmerized by this little American family, refugees of the war they had valiantly fought and won. We spoke not a word of English, of course, but Mama was suddenly euphoric. Finally hearing the easy twang and rhythm in these gruff American voices made her shy and halting. After so many years, would she even remember how to speak English?

These brave soldiers turned their attentions to us, a little band of French-American children, to teach us a few words of this new language, to introduce new foods to children who had never seen an orange or a banana, to teach us not to eat the skin, but to peel the fruit for what was inside.

We celebrated Betty's fifth birthday on this big boat, with soldiers and captain and crew crowded around to join in the festivities.

It didn't take long to learn the new language, to acclimate to the wonderland that was America, a new and glorious home. Rona, eleven years younger than her oldest brother, was always separate from the rest of us, as we all began the process of assimilating in school. And from the beginning, she was American, while we had to learn how to be so. She simply grew up into her new country, while we were constantly stumbling, eager to be just like everyone else. When I was eight, I came to America and learned a new language. When Rona was eight, she watched "Howdy Doody" on the neighbor's new TV set. She would always be more American than any of her brothers and sisters. She knew no other life than the American way of sliced bread and cereal in a box.

The letters gave substance and balance to all that I had been reading of Mama's journal. Her voice had carried over the pages, infused with her hope and the love for the man she married. But it was always her voice and her understanding that came through. Their complicated journey together throughout the years of war and its attendant challenges always seemed to be from her perspective. But now, here were some letters from Papa.

I knew so little and understood nothing at all…

Betty had brought the letters over. Betty was the archivist, the lynchpin for the scattered family. It had always been Betty who stayed connected. She always had the latest news, even about the distant cousins still in France. Somehow, while her brothers, her sisters, and her parents stumbled through their lives in self-centered separateness, she came to represent—for everyone—a solid and secure base. She collected Papa's paintings, after he died. She retrieved Mama's letters, after she died. She gathered her brothers and sisters together to distribute the paintings, but she kept the letters for a future time, to be catalogued, and copied for her scattered siblings.

I offered to make the copies on our big office copier that could churn out batches of documents quickly. Betty came with two large file boxes.

"Wow! I had no idea there was so much stuff..."

"It's really not so much, once you realize this represents their entire life together. And there's a folder of your letters as well. She kept it all." Betty continued, "I was really moved when I read the letters from Papa. He loved her so much..."

"Really? I had the impression that he was quite self-absorbed."

Betty studied me, her older sister, wondering, as she often did, when did I become so...cold?

After Betty left, I settled in to read these letters for myself—to begin to unravel the mystery of my parents' life together.

I pulled out the first letter from Papa, immediately realizing that most of these letters would be one-sided. There were none from Mama. Betty had carefully catalogued each letter that Papa had written to Mama; post-it notes with little comments in her strong, open handwriting fluttered to the desk as I started to read. The fragile air mail paper crinkled as I carefully moved the letter closer to the strong light. Some of the words were faded and no longer legible and I barely made out the date, Thursday 27th—but what year? Betty's post-it note guessed: wartime?

"Dearest," he began and I was immediately surprised. I had never seen displays of affection from him, of that I was quite certain. He continued, *"I am anxious about news..."* The next two paragraphs had faded to ancient vapors. I continued to read. *"I do the accounts like clockwork now and I think it saves money."* I

smiled as I remembered Papa's absolute abandon when it came to keeping track of money. Mama must have gently scolded him. *"The trip to Paris seems very useful,"* he continued, *"I don't dare to say anything until it really is true, but all prospects are good. I miss you so, dearest—I just dive into work, but sometimes the inspiration does not come right, as you are away. I will be so glad to get to the chalet to see you all again. Write to me often—you have so much more to say than I have. Love to all. Your, Paul"*

This must have been written sometime between 1941 and 1945, probably when he was traveling, as he tried to successfully bring to fruition at least some of his visionary dreams. The letter would have been written before Mama went to America with all of us in June of 1946. And it was summer so this was also before Rona was born in December 1945.

I sat at my desk, the letters scattered around me in small piles, sorted by year. The past drifted up in a fragrance on the thin sheets of airmail stationary, which fluttered like autumn leaves. As I read the letters, my fingers caressed the paper, as if I might somehow recall the presence and the mystery of my parents; if I could only read the faded words, or understand the depth of the language as Papa went from English to French and back again—even as he tried to communicate his longing and loneliness.

> "Dearest, These last days were not cheerful, and any letter I would have written would have been anything but happy. Our anniversary and then your birthday, and I had planned for months to be with you then. I have had awful days and nights. I have been trying so hard to make something happen—to no avail, I fear. For instance, I saw the director of the gallery finally, after making an appointment which he did not keep. I waited until 7:00 to see him, just as he was going home. He at least looked at my paintings and acted amazed. He is sure of success and says he will open his gallery for me in the fall, as it is now too late for the season."

As I read, I felt his frustration and discouragement as a mourning note over the decades.

I continued reading,

> "It is so nice to talk with you, the only one with whom I really talk—and you can see by the scarcity of my letters that I don't talk much. You letters are the only nice ones, and they are so wonderful they make me gurgle inside like a proud turkey, and every time I try to be half as nice in a letter to you, the words get strangled in my throat. I need you so, my sweet Liv, I ache for you all day and night long. Let's be patient, dearest love; we are always together and will be nearer soon. Happy birthday to my dearest bride."

Dim memories began to surface, as I tried to stitch together what I barely recalled, and the fresh reality of the words that marched across the pages I read. In the next letter, we had all left France and had resettled in America. Papa stayed behind. As a child, I had barely questioned this arrangement, since Papa had so often been gone from home. Now I began to understand the tension between my parents.

> "August 30th, 1946. Dearest all, Welcome to your new home, which Papa hopes to know soon. When? Nobody knows. Send me pictures of it. This will leave you time for the chalet to be remodeled, cleaned, deodorized, X-rayed, and bathtubbed." His sarcasm was explicit. "It is much less hopeless than you may think, as Belleville is definitely taking shape, and money will be flowing into Papa's hand before long. It is not so dumb as you may think to have bought the Muffat chalet (with the advance Lindsay gave me). It is a priceless place, according to Col. Peter D. Lindsay." His hurt pride was evident in his next comment. "If Mama still had a poppyseed of confidence in Papa's sense of business (but she does not), we could make many more exciting projects."

His letter went on to describe how he was called upon to host many important guests and take them on tours. He complained that he felt as if he had become a tour guide—but he needed to do this because these people were potential investors in the development of the ski resorts that were taking shape.

I was always mystified by Papa's lack of success in all his

business ventures. His ideas were visionary, but never seemed to amount to any money in his pocket. It was as if there was always someone ready to capitalize on his efforts—before he could secure any return for himself. As many times as he was taken advantage of, he always came back with a renewed hopefulness, never ready to give up or give in. His letter finished with a plea for Mama to recapture the hope she had always invested in him.

> "Don't worry, Liv dearest. Even if there is not the slightest poppyseed of confidence left, I really believe (there he goes again) that next year you may see some of your dreams come true. We are in full storm now, and the ship has to keep her way. Take it easy, and when you come back, you will sleep in a new room, and the big fireplace will heat the whole room, and both our hearts. We will have so many things to tell each other then. And don't worry. We shall have wood. Big logs from the forest, still covered with moss and lichen."

He closed with a note to the children.

> "Love to you all. I am always with you and wish I were with Mama, to hug her and kiss her eyes to dry out the tears. But our two undersized boys will replace Papa."

I remembered that Paul and John had shocked the American relatives who had taken us in when we first arrived. Both older boys were malnourished and small for their ages, with the sign of rickets that had given them sunken chests. They were embarrassed and Papa was furious that they should be singled out as puny as a result.

I was also surprised that Papa expected the family to go back to France to live. Even though I was not quite nine when we made the trip to America, I had always understood the finality of that voyage. We would be going to America to stay.

— 17 —

NEW LIFE

It hadn't been hard for Mama to readjust to her familiar life in America. She bought a large house in Connecticut, using her father's inheritance, so that her children could begin the process of finding their way in this strange new land. We arrived in late spring, and had the summer to begin our baptism as new Americans. By the time school began in September, we were all speaking English except Rona, who was barely a toddler. But we were still kept back a grade—I guess because the school thought we hadn't been getting a good education in France.

We learned to chew bubble gum; we learned to ride bikes; we got excited about baseball and decided the Brooklyn Dodgers were the best and Pee Wee Reese was the best of all baseball players; eventually, we went to our first movie, "Red River" with John Wayne and Montgomery Clift, and I decided I would marry someone just like him one day.

In 1948, Papa finally rejoined us. By this time, none of us were speaking French anymore. It had only been two years since he had seen his family, he thought, but we were all so different now that he barely recognized us, though Mama, as always, had that sweet innocence that he had so loved so many lifetimes ago. We had all been through so much, these last ten years, and she had always endured the trials with grace and forbearance, he thought. Now, he saw that she was home at last, where she belonged, near her sisters, in a land she understood better than he ever would.

"Do you like the house, Paul?" she asked him timidly. "I tried to find something that would grow with the children, but would give you enough space for your studio." She took him by the hand now, eager to show him around. We buzzed like bees, eager to share in this momentous homecoming. Papa left his large suitcase by the door, almost as if he might leave as suddenly as he had come. Dark brown leather, scratched and scarred, weathered and somewhat limp, the suitcase was covered with travel stickers, places that reflected his odyssey through his peripatetic life.

He took Mama's hand and let her lead him, suddenly shy, as if he would bolt if she let go. They went through the dark-paneled hall, its hardwood floor lustrous with fresh wax—we had spent an hour in our woolen socks, skating rhythmically over the floor in a game that she invented to get us to help her with hard housework. Now, we all hung back, needing permission to be part of Papa's greeting party. Mama nodded an okay and we dashed ahead to be the first to see Papa's expression when he would see his studio. The room at the end of the long hallway was softly lit through the windows that all faced north—the perfect orientation for his drawing board and his easel. The room was longer than it was wide and the wall opposite the windows was banked with a series of bookshelves. As if waiting for him to fill it with his personality, the room was quite empty except for a large oriental rug on the floor, subtly patterned in muted colors.

"Do you like it?" she asked again.

Now he let go of her hand and hugged her to him. She melted into his arms and began to cry.

"Shh, Shh," he kissed the top of her head and we gathered around in concern. "It's perfect. You did so well. The light is just right; it will be a wonderful place to work."

"We've all missed you so much. When you said you were coming, we all dashed around like crazy people to get the place ready for you. Didn't we, kids?" Mama had already lapsed into the *argot*, the slang of America, he realized.

"Why don't you show me the rest of the house? I'm curious; do you all have your own rooms?" He addressed his gathered children and we erupted with fresh enthusiasm, eager to show him that we did, indeed, have our own rooms.

Papa filled the house with his presence, as he had always filled every space he had ever come into. It was as if even six noisy children could never be enough to still the echoes.

We ate in the dining room that night, rather than the kitchen, where we had always eaten before Papa came. He had a gift for each of us; something that he knew would suit each perfectly. And how did he know to give Paul an airplane model, precision-scaled and even with the glue that he would need to put it together? John got a microscope, small enough to have been able to fit in Papa's suitcase; I, of course, got a pad of water color paper and a small set of water colors—in tubes, not like a kid set. Peter got a bag of marbles, including one especially large and colorful one. How did he know that his favorite game was playing marbles with the little boy who lived next door? Only he could never play with marbles of his own, so he could never practice shooting them out of the circles the way you're supposed to do. Peter looked at his father in dumbfounded amazement, his tousled white-blond hair a crown above his so large brown eyes. His pants were too big, a hand-me-down from brother Paul, and his cinched belt had a tongue that hung down. Peter always seemed hastily put together, as if his body didn't quite know how to be nine years old. Papa looked tenderly at Betty, whose serious brown eyes continued a methodical examination of this strange man, whom she barely remembered as her father. He handed her a doll, whose porcelain face looked placidly at her new owner. Betty took the doll and hugged it close, never taking her eyes away from her father.

Rona was not quite three, and the one that baffled him the most. She had been a sickly baby when he last saw her and he had feared that he would never see her again. She stared up at this stranger, her dark bangs straight across her forehead, a scowl of disapproval in her intense gaze. He reached for the last gift, a small recorder, and handed it to Rona. She fingered the holes with both her hands, her small fingers dancing over the length of the small wooden pipe.

"Do you know what this is, Rona?" he asked her, squatting down to be at her level.

She nodded, and put the recorder to her mouth and tried to blow. A reedy squeak ensued and she grinned with pleasure.

"I'll teach you to play this. It's a recorder. Would you like that?"

She nodded again, and began to laugh with pleasure. She ran off with her treasure, squeaky notes following her. Papa winced at the sound, but smiled.

Later that first evening, after all the commotion had died down and we were finally in our rooms, Papa settled himself into one of the chairs in the living room and waited for Mama to join him. The clattering in the kitchen stopped and she came in, wiping her hands on her apron. She moved to the chair nearest him, but he motioned her to him. She sat on the arm of his chair and let her hands rest in her lap. He put an arm around her.

"This is a fine house," he said again. He reached up and brushed a stray wisp of hair from her face. "The children seem very happy, well adjusted. Do they ever speak French anymore?"

She shook her head and reached into her pocket for a cigarette. She gave him one and he lit them both. They were silent a few moments.

"Too bad," he said finally. "They will regret it someday."

"Yes, that's true. I tried, at first. But they were so eager to embrace their new life. And Sally Anne was getting teased, so I gave it up." She hesitated before continuing. "Do you think you will be staying, now? You said in your letters that Christian is going on with the ski resort. So it will be built?"

"Oh yes. But I probably won't need to go back for a long time. It's well under control. It will be a very profitable venture, but it will take time before we see any money come out of it. We've just finished the planning stages for the first phase. So, to answer your question, I've had an offer to join a firm in Manhattan."

"Why, that's wonderful! Design? What? Tell me about it." Mama was excited. She got up and went to a cabinet near the fireplace. "We should celebrate. How about a brandy? I have some Courvoisier." She brought over a bottle and two snifters and poured a little in each, setting the bottle on the coffee table.

"I think it will be good. It's restaurant design, which could be quite challenging." He sipped and watched the clear amber liquid coat his glass in a golden fall.

"I can take you to the train station, like all the other wives whose husbands work in the city. And I'll bet you'll meet a lot of other interesting people, even on the train—and of course at your work. It will be a wonderful opportunity, I'm sure."

He looked at her quizzically. "What do you mean by opportunity?"

"Oh, I don't know," she stuttered, "I mean, you won't be stuck here, like we were stuck in the Alps and you always had to go off far away to get any work. This will be close. And it will be steady… and secure. We can be a family…for sure now."

He shivered slightly at the picture of getting on a train every morning, at the same time, then coming back home on a train, at the same time, and spending his days in a teeming city which was not French, and therefore foreign. But he'd get used to it. He had to settle down, finally. He was almost forty, had a wife who adored him, had six growing children, each as different as individual snowflakes—and he had a promising job with people who respected his work. Maybe finally, he would be happy, he would be successful. No more chasing empty dreams that vanished in a puff of smoke. Liv didn't need to find out that he had been told he would no longer be needed for the project at *Belleville*. Better that she should believe that he left voluntarily. She didn't need to know that he had been elbowed out of what was to become an extremely lucrative investment at *Méribel*.

In truth, he was coming back to Mama defeated by every venture he had attempted in France. He felt a complete failure—as a man, as an artist, even as her husband, when he finally recognized that it was Liv who had been his principal financial backer in all his ventures. He would try to make this a new beginning—to a better future.

And when I think of those years and what it must have been like for Papa, I find myself comparing his circumstances to the way Joe's life has gone. Both these men grew up in privilege, with much positive support from their parents. Papa was encouraged by his mother, to believe that he could succeed at anything he set his mind to. And she was always there to support his efforts. Joe had the same sort of encouragement from both his parents. He could do anything he wanted to do, they always assured him.

Yet, when it came to interfacing and succeeding in the wider world, both men were surprised to find that their talents would not necessarily be recognized, much less appreciated. Not only that, but if they were successful, their trust and naiveté made them both easy targets for any entrepreneur who might want to appropriate the ideas or concepts they had. Unfortunately, the results were invariably poor copies of what might have been.

Today, I suffer for Joe, as I am helpless to pull him out of his deep despond. "I'm in my seventies," he'll cry in frustration. "I watch all these young men pass me by—they get all the good commissions, all the awards, all the fame. And they're using ideas I developed thirty years ago! When is it my turn? Will we never get our house on the water?"

As for me, I think I must have learned well from Mama. I can be as frugal as she was, and not really care if we ever get our house on the water. I don't think I ever expected much, and I don't think she ever expected much. She taught us all, by her example, that happiness didn't depend on how rich we were in our pocketbooks, but rather, how rich we were in our hearts.

We settled into a reasonably pleasant routine, in those first days when Papa was with us finally. He seemed to enjoy the restaurant work which gave him a chance to explore avenues of art that had escaped him until now. He did large murals for one restaurant; he designed the fabrics for another. Each had its own set of challenges. His secret frustration, one that he dared not share with anyone, was that none of this work had his name attached to it. He was working for someone else's benefit. He felt more and more like a cog in a giant machine of enterprise, walking from the train to the office building, then back to Grand Central Station at the end of the day with all the other tired men, to get on a train to the pretty little town where the wives would be waiting in the station wagon to take them home.

His escape was his piano and his studio. The piano had been Mama's special gift for him. She had insisted that his treasured piano should be shipped from France, to stay in the family forever. Her father's inheritance could make that possible.

"I could see you were getting a little restless," she later told him, "and you seemed sad, as if something important was missing from your life. The children and I weren't enough, and your job was becoming just a job, I think…"

"Well, it is hard, sometimes. But it never has to do with you and the children, please understand. And the work has been quite absorbing, as you know. But you're right. I have missed playing, more than I ever thought I would."

"I have missed your playing as well, and so have the children. Do you remember how they used to love to fall asleep as you played? They loved most the Schubert piece that described the father taking his sick boy on his horse—rushing to the farmhouse in the storm. What was the name of that, I don't remember…"

Papa smiled, his eyes softening in memory. "The Elf King. The Goethe poem set to music."

"That's it. You played, and you looked at the children as you spoke the words. And they were enthralled. Do you remember the poem?" Mama looked at him with the same expectation we had shown him in the chalet as we gathered around his piano in silent wonder.

"I probably don't remember the words, but I certainly remember the music."

"Would you play it now, then? I can get the children to come near the piano, as they used to."

She called for us all to come in and we gathered near the piano, but not too near—we remembered that he didn't like being crowded.

Papa rested his hands on the piano keys, his long fingers caressing them lovingly. He looked at Mama a long time, as if once more recognizing the gift she was to him. He turned and waited for us to stop fidgeting. We were all quiet, waiting for this special moment. Mama stood by the piano, one hand resting on the lustrous mahogany case, as she knew the music he played would transfer directly to her heart. She smiled, and waited.

Paul locked eyes with her, and then he bent his head as if to lift the notes as he spoke the words, which in fact, he remembered well:

> Who rides, so late, through night and wind?
> It is the father with his child.
> He has the boy well in his arm
> He holds him safely, he keeps him warm.
>
> "My son, why do you hide your face so anxiously?"
> "Father, do you not see the Erl king?
> The Erl king with crown and tail?"
> "My son, it's a wisp of fog."
>
> "You lovely child, come, go with me!
> Many a beautiful game I'll play with you;
> Many colourful flowers are on the shore,
> My mother has many golden robes."

"My father, my father, and don't you hear
What Erl king is quietly promising me?"
"Be calm, stay calm, my child;
The wind is rustling through withered leaves."

"Do you want to come with me, dear boy?
My daughters shall wait on you fine;
My daughters will lead the nightly dance,
And rock and dance and sing you to sleep."

"My father, my father, and don't you see there
Erl king's daughters in the gloomy place?"
"My son, my son, I see it clearly:
The old willows they shimmer so grey."

"I love you, your beautiful form entices me;
And if you're not willing, I shall use force."
"My father, my father, he's grabbing me now!
Erl king has done me some harm!"

The father shudders; he swiftly rides on,
He holds the moaning child in his arms,
is hardly able to reach his farm;
In his arms, the child was dead.

The piano hummed under her hand with the last notes. We were all silent, transfixed as we had always been. I watched, as they lost each other in a long gaze of intimate secrets, as memories and sensibilities overtook them both in a flood.

Word began to get around that there was a concert pianist living in their midst. Papa was never clear as to where the rumor began, but he was flattered. It was a little like the old days when he played for the soldiers on their way to Switzerland, and the special guests, future investors, friends of Lindsay, his English friend who had the vision to develop the Alpine ski resorts. They were always so grateful for the culture, it seemed to him.

He was asked to do recitals. He and Mama were frequently invited to parties where it was understood that he would play for the guests.

Papa began to hate the circuit. There was too much drinking, and very little interesting conversation. He began to despair as he thought of spending years doing the same thing over and over again.

He became increasingly despondent and Mama knew it would not be long before he either left by himself, or gathered up his whole family to find another adventure somewhere else down the road of life. He began to explore the possibility of teaching, or maybe writing. He was not meant to live the life of a drone, as he put it. The endless cycle of home to train, to city, to train, to home, to other homes for endless recitals with gushing, drunken guests left him feeling as if he had been gutted and only the appearance of a shell remained, not unlike the stuffed heads of the magnificent animals mounted in Dr. Moline's gallery, whose blind eyes could no longer speak.

Yet—he was tormented to see that this was such a happy place for his wife and his six children. We had nested in, found our comforts. We had established roots that were going deeper into the soil of this New England town, finding friends and making our own adventures, even as he was feeling more and more alone and lonely. Even Mama, now that she was close to her sisters, had established a way of life that didn't necessarily include him.

In desperation, he began his quest alone, not involving anyone in a new seismic move, yet once more. He would simply explore the possibilities—what might be out there, waiting for just his particular talents. He wrote letters to universities, detailing some of his revolutionary thinking as it related to archetypal patterns in different cultures and how different peoples discovered and developed solutions to better deal with their environments. He compared himself to Frank Lloyd Wright, as a visionary humanist on a quest to do more intelligent design, to teach philosophies for better buildings. He wrote, and sent his letters out, hoping somewhere there might be an enlightened soul who would rescue him. He was in a bog of quicksand and needed to have someone extend a branch he could cling to, that he might pull himself out.

As an undercurrent in his desperation was the knowledge that he could always go back to France, to paint, to travel to the sundrenched hills of Spain or Italy, or maybe back to Brazil, where he had been last year. He could leave all this behind. But that would be admitting failure, and that he could never do. This time, he was going to make things better for his family. Mama deserved at least that. He would succeed in America—as he had not succeeded in his homeland, France.

— **18** —

PAPA

Spring 1951: Papa became more and more morose until even his piano wasn't enough to lift his gloom—and then, everything changed.

He was ebullient, more keyed up than I'd ever seen him, unrestrained in his excitement. He waved the letter in Mama's face. "I did it! I did it! I'm going to teach! Gather everyone around," he commanded. "I have big, big news for everyone!"

He sat us all down in the living room and we waited expectantly—even Mama, who looked as mystified as the rest of us.

"I have been trying—for the last six months or so—to find something better to do with the talent God gave me than to be a drone, a cog in the giant machine of commercialism. Liv," he turned to her, "I know you have done the best you could to keep me happy. The piano has been a Godsend, believe me."

She reached out her hand and touched his arm, as if to interrupt.

"No, no. Let me go on. The thing is, I had to do this by myself. Find a way out, I mean. I've been writing letters to colleges and universities, trying to interest them in some of the things I've been working on—some of the plans and ideas I developed in France. I never dreamed it would come to this. I was thinking of a lecture series, or something like that. But I got this letter today—I can't believe it!" Now Papa was laughing in excitement and we all joined in, because his joy was contagious.

"I have been offered a teaching position—can you imagine? They want me to teach young architectural students about my ideas—you know, like our influence on the environment and how we can do better planning, how we can be better." Now Papa was stumbling over his words, trying to get his message across to his young American children who could no longer speak French—though we would surely have understood if he had lapsed into French. "I only hoped to do a series of lectures, but they want me to *teach! Architecture! At Notre Dame!* Can you imagine what that means for us? Liv, it means you will never have to worry about finances again. And for all of you—it's a fresh new world—almost as big a change as when you all first came to this wonderful country!"

"That's, that's very exciting..." Mama stumbled. "Why didn't you tell me you were doing this?"

"I didn't want to get your hopes up." He dismissed her and turned to us. "You'll see. This is going to be the adventure of your lives."

"Where is Notre Dame, anyway? What kind of a school is it?" I asked, not quite sure I liked this whole idea—except that I'd never seen Papa so happy about anything.

"It's a Catholic University for young men—in Indiana. It's very prestigious, with an excellent academic reputation."

"But we're not Catholics. Doesn't that make a difference?"

"Obviously not." Papa was getting a little irritated at what he saw as a lack of enthusiasm from his gathered family.

"Indiana?" Paul piped up. "But what about school, and what about my friends? We love it here. And Mama's sisters live here..."

"And this house is so great—with the woods behind it, and the caves to explore, and all that..." John chimed in.

"Indiana's in the middle of the country, isn't it? It sounds dull. We'll never make friends there—unless they're country hicks. Yuck." I grimaced.

Paul, John and I were the teenagers, the ones most loath to pull up roots once again. We vividly remembered the frenetic wanderings of our childhood in France. Peter, Betty, and Rona only saw this as a grand new adventure—going someplace they'd never known. Mama was quiet for a long time, letting us all voice our loud opinions first. Then, she looked at Papa, and smiled, as she caught his vision—yet again—and embraced this new and wonderful dream.

"I know you haven't been happy here," she said, "It's been difficult for you to fit in with the people we've met. You think their lives are unbearably shallow and you're afraid you could become like them. I know that would be impossible, but I can see you've been slowly suffocating here. This is without question a very good thing. You were meant to teach, to write even—I'm sure of it. You have so much to say." She laughed and turned to us, all in various stages of perplexity. "It will be another grand adventure. Just you wait. You will be so glad Papa made this decision! Paul, when do we leave? I'm so excited!"

"I thought we might turn this into an odyssey, a way of seeing a little more of this great country. You children have no idea what lies beyond this tiny little enclave on the coast. We can take our time crossing to Indiana. We'll stay in motels as we go along in our new adventure, exploring everything along the way."

Mama's practical side was always in conflict with her dreaming optimism. "It'll work out," she said with new determination. "It always does. Besides, Paul, you'll be so happy—doing what God intended you to do—and getting well paid for it—after all these years. Let's get to the planning, everyone!"

Before we left our house, our wonderful home in Connecticut, I took one of Papa's Exacto knives and carved my name into the underside of one of the bookshelves in his studio. I wanted whoever moved in there to know that this would always be our house, even when we no longer lived there.

In fact, our trip turned into a memorable vacation. For the first time in our lives as a family, we were traveling without fear—indeed, with great anticipation. We were all together, for once. And Papa was so happy, so proudly excited to be doing this wonderful thing for his family. Papa bought a big Chevrolet van to go with our trusty station wagon. And wonder of wonders, they bought two travel trailers that would be towed across country—like the pioneers in their covered wagons. As always, with Papa, life was a grand adventure, to be embraced and treasured. He explained,

"We're taking our home with us. We can be explorers and vagabonds—never the refugees we once were!"

We took detours of exploration. The weather was consistently perfect summer sunshine and soft breezes.

We stopped at a farm for a picnic one day, and Papa asked the farmer if we could sit under a tree in his meadow. The air was redolent with the piles of cow manure. Papa breathed deeply and grinned. "Isn't this wonderful?" he exclaimed. "Just like the chalet."

Indeed, I was reminded of our soft meadow grass, high in the mountains, dotted with the intense blue of mountain gentians and the soft buttery yellow of the wild primroses. I took off my sandals and wiggled my toes in the soft grass and laughed with Papa. He took my hand, impulsively. "Come on, Sally Anne!" he said. "Let's go ask the nice farmer if we can have some fresh milk from one of his beautiful cows!"

The farmer took us to his cow barn where the afternoon milking was going on. Coming in from the bright sunlight, the air in the barn was filtered and soft, with dust motes dancing along slanting beams of light streaming through the cracks between the boards. The soft sound of hooves on thick straw, as the cows settled in, was a counterpoint to the whoosh-whoosh of milk going into the bucket. He didn't have many cows, and preferred the time-honored way of milking by hand, rather than lining them up and plugging a machine into their teats. He offered us each a pail and asked me if I wanted to milk with him.

"I've never done it," I said. "I don't know how."

"Oh, it's really easy. Watch me and do the same thing. Grab a stool."

"Is it okay, Papa?" I asked.

"Of course. We'll do it together."

Once I got the hang of it, I wasn't scared anymore. I sat on the stool, with my head against the cow's side, feeling the rough but still soft coat against my forehead. I pulled and squeezed on a teat the way he showed me and the milk magically squirted into the bucket I held between my knees. I was surprised to see all the foam. I was also surprised that it smelled like the cow—and it was warm.

Very proudly, I took my bucket and walked back with Papa to our picnic under the tree. Mama dipped our cups into the milk and we drank it with the sandwiches she had made. Even now, I remember the thick, rich warmth of that milk—unlike any I have had since.

Memories of my father are inevitably linked to singular experiences with food: a lunch of asparagus in Paris, a cup of thick warm milk. His passions are in my blood as well.

Papa had given me a Kodak Brownie camera so that I could document our adventure from Connecticut to Indiana. I still have some of those three inch square images, black and white, with the borders decoratively crimped. In one, everyone is lined up on a beach somewhere, sitting on a log. Everyone except Papa. I must have asked him to shoot the picture with my camera. He took another one of just me, sitting on a big rock, looking out over Lake Michigan, big pine trees in the background. Why don't I remember the circumstances behind these ephemeral images—snapshots of a glorious summer?

We initially rented a small house and crowded together with the two travel trailers, until Papa could have his dream house built. This wasn't much different than it had been when we were all shoehorned into the chalet—except now we were no longer small, but were growing teenagers, all elbows and big feet ready to bump into everything. But his house would be the way he dreamed it should be, set into a wooded glade, overlooking a placid lake.

As if it was yesterday, I can walk through that wonderful house with complete familiarity. I dream about it sometimes.

Perched on a gentle slope, at the base of which was a spring fed pond that led to the lake beyond, the front was almost entirely glass, with a deeply overhanging roof shaped like a wing poised for flight. The north side of the house, which was the entrance, and faced the wooded gravel driveway, was nearly windowless except for a long shallow bank high on the face, which brought the good light into Papa's studio space.

Mama had been integral to the planning process and had developed the basic layout, knowing precisely what would be absolutely necessary and what would be left to Papa's architectural genius. The plan consisted of two giant rooms, offset from each other by a graciously inviting entry. In the late fifties, such an open plan was rare, and even unique. The first large room consisted of Papa's studio as a long bank of drawing board, with cabinets below, and bookshelves and windows above. The floor was radiant heated concrete. Using the center post of the south-facing wall of windows as a sundial, Papa painted a map on the floor with rays marking the hours of the day. He built a planter in the floor, against the windows, large enough to accommodate an avocado tree at one end and a coffee tree at the other. Their bedroom, which was also his music studio, was at the far end of the room, where the ceiling was lower for acoustical reasons. They slept on a pull-out sofa and closed the room off for privacy with a velvet drapery—just as they had done in the chalet. The other end of the room was the main seating area, with built in cushioned benches nesting against the large fieldstone fireplace, where Papa hung the eagle that had finally been caught and stuffed, that had threatened Betty's life when she was an infant sunbathing on the terrace in the chalet.

The other large room was for Mama and us children. A large open kitchen was defined with a generous bar counter. This separated the kitchen from the chemistry lab area, specifically purposed for the many scientific experiments that John and Peter loved to do. Opposite this, was bench seating and the dining table. This whole wall was also all windows and faced out over a roof garden for all of Papa's vegetables and amazing strawberries. At the far end was the entertainment room, with built-in seating and a wall of cabinets that housed the black and white television set—our first. The back door led to the two travel trailers we had kept since leaving Connecticut. The smaller one was for my brothers, and my sisters and I had the luxury of the larger one: 10'x50'.

It may seem odd today, to have such an arrangement. But our parents knew we would be moving on in time and this allowed them to have the home of their dreams, for themselves. They also encouraged independence in each of the six of us and were ready to push us out of the nest the moment we tested our wings for flight.

Papa was like a tidal wave that swept up everything in its path to carry wherever it might land. And in fact, they had both dreamed of the day when he, as an architect, could actually manifest his best ideas and put them in place in their home. And he was so happy—finally. I think too, that she was relieved to have him stop his wanderlust. He was home now. He seemed so energized by his teaching, by the enthusiasm of his students that he began to think of writing a definitive book, one that would capture his imagination and harness his passion. Mama went to work as well. Now that we were all in school—even little Rona—she could venture out herself and do something that would test her agile mind. She taught French at the local middle school and became absorbed in her new work. As always, she was the hub in all our lives, the one to turn to for help, advice, comfort and counsel.

When we moved into our new home, it was finally clear to me that Mama and Papa were critically connected, so essentially joined that where one left off, the other began; one's vision was realized and understood by the other; together, they were a formidable whole. Mama was the editor for his wide-ranging book on architectural archetypes. When *"What is Design?"* was finally published, it became a cult classic for decades after it was out of print, as the touchstone for a burgeoning sustainability movement. As he worked out his vision for a chapel at the women's college next door to the university, it was Mama who helped him stay grounded with a definable budget. And it was Papa who encouraged her to teach, who was always there for her when she needed his encouragement and validation in all she did. He recognized her gifts, so different from his own, just as she had always understood his vision.

Among my fondest memories is that of Papa, sitting alone in the center of his sundial, looking out to the lake beyond. On the small table before him, he has set his special lunch, the same every day, summer, winter, spring or fall: a helping of spaghetti, topped with a bit of sautéed tomato and onion, and an egg. I can see him pierce the egg, to let the soft yolk spill over his feast. He has a crystal goblet of wine to sip as he thinks his thoughts and surveys his peaceful domain. This is his time. Sometimes, he varied this with a salad and an avocado, filled with vinaigrette, into which he can dip his bread.

When *Mamette*, our grandmother, came to visit, I was to keep her company while she ate the same solitary meal. I looked at her avocado longingly, wishing she would give me a taste of it. But she never did. Oddly, Mama was never a part of these quiet, solitary lunches. Somehow, their rhythms, separate as they were, seemed to suit them just fine.

The house was the nest, the castle, the fortress, and the safe haven that had eluded them until now. No more refugee wandering, no more distance between them, and a longing to be together. They were one now, building their future, guiding and nurturing their children, dreaming a dream that seemed to finally be a reality.

– 19 –

PARIS

The end of January. Only two months to go before spring… Already, the tiny birds have begun to come back and I can see them flitting through the branches of the giant chestnut trees outside my office window. When I went to the mailbox the other day, I noticed the first tulips beginning to show, like little green ears poking up from the rich black earth. Even the cherry tree is timidly sending a few blossoms to herald the coming season.

Winter in Seattle isn't bad. Just wet. Not really cold, just grey. But I miss the sun and how it plays musically throughout the house, sending rainbows and shadows playing on walls and cabinets, in lively quiet travel as the day progresses.

If there is anything I am most grateful for in my marriage to Joe, it is his love of light, in all its possible permutations. He is fascinated by the play of light and shadow and has made it integral to all his very original interior designs.

For both of us, this is our hardest season to get through. Joe is especially affected, though he only occasionally lashes out in impatience at the dreary tedium of wet, cold and grey winters. He is a California boy, used to being barefooted as much as he can politely get away with, used to open doors that welcome warm ocean breezes, used to dreamy afternoons in a hammock in the shade of a fragrant eucalyptus tree.

Winter is a season of endurance, and a quiet time. The house is silent as we work in our own office spaces, as we wait for the sun to bring vitality into our hibernating world.

My thoughts now drift to the distant past, to the winter in Paris with *Tante Marguerite* and her husband. As Papa's sister, she was eager to introduce me to my French heritage.

After two years in New York at Parsons School of Design, Papa felt I needed to finish my fashion studies in the heart of the fashion world in Paris. Of course, I embraced this unique opportunity.

I remembered the trip we took together to Northern France in the little *Deux Chevaux,* with my uncle hunched over the steering wheel, cigarette dangling dangerously from between his clenched lips, as he tried to coax the little car up a hill.

I sat in the back, my migraine so intense I felt as if I would throw up.

"I have just the cure for you," he said finally. "We will have oysters for lunch. I promise you that will make you feel better."

"Oooh…" I moaned. "I can't possibly eat anything. And oysters? They're so slimy…"

"You've never had one, have you?" *Tante Marguerite* asked with a smile of understanding. "*Stephane* is right. It will make your headache vanish."

We sat in the small café, choosing a table by a window. I felt blinded by the white linen cloth so I looked out to the grey winter day instead.

The oysters were brought on a bed of ice on a large platter. Slices of lemon and a mignonette sauce were the only addition.

I watched my uncle squeeze the lemon over the glistening oysters. He picked up one of the shells, took a small fork and pierced the oyster, then dipped it in the clear mignonette. He popped it in his mouth and slurped up the remaining essence in the shell. Finally, he broke off a piece of fragrant and crusty bread to eat.

"Now you know how it's done," he said. "So eat!"

Gingerly, I followed his lead and let the oyster slide into my mouth. I closed my teeth on its tender life and was astonished at the flavor. It was as if I had swallowed the soul of the ocean and all its primal goodness. I ate another, and another—and slowly realized my blinding headache had vanished.

I loved Paris as I gradually learned the *Métro,* navigating from the *Gare St. Lazare* to get the right route to my school. My aunt and uncle lived in the suburbs, near where Claude Monet did his magical paintings in his gardens at *Giverny.*

I loved being alone, discovering places and treasures by myself. In the beginning, I struggled with what had become a new language, but within a week or two I was completely at home in my new environment.

With my aunt and uncle, we explored *Versailles* and my favorite, *le Petit Trianon,* the little palace that Marie Antoinette had fashioned for herself. I walked through the *Bois de Boulogne*, loved walking along the *Quais* by the Seine.

I made no friends, but I didn't care. Paris was my friend, my ardent love. I wanted to stay here a long time—even after I finished school. I wanted to fashion a life for myself in this country that felt so much like home and was familiar, yet utterly foreign.

I stayed in a small attic room in the gracious and comfortable house of my aunt and uncle. My dormer window looked out on a small enclosed garden, now sleeping in the soft winter light.

I wrote letters home, thanking Papa and Mama over and over again for making it possible for me to be here, in Paris, studying fashion design in the fashion capital of the world. Not until years later did I ever fully appreciate the gift they gave me. I wrote to Mama most often, because I felt so close to her. Papa was still an intimidating force, hard to understand and even harder to please.

I had always looked forward to hearing from her.

And at first, she was full of encouragement, full of excitement for me. She wanted to know all about what I was doing, and what I was learning. And she was full of news from home, with funny little stories about Rona and the news that Betty would be going to music school after all. She mentioned that Paul and his wife Audrey would be having a baby soon. She would be a grandmother! She noted that Peter was in Germany now, in the army. Maybe I could be in touch with him. And John was teaching in Minnesota, even though he didn't have a teacher's degree. She found that to be quite remarkable and wonderful. Then, gradually, I realized the tone of her letters had changed.

She wrote about Papa. She was worried that he was spending too much time on the California project, a ski resort he was proposing that would eclipse the aborted *Meribel* that was now being finished so successfully by others. She had misgivings about its efficacy. It seemed "pie in the sky" she said. She wanted Papa to finish his book; she wanted to continue editing it but he was brushing her off.

Mama sounded lonely. Her brood was leaving the nest, one by one; her only company now was Rona—who could be a typically unpredictable teenager.

I thought about how she had been that summer, before I left; how she seemed a little lost—as if her world had somehow crumbled and she was no longer sure of her bearings. I had missed so many opportunities to spend more time with Mama. Maybe I could have reassured her a little. But I was too full of myself to pay much attention.

But I realized how much I missed Mama. She had always been so important to me. She was a counselor and a mentor. Her gentle words came to me as life lessons. She taught me by example. I think I needed to go home—for me, as much as for her.

As much as I loved the life I was carving out for myself in Paris, I also was aware that I had come here to escape—maybe redirect my steps from the path I'd been on. I really felt out of my depth at the fashion school, as I had feared I would, despite Papa's effusive confidence. *Tante Marguerite* and *Oncle Stephane* were really sweet and had been very generous with me—but it was time to go home.

I wrote to Mama.

> Please tell Papa how sorry I am to disappoint him—again. I would really like to be home for Christmas. I miss you terribly, and feel a little lost without being able to talk face to face with you about some of these things that are bothering me so much. I need to spend some good time

with you. Letters just don't seem to be enough. I need to make some life decisions and I could sure use your motherly advice. You've always been such a good counselor for me. I trust your judgment. Would it be okay for me to come home? Please tell Papa how sorry I am.

Papa was disappointed, Mama wrote back, but they would be so happy to see me, she said. She said she had missed me more than she thought she would.

I was relieved that it was Mama who met me at the boat. She had come to New York by herself. We were going to make a grand occasion out of this homecoming, she said.

"We're going to stay at the Waldorf Astoria for the whole weekend," she said. "Just you and me. I came early and spent a few days with my sisters; Paul and Audrey will be coming later so that we can all have Christmas together. Only Peter won't make it. He's still in Germany. But I wanted some special time with you."

That was probably the best time I ever had with my mother. She knew New York the way I knew it—as young students exploring the vitality of a vibrant city. When she was young, she said, she came into the city to go to the Metropolitan, for the theater, for shopping at Bergdorf's. So we did the same things—together. We even went into the Village, and sat on a bench in Washington Square and fed the pigeons—even though it was really cold. We had a fabulous dinner at the Ritz. She pointed out the clock that is so famous. Her eyes danced and she laughed with joy. I had never seen Mama so free. We finally went to Grand Central Station, so familiar to both of us, to take a train home to Indiana, for Christmas with the whole family.

When I came home that Christmas, I had special gifts from Paris and New York that I'd gathered for everyone. I was especially pleased with an LP I had found of Van Clyburn playing his winning work at the Moscow Tchaikovsky Competition only a year earlier at the height of the Cold War. I thought Papa would be so pleased that I had found a perfect gift for him.

He looked at the album cover, then frowned as he scoffed, "Van Clyburn? You can't be serious, Sally Anne!" He tossed the album to the nearest table and said, "he is a very mediocre excuse for a pianist!" He strode to the piano and scowled at me. "This is how this piece should be played! Listen and learn!" He played the piece with passion and energy, daring his stunned audience of a family to appreciate his artistry and interpretive zeal.

That episode reminded me finally of who my father really was, who he could be from one moment to the next. I stole a look at my mother, to gauge her reaction. She appeared to have shrunk into herself. She sighed and quietly left the room to remove herself from the all too familiar storm of her husband.

I realized this was not the first explosion of temper from Papa. And it began to make sense to me that her letters had taken on an air of timidity.

And of course, as was typical of Papa, the storm passed as quickly as it had erupted and we ended up having a lovely family Christmas after all, though somewhat disjointed and forced.

In time, I married one of Papa's architectural students, possibly, in hindsight, because we both were in such adulation of my father… so I left home as well, and for the first time in my life, I began to realize the depth of Mama's gift to me. All I am, as a wife and mother, can be traced to who she was as my own mother. Certainly, I've had my own way of doing things, but in the back of my mind, I could always ask the question: "How would she have handled this?" And my own children, now grown and with children of their own, can ask themselves the same question. We may put our own stamp on our families, but we are all part of the rich tapestry that is our heritage.

My daughter once said to me, when she was a frustrated young teen, "Mom, I don't want you to be my *friend*. I want you to be my *Mom!*" And now, I know beyond everything else, that I will always and forever be *Mom* to each of my three grown up children. They may disagree with me, they may be angry, or resentful, or think I'm foolish—or whatever. But I will always be their only Mom.

I'm certain that if I could talk to Mama today, she might say the same thing to me. I'm sure that I broke her heart in many pieces, many times, but she would still say to me, "I am Mama, and will always be so."

I believe that a mother's heart will only craze, like a lovely antique vase, but will never crack and break into pieces because the bonds are too permanent, too strong.

– 20 –

HOUSTON

The rain drums on the skylights. The rainy season insists its presence with predictable regularity. I know that since we put in skylights, I've become aware of weather patterns as never before. Scudding clouds punctuate blue skies and cast occasional shadows; bright summer sun warms my back when I sit at the kitchen bar. And now, the skies are uniformly grey. When the rains come, the sound on the skylights becomes amplified, and works its way as a steady counterpoint to the rhythmic blood pulse in my head, for once blocking out the ever-present tinnitus that has become increasingly maddening. I have a headache again, just enough to be an unpleasant distraction.

Joe is working on his website and is rummaging in the attic, in search of images to scan. There was a time when he asked me to be in charge of his marketing efforts, but I could never wrap my head around such an endeavor. Now, he has stopped asking me, tacitly accepting my lack of enthusiasm. The musty attic smells, redolent with the scent of old paper, dust, and fabric drift toward my office, like an ancient history being unearthed. Joe often laments his dearth of editorial "ink" over the years. Yet now, the quiet is punctuated by his exclamations as he discovers long-forgotten magazines and books that have featured his work.

We've been married more than three decades. As if lifting a heavy blanket from my shoulders, I am freshly grateful for the easy love we share. Over the years, Joe has gradually begun to melt the icy cold at the core of my being. He has, over time, begun to crack the hard carapace of protection that I have fiercely erected around my heart. He has never insisted himself on me, but has rather encouraged me to bloom slowly like an opening rose. He has always accepted me, even in my harshest coldness—as an icy wind that only he can warm.

Even as he is transparently honest and forthright, it doesn't seem to matter to him that I am so often a closed book. He travels through his life with his heart and all his thoughts out in the open for all to read. As a man truly without guile, he is always surprised at the perfidy of others—especially colleagues.

Joe talks of the "rip-offs" he has experienced throughout his career as if he had always expected that he could trust others to be true to their promises. "We could have had our house on the water if only…" he would complain wistfully.

But I have witnessed, and experienced deceit most of my life. My father was crushed his entire life as he tried to make his ideas understood and accepted. Was it the lot of an artist to strive unsung throughout his life, only to be recognized when it was too late to be appreciated?

I affectionately call Joe "Paisan" when he wears his hat—which is whenever he is outside—even in the rain. Square and stocky, not much taller than me, he has the solid build of someone who could do heavy physical work. Big hands, big feet, a powerful back and forearms, he can embrace me in a bear hug that envelops me in safety. More than anything, I feel secure in his care.

His grandparents came from Sicily but with blue eyes and blond hair, always in disheveled ringlets, to call him "Paisan" might have seemed a little out of character. Everyone is his friend. A walk in the park—or anywhere—could take a long time as he engages perfect strangers in lengthy conversations. He is a friend to all the neighbors. I love watching him from the window as he stands on the sidewalk, talking at length with someone, laughing his big hearty laugh, gesturing enthusiastically.

Joe is loving, forgiving, genuine and open. He is all that I cannot be. With Joe, what you see is what you get. I love him with a peace that I have never known with anyone.

My thoughts drift back, continually making the comparisons— and differences between these two artists: my father...and my husband.

We were a family, whole and complete now. It seemed as if the days of wandering, of being uprooted and transplanted like potted seedlings might finally be over. We, as children, had always embraced the changes and new horizons, but Mama could now breathe a sigh of relief that this time would be different. Papa would be home to stay, finally.

Together, they began the plans for the house they had dreamed of building for so many long years. They found a piece of property on a small lake, just outside of town, close enough to the schools that we would all be attending. They kept the two travel trailers that had been our "covered wagons" in our trek across country. They would be placed on the property, adjoining the new house and would serve as dormitories for us kids. We were delighted with that idea, relishing the autonomy and independence we would enjoy: one trailer for the brothers, the other bigger one, for the sisters.

We all flourished in our new high school, one after the other following in the footsteps of the sibling that preceded us. I struggled with math and science and was criticized by the teachers for not being as brilliant as my two older brothers. We all went into the choir, one after the other, loving to sing as if we were the family Von Trapp. I loved speech and drama and got parts in all the plays, went to contests throughout the state.

Mama taught French in the junior high school. We often met after school and shared a couple of cookies before going home. We all got after school jobs and did all the extr-curricular stuff that made high school interesting and challenging. But none of us made many real friends. We were thought of as a little different, maybe even as somewhat eccentric, the kids of the French professor who taught at Notre Dame.

Papa often hosted parties for "his boys", the students who adored him and his magical ideas. He would prepare big T-bone steaks in a very hot iron skillet, laying the still sizzling steaks on a large chunk of butter in a platter; he de-glazed the pan with wine and poured that over the steaks, turning the pan upside down over them to retain the heat. The conversations at these parties was lively and fascinating and we all participated.

In time, I married one of these students in the chapel that Papa had designed, with the high school choir singing "Ave Maria" from the balcony behind us.

Heady, glorious times that we should have anticipated could not last...

Papa was inexplicably terminated from his teaching position at Notre Dame, soon after he finished work on the chapel. I thought he had tenure. I didn't think they could do that. He refused to discuss it with anyone—not even Mama. Politics was all he would ever give as a reason.

The dean at the school was apologetic and circumspect. The decision had not been his too make, he insisted. So he helped Papa secure a position at a college in Houston—for less money and less prestige, but at least he wouldn't be completely cast adrift. We were all incensed, but I think Mama was devastated. Her world was tumbling—again.

So many times, just as her little space on the planet seemed secure, Papa had yanked her up again, a tender young shoot putting down roots in one garden after another. Yet, with the resilience she had always demonstrated, she lifted her chin and carried on. She would find a new teaching position for herself; Rona would go to college locally—there wouldn't be enough money to send her away. She would have to live at home and Mama was sorry about that because Rona would miss out on the away from home experience the rest of us had enjoyed.

They had to sell the wonderful house, of course. Years later, we found out that it had been razed to the ground to make way for a condominium development.

They started over in yet another new place, this one more foreign than any they had previously landed in. The letters Mama wrote me revealed an uncertainty that reminded me of the letters she wrote when I was a student in Paris, so many years ago. She had always been optimistic about every change that Papa brought into her unpredictable life. She even seemed to thrive on all his new adventures for the family, taking every new step as a personal challenge. This time, it seemed more daunting.

As proof that Papa was wrongfully terminated, many of his former students followed him to Houston, eager to continue learning under his inspiring vision of a better world.

Papa traveled a lot that first year, even though this was a new school for him, a new test. He was well-enough respected that he could design his curriculum and his schedule. His students adored him and he thrived on their adulation. Mama told me of her new position at the local high school where she was teaching French. She said Papa was doing well at the college, though she still didn't know why he was let go at Notre Dame. He still refused to talk about it beyond saying it had been political and he just wanted to put it behind him. She talked about the house they had bought in Houston, in a quiet neighborhood near Herman Park, which reminded her of the house we had lived in when we lived in Darien. Lots of windows, big rooms, comfortable and gracious.

She said she missed me terribly.

Mama seemed sad to the point of despair. And, I thought, she sounded frightened. This wasn't like the fear or insecurity she had felt during the war. That could be explained and understood and even quantified as the indomitable force of catastrophic war. Such an event was so large that Mama could realize that it really had nothing to do with her. But this was different. She searched her every action to try to find a reason for her sense of abandonment. She said it was her fault that Papa was so distant, always eager to be gone. She must have done something; said too much, not been sufficiently affectionate…it must be her fault that he stopped loving her. Was he having an affair? Was he really not going to all these distant places, like Brazil, or Spain, or even France? Was he using the money she so easily gave him for another romance? And yet, she knew he was off on these distant journeys because when he eventually came back from his trips, he always had something to show for it.

Mama even got quite intimate with me as she tried to explain her malaise.

She said that sometimes she felt a physical ache overcome her entire body when she remembered Papa's long expressive fingers as he explored her body with easy familiarity. She was the piano that he played with such obsession, pulling the notes to inexorable crescendos of passion. She had never questioned his love for her when they lay locked in spent embrace. She felt complete, as she knew that she too had satisfied him to his core.

Even if Papa came home before Christmas, even if he stayed home this time, what would it be like to have him in the house again? Could they be lovers again or was that a dusty memory of years ago? Mama dreaded the storm cloud she knew he would bring, and with it the mystery of its source.

– 21 –

DISCOVERY

May 1964: It was hot and muggy again. The two weeks of spring were over and the summer heat was creeping up, even though it was only May. How was I going to manage another pregnancy in the abominable Houston heat?

We had moved for job and family and I realized that it was only family that could keep me here. Of anywhere I had ever lived, this was decidedly my least favorite.

I was on the patio with the children. Mark especially liked the pill bugs and would follow them with fascination, occasionally putting one in his mouth. I took to putting a bell around his neck so that I could keep track of his wanderings. If I didn't hear the bell, he was too far—or in some kind of quiet mischief. Kim was always so absorbed in her solitary games that I never really had to wonder if she was in trouble, though early one morning, a neighbor had called to say she had come to the door in her nightgown asking for a bowl of cereal.

The planter was a riot of color, the moss roses cascading down its brick sides. The rosemary had not been a good idea; as I had suspected, it was too humid for a desert plant to thrive in this climate. I often brought my sewing outside with me so that I might have something to do, even as I was watching the children.

Mama's car pulled into the parking space in front of the planter the sun glaring like a searchlight on its windshield. "Gammy!" Kim cried out with glee, running to the car.

"Kim!" I called, "Look both ways! Hi, Mama. What brings you here today? I wasn't expecting such a nice visit. You always call first."

Mama had gotten out of the car and was greeting Kim tenderly. Ever since we had moved to Houston, Kim was her singular obsession. Perhaps because she was approaching four and was much more entertaining than her obstreperous little brother, Mama could easily find ways and reasons to come spend time with us. And I was always glad to see her. In many ways, we had become each other's closest confidants. I turned to her for advice with the children and she turned to me for counsel in trying to better understand and communicate with Rona, now a wildly independent eighteen year old in her first year of college. She lived at home but was rarely there. Mama worried that she might be getting out of control, yet could do nothing. Papa had been gone several weeks. He wrote Mama a little note, letting her know he wasn't sure when he would come home, which only intensified Mama's wildest fears. And how could he stay away from his teaching so often, she worried.

"Mama, what's the matter?" she had been crying. Her eyes were still teary and her cheeks were bright and flushed. She brushed stray wisps of hair from her face, and her lips trembled as she fought to keep back her crying. I wrapped my arms around her and held her close, aware of how small and fragile her frame was. When I caught myself complaining about my lot in life, I thought of Mama, who had been through more than I could ever even begin to fathom. As the stories had unfolded over the years, and she invariably spoke calmly of the momentous, often painful journey of her life, I greatly admired her and was humbled. Now, we sat together in the plastic lawn chairs I'd gotten with my S&H Green Stamps.

"What's the matter?" I asked again.

"I think I need something to drink. Could you fix us some iced tea...or maybe coffee...? I don't know..."

"Sure, Mama. I'll bring it out. Just sit tight. I'll be right back."

"Thank you, dear. I'll watch the children."

I hurried inside. I chose to make iced tea, since a cup of coffee from the electric percolator would be bitter and stale by now. I came back out with two glasses and a pitcher of iced tea, which was already sweating in the morning heat. The ice tinkled in the glasses as I poured. I went to the planter and picked a few leaves of the fragrant mint I had tucked in with the moss roses and dropped it into our glasses. I added the slices of lemon.

"Do you want sugar too?"

"No thank you, dear. This is lovely…" Mama sipped her drink, sighed and tried to compose herself. "You always do such a nice job of presentation, Sally Anne."

"Thanks, Mama. That means a lot to me. Okay. I'm listening. What has happened?"

"It's your father. It's Papa …"

"Is he all right? Did something happen to him? Is he back home?"

"Yes, he came back the day before yesterday."

"Why didn't you tell me?"

"I was going to, but then…"

"What."

"He's gone, now."

"Mama, you're not making much sense. What's going on? He's gone? Where?"

"I don't know." Kim tried to climb into her Gammy's lap. "Not now, dear. Go play with Mark, why don't you?" She gently moved her off.

"He left something."

"What is it?"

"He didn't mean for me to find it, I don't think. But maybe he did…"

"Can you tell me?' I was growing concerned as Mama stumbled to get her story out. I reached out my hand and touched her shoulder, as if trying to get her attention, even as I was also trying to comfort her.

"He wrote a poem. I don't think I was supposed to find it. But he left it in plain sight, as if he wanted me to find it."

"What was the poem?"

"It was very explicit." She blushed crimson. She closed her eyes.

"Go on..."

"It was a love poem..."

"He's having an affair?"

"I guess so. Maybe so. Yes. But he's not in love with a woman..."

"What are you saying?"

"His name is Mario. That's why he's been gone. And I think he's going to Spain now. He's going to bring Mario to Houston..." she had taken on a listless, emotionless cadence to her speech, as if reciting names from a phone book. "I guess I've known this about him all these years, but haven't wanted to. I remember Serge...and Christophe... tried to tell me. I think he does love me, in his own way. But there's this other side...He's very passionate, you know. Maybe it's too much. I don't know. What can I do? What will happen now?"

I felt that anything I might utter would be the wrong thing to say. I was trying to make sense of what Mama was telling me, but images kept getting in the way, as well as every memory of Papa. How could we all have been so fooled? And how did he manage such a duality? Mostly, I thought, what now?

"I think I could accept this more easily if Mario was Maria, if you know what I mean." Mama chuckled without humor, "Was I so sexually inadequate? Maybe if I had been more attentive to his needs, if I had shown him more passion—but he always knew I loved him completely."

"Oh, Mama...there has never been any question about your love and faithfulness," I was finding it difficult to speak. "I'm amazed that you put up with so much for thirty years. He never appreciated you enough!"

"I feel inadequate as a woman. I have been passed over, not for another woman—I think I could understand that—but for a man!" she returned to her first regret, "what does that say about me?"

"Mama, you have been my most important model, all of my life. Even as a little girl, I wanted to be more like you. And it was so obvious that you and Papa had a passionate life—even when he was so difficult."

I paused, and then went on as if suddenly making a unique discovery. "We've all been fooled, and you most of all. But how could you not? The two of you had such a unique relationship. It could have turned out any number of ways. Thirty years!" I exclaimed.

"Sally Anne, how am I going to go on, knowing that he is in the same town, maybe even the same neighborhood, with his lover? And what about Rona? Shall I tell her the truth? What can I say to her? She's too young to know this kind of thing…"

But maybe we could keep this a secret between the two of us? Did anyone have to know that Papa was having an affair with another man? Could he not have left Mama for another woman? Was that not more plausible, more acceptable?

"Mama, why do you have to tell anybody about this guy?" I broached the impossible.

"I can't do that! At least the family has to know. I have to tell the boys, Paul, and John and Peter. And I have to tell Betty. She needs to know. And of course, Rona."

"I don't see why this can't be a secret between us. What harm would it do? Seems to me it would be more damaging, and definitely more hurtful to tell everybody. What would that do to our image of our father? It would be easier to accept if we just said that you were getting a divorce because he was having an affair."

"Divorce? I hadn't thought of that. Maybe he can just be gone. He's gone a lot anyway."

"Mama, I don't understand you sometimes. You've spent most of your adult life supporting him, protecting him, and now that he's done this awful thing to you, you still manage to stand by him."

"I still love him…" she started to cry again, her whole body shaking as she tried so hard to suppress her tears.

"Gammy. Don't cry…" Kim came to her grandmother, and patted her knee tenderly, in the childlike innocence of making a hurt go away the way Mommy did when she skinned her knee.

"Oh, Kim …thank you. That makes me feel so much better." Mama wiped her eyes with her hand and lifted Kim into her lap, needing to embrace the tender purity of her granddaughter. She turned back to me with renewed strength and resolve. "I will tell the others, in my own way, in my own time. After I tell Rona, she will be devastated. I want you to be there for her. Will you do that?"

"Of course. But what's your plan? What are you going to do?"

"I don't know. Yet. But it will be clear in time. Everything always has a way of sorting itself out."

I realized that this was Mama's singular coda: everything always has a way of sorting itself out. How many times in her daunting journey with Papa had that not been the case?

— 22 —

BETRAYAL

I knew I was pregnant again. I wouldn't tell anybody, not even my husband, not even Mama. This would be my secret for a while, maybe something like forgiveness from God for the awful thing I had done to exile my father. This child would be a gift of healing—especially as I would be having my baby near Christmas.

After Mama left that afternoon, after I had assured her that indeed, it would all work out, I continued to sit on the patio, unseeing, almost unaware of my two lovely children, innocently playing in the cooling afternoon.

A flood of confused memories swirled in my mind as I looked back over my life, trying to piece together something that might begin to make sense. Was there anything I could grab onto and hold and say to myself, "this was it, this was the time I knew something..." And of course, I could only remember the peripatetic journeys of my father over the years. How often was he home, really? And yet, I knew this was a fool's errand that would never lead me to any enlightenment at all. I could only remember how much I loved my father, and how he always seemed to make a point of paying attention to me, of listening to me—as I knew he did with each of his children. He loved us all and cared about the dreams that we had for our lives and what we might do that would be grand and wonderful, because we were grand and wonderful.

And, despite the distance I saw growing between him and Mama, I also knew that he loved her as he could never love another woman. So, what was this dichotomy? What drew him away, and had drawn him away all these years? I would certainly never understand, but I knew he had hurt Mama in a way so profound, I could not forgive him. He had to pay, I thought. It was too unfair. I would go to the dean myself, because I knew she never would. She would move on as best she could and swallow her hurt, her pride, herself. This was not a secret to be kept just within the family. I would have to expose him, and I knew that he would be fired, as a result, because no school could harbor a homosexual, not in 1964.

Taking it upon myself to do this would horrify the whole family, I knew. "How could you do this?" they would all say. "What makes you the arbiter of justice? What about Mama? Don't you think it's her decision to make, if any?"

But I didn't think the reaction would be so swift, so final. It felt as if a bomb had gone off in our midst, exploding all the love and joy of our family into a million shards and pieces.

We left Houston. Philip had lost his job in the architectural firm and there seemed nowhere else to go. A curtain went up and I was left outside. Mama couldn't believe what I'd done, and all my siblings were horrified. My precious sisters were married without me. I had planned on making their wedding dresses...

We went to Illinois and lived near his parents and I watched my children grow without their grandmother, without any of my family. I closed in on myself, growing away from this man I had married. I felt lost and forsaken, bereft of all that I had held dear. I tried to form new alliances with his mother and all his siblings, especially his one sister and his youngest brother. It was the time of the Vietnam war and all the protests, the feminist movement and women's liberation. I got involved in protests to pass the ERA amendment and we wen on peace marches, even to the one in Grant Park at the time of the Democratic convention.

Gradually, a bit at a time, I reconnected with Mama and Rona, and big brother Paul, who was all set to go to Israel to live if Nixon won the election. We were still distant and apart, but we wrote letters and that helped. I came to call these years the Wilderness Time.

— 23 —

FORGIVENESS

I'm at my desk, lost in thought; the letters Betty brought over in two big file boxes lie scattered around me. The sun is shining, for a change, and I yearn to do some yard work today. The beds are overgrown with dead brown stalks; the roses should be pruned now. It's the tail end of winter and the promise of spring is evident, even in the fresh softness in the air.

But the letters have drawn me in anew, awakening dusty memories I thought I had vanquished long ago. And I realize, as I read, that I may finally bring full closure to the lingering pain of my guilty past.

Papa began,

> On the eve of my departure from Houston, I thought I would send you this message from one artist to another to tell you again, once more, how much confidence I have in your extraordinary talent.
>
> You may have doubted me—and this touched me more than any other criticism—but I never doubted about you. I know how few men are gifted as you are, with intense creativity and at the same time such a complete command of your hands (I remembered watching the sure deftness of his line work...)such a constant drive toward perfect craftsmanship. This gift of God has its curse, as you are aware of what you are worth. Believe me, I have been through that myself, and am still in the same boat. It took me no less than the shocking experience of the last

6 months of solitude to put into me less arrogance, more patience toward other honest and dedicated comrades at arms who cannot be held responsible for what they do not know about art and creativity, and for what God has not put into them.

As I told you when we last met, patience is the hardest of all virtues—and it requires first to understand other people's thoughts, even and mostly the unexpressed. And this is most difficult for an artist who lives wrapped up in his own work and always believes that he is right, and that his solution is always the only solution.

All I want to say is that I respect and admire your art, as much as your course in facing this beginning of your life as an artist.

I know you don't hear many people say anything good about the very best things you may do, and I know how discouraging it is to work in this void. But this void proves your worth, as it shows also that you already are on your lonely way ahead of the crowd.

You have the blessing, however, to have in Sally Anne, another artist who knows your worth. She brings you, I am sure, the same kind of inspiration that Liv brought me through selfless dedication and the only valid kind of encouragement: the one based on the genuine and direct appreciation of successful deeds, as well as mistakes and failures. Even though we men may resent the criticism of a woman toward out work, we must never underestimate the keenness of their intuitive judgment. I had more damning criticisms from Liv—which I resisted hotly at the time because they were so true—than from my comrades in arms, in school, or later in life—believe me!

Now, "why should he write me all this?" I can hear you say. Just because I think you are among the extremely few God-given creators in this world, and I don't see why I should not tell you so.

I wanted to keep this message strictly as a talk between two artists who understand and respect their own work, but I could not close without telling you how thankful I am to God that from the misery which I brought about to my wife, was born a closer understanding and kinship between the rest of the family. I am mostly relieved because I know how close Sally Anne is to Liv, and all the good that may grow, stronger with the years, from this closeness for both of them.

Once we are rushed by destiny into solitude, we come to realize that true love and friendship are after all the only things that matter in life. The world is made up of lonely people who only wait for a word or an outstretched hand to give forth their riches from which we gain so much more than what we think we give. The world is so direly in need of dedication of individuals to other individuals, or tolerance, and true humble respect. This spirit is the only way to bring peace to the world, and make it all possible for great things to dream.

I wish both of you all the luck and the love you deserve, and that it should grow into your children, so innocent of the world ahead, and so confident in yours.

God bless you both.

Paul

I was astonished by his words. After what we had done, how could he be so gracious, so loving, so forgiving?

Where had this letter been? How did I not know of it? Would it have made a difference in my understanding, first of my father, and finally a different view of my husband? How loving Papa was—and forgiving. Or did he not know of the deceitfulness when he wrote this?

I mourned as I had never been able to until now. My father was gone, forever gone; and I couldn't, would never be able to express my sorrow for the tragic end to his life and my role in his lonely path.

But I never cried anymore. If I could have, my tears might have begun to melt my stone cold heart.

The next letter I read was from the dean of the college:

Paul, I have been informed of your serious personal problems. Unfortunately, this affects the College. Apparently there is substantial proof behind the accusations.

Unless you can prove otherwise, I must ask you to send me a note resigning from the College.

This grieves me to write this letter, because Paul, I have great admiration for your talents and skills, as well as your dedication to teaching. You will be a great loss to the College.

Best of luck.

The last letter in the group was the most difficult, but not only because it was written in French. This was the first, I guessed, of many letters he wrote to Mama after his "outing". As I laboriously translated, I was overwhelmed by the depth of the love that still burned between them. They were divorced; he was in Spain with his lover; but there was only one person who had ever mattered, in all his life—Liv, his one true love.

Chère Liv, he began, dear Liv,

> One letter from the dean in response to my own led me to know who it was that betrayed me—"close members of your family".
>
> I have to say I was absolutely frightened—and heartsick. Do they understand the gravity of their actions? Not only does it mean the end of my teaching career—but even makes it not possible for me to make a living anymore. To protect themselves—and the College—they destroy me, without recourse.
>
> What possible good thing can I write to you? Evidently, no one can show me the same understanding that you have shown—with such elegance and heart. But what has happened is not, after all, fatal.
>
> I have no one else but you now, in whom I can have true support. And, as a matter of fact, I well know that I have never had anyone but you. I know now, that I can only trust you, you who are on the other side of the ocean.
>
> Thank you for your good and long letter.
> Je t'embrasse (I kiss you, I embrace you…)
> Paul

All the guilt, all the sorrow, all the loss that I had closeted in the deepest recesses of my being finally came out in a moan—not a cry. As if the hand of God reached into my heart and at last opened it to begin a healing process, I began the long course of letting go.

How was it possible that I had known so little about my parents? How could I have been so misguided all these years? The letters were gradually revealing Papa's profound love for his wife. Mama had often talked of the passion that was such a fire between them. But that was always Mama's point of view. Papa had seemed stern and distant most of the time; and I thought the reason for his frequent and long absences was his need to get away from his family. It was a revelation to read his constant trust and devotion to Mama. She was his muse—and his true love.

My oldest son is 52 now, a year younger than Papa was the last time I ever saw him. He was so young…I reflect on my squandered life and all the missed opportunities to somehow find forgiveness that would finally assuage my guilt in the final treachery so many years ago.

It's too easy to blame my first husband, the artist Papa extols with such grace. It's too easy to blame our actions on our youthful outrage over my father's actions. We can say that in 1964 homosexuality was considered an abomination, worse than pedophilia or rape or other violence. We can say this…and I did. I was the "family member" the dean spoke of so guardedly.

But the truth is that I have carried the guilt of this terrible action like a leaden weight on my soul. It has shaped who I am, though I may deny it and say that my conscience is clear, and I feel no remorse. But oh, how I hurt inside…If I could change the past… how often I have thought with desperation.

Both my sisters, Betty and Rona, were married the next year. I had always thought I would design and make their wedding dresses, but we never even went to their weddings. I spent less and less time with Mama and we finally simply left Houston. Mama and I wrote letters, somehow avoiding any discussion of the cataclysm that was central to all our lives. I was to blame for Papa's departure and my actions were incomprehensible to the rest of the family. How could I have done such a terrible thing? How was it any of my business to take it upon myself to be the moral arbiters of the family? Was it not up to Mama to decide if any action was to be taken?

I never cry anymore. I feel as if all my tears have been used up to be replaced by the dry desert of my soul. There seems to be no further way to express sadness. It is clearly too late to hit a reset button for my life, and even if I could, I probably would still repeat all the steps that have finally led me to where I am now, thinking about Papa and the path he had to take that had led him to where he finally landed.

— 24 —

SNOWBOUND

The ghosts of Christmas past always haunt my present, forever reminding me of the shoals and reefs my little boat of life has managed to avoid—and the storms that I couldn't. This, the strangest Christmas for being trapped without the warmth of family, has left me bereft of new images to supplant the old painful memories.

Joe and I have been snowbound since well before Christmas, as has everyone else. Seattle doesn't handle snow well and has too few plows, not enough manpower, and is always surprised by the mighty hand of winter. The snow has come in waves, never relenting enough to make headway against the deepening drifts. I think of my two sisters, each alone on this Christmas day, each trapped in immobility. At least, I have Joe, my rock in every storm.

We sisters have talked together, somehow keeping company in our separateness. The small presents we have for one another stay unopened, waiting for a thaw to bring a long overdue visit. Christmas trees are lit brightly to lift the gloom of no sharing eyes. Cookies are growing stale for want of mouths to take in their sweetness. There are no children, even, to romp in the snow and make snow angels.

I think Rona doesn't really want to see anybody, even if she could. She limps through her house alone, sits gingerly in her easy chair and watches the Hallmark channel day after day, trying to ignore the sciatica, or whatever it is that gives her so much pain. She has talked to everyone, endlessly, until she may think she's making a nuisance of herself. She tries not to be lonely. She tries to not show it to others in her voice on the phone.

Betty, who always makes lemonade out of lemons, is wearing down into simmering annoyance now. "This is surreal," she says in disgust. "I've never experienced anything like this. I can't even imagine it in my worst nightmare! I've shoveled the driveway four times now. Four times! I tried to get out yesterday so that I could see Wayne at the Veterans' Home. I couldn't get past the driveway—and with all-wheel drive! I have no more fresh vegetables. Lots of other stuff—in my World War III pantry, as Kim calls it, but I can't even have a salad!"

"Next year, you should bug out sooner," I suggest, "you should plan a visit to your daughter's in South Carolina from Thanksgiving until after the New Year. Get out of all this aggravation.

"That's what I was going to do, remember?" Betty says with exasperation. "I had the ticket and everything—but we're snowed in!"

Since Wayne's stroke on Thanksgiving several years ago, I have grown to love and appreciate my younger sister, Betty, as if I were newly discovering her. We had never lived close to each other and had grown distant over the years—especially me, given my characteristic propensity to dismiss anyone I didn't see often—even my brothers and sisters. After all, how long had it been since I had talked to any of my three brothers?

"Of course, they could call me just as easily as I can call them," I thought. "But it takes someone like Betty to keep a family connected."

Of course, Mama had been the one that kept the ribbon of family connected first. Then it should have fallen to me to pick up the ribbon, but after the "wilderness years" as Mama and I had called them after we left Houston and moved to Chicago, far from brothers and sisters who were still horrified by my betrayal of Papa, it was Betty who continued the ties. "And Kim is doing it now for her brothers and her cousins, just as her oldest daughter is beginning to pick up the first threads for her generation." The tapestry grows and takes shape, generation by generation.

Is this how we create oral histories? From mother to daughter with a yearning to maintain a connection to shared memories, shared pasts? There always seems to be one person who has sufficient interest. In our family, it's always been Betty.

Of the six, Betty was the only one to pursue the passion of music throughout her life. She married a jazz musician, but her own expression was in her voice. Just as Papa had recognized long ago, she sang with the purity of an angel. But rather than move into performance, she resolved to share her love of song through teaching. She became known and recognized as a premier choral director, and was frequently called upon all over Texas, where she and Wayne lived for many years, to do clinics and to judge high school choirs.

She traveled a lot. And when she wasn't traveling, she was consumed with the work of perfecting her choirs. Wayne taught as well, and then moved into retirement. Betty had married a much older man.

Their comfortable routine was shaken and altered dramatically with his stroke. They moved to Bremerton to be closer to family. Travel was out of the question now. Even her work was put on permanent hold. Her consuming task would be, from this day forward, to care for Wayne, however she could manage it.

"Betty," I called her one day soon after Wayne came home from the hospital. "How are you going to care for him? He can't walk; he has no function on his left side; he can barely talk!"

"I'll figure it out, day by day. I have to. The physical therapy people will train me to do transfers—to get him from his chair to the bed, or to the bathroom. I can retro-fit the house, can't I?"

"How characteristic of you," I said. "So stubborn—obstinately refusing to be defeated in anything. The eternal optimist."

And Wayne valiantly tried to get better—insisting that he would walk again. But the therapist sighed and shook her head, knowing that would never be possible anymore.

Betty and Wayne lived a ferry ride away. It was never easy to visit back and forth, and had to be thought of not simply as an afternoon or a morning visit, but an all-day affair. At first, Betty ventured onto the ferry, wheeling Wayne and carrying all the paraphernalia that he needed. She even took a few trips with him to see their grown children in other states. But that began to be an arduous ordeal that left both of them utterly exhausted.

I visited as often as possible, often taking the ferry with Kim, who adored her Auntie B. But we all worried about Betty, concerned that this would become too much for her to continue much longer.

One day, she slipped and fell on the ice in the driveway, bruising her thigh with a giant hematoma.

"You can't do this anymore!" I tried to tell her. "Isn't there something else that can be done? He should have a professional caregiver. You're not strong enough to keep doing this. What happens if you get sick? Are you going to try to keep taking care of him, no matter what?"

"Until I can't anymore, I guess." Betty was resolute. "What would you do if something happened with Joe? Would you just walk away? Or dump him in a nursing home?"

I didn't want to think about what I might do.

But soon enough, Betty had to face a new reality. Wayne was hospitalized with a severe infection that left him even more weakened. Finally, to everyone's secret—and not so secret—relief, Betty would no longer be able to care for him by herself. He was moved to the Veteran's Home, and now Betty was alone in her big house, just as Rona had become solitary in her life after she lost her cherished husband, also much older than she was.

Betty, in her uniquely stubborn fashion, was undaunted at the new twist her life had taken. She would no longer be able to afford to do all the nice things she loved, now that she and Wayne were on Medicaid, but so what? She could get used to anything; and she would overcome if at all possible. She would still be able to do voice clinics, so that was a good thing. She would visit Wayne several times a week and watch movies with him in his room. That was a good thing too. She'd be able to visit her sisters more easily than before and she certainly looked forward to that. She might even be able to visit her daughter, knowing that Wayne was in good hands.

But she would miss him. She would miss not taking care of him, as she had for all the years they had been married—even before the stroke. They had been married over forty years; she knew him better than anybody. And he adored her with such complete abandon that she sorrowed at the loss of being together as they had been.

I am realizing anew that we are all getting older, as our families go on without us. We can sit alone, parked in our respective houses, knowing that our children and our grandchildren are making their own Christmas memories, just as they are building on times past, in distant and disparate places. "It feels like a letting go," I mutter to myself. "We're holding a ribbon that our children have released so that they can have their own traditions…" I look at the Christmas tree, brightly lit and hung with ornaments that span nearly fifty years: blown eggs that my children and I decorated together. "There's the goofy face that Sean drew, and the beautiful face that Kim etched, and all the ones that I made…" And the grandchildren have their own ornaments displayed as well: a snowman doily with a face carefully drawn by Mark's four-year-old, and Erin's beaded iguanas trailing long ribbons. Every ornament has a history and the history is the story of family and love and warmth. Finally, it occurs to me that nothing on the tree came from Mama or from my own childhood.

And I understand the symbol of the ribbon.

— 25 —

THE BOX

The cardboard box was layered with a fine film of attic dust. Even though I moved it carefully, little dust devils settled on the cabinet around the box. The edges of the cardboard lid were curled with age. I hadn't visited the contents since we had moved here many years ago and put the box in the attic, with all the rest of moving detritus that could be put aside for later decisions as to what to do with it all. The box would have stayed in its forgotten corner except that this was an exceptionally hot summer. After the major remodel of the house, our contractor had warned that the attic heat would cook anything we might be storing up there. I didn't care about most of it, except that this was where Joe had all his old 35mm. slides. They would have to be stored in his archive closet.

I am not a saver of stuff. So when I saw the box, I decided this would be the time to sort and toss—mostly toss, I thought. I wasn't surprised that I remembered all its contents. This was memorabilia of my own life, from my high school days up until I met Joe. I had already culled the contents many times, and all that was left, I thought, would be mementos that might mean something to my three grown children.

There was my high school senior year book, and the varsity letter I got for being president of the Honor Society. There were my various ribbons for the speech meets and the debate team events. I carefully unwrapped the tissue that protected the christening dress

I had made for Kim. That would go to her, of course. Newspaper clippings that described my success in New York, others that announced the coming marriage of Sally Anne, daughter of acclaimed architect and professor at the University of Notre Dame. And there were the letters.

This was the sum and substance of all that I had chosen to save over the last fifty years. I had another box which contained photographs. A third box was labeled "kid art" and was my treasure trove of all the childhood drawings done by the children. My last box contained what was left of Mama's things, hastily collected after she died. This box was still unsorted, still partially sealed from when I had filled it long ago. I had already brought the photographs down from the attic, so the remaining two boxes would stay where they were until I had the time and energy to revisit this part of the history.

There were three packets of letters, neatly held by thick rubber bands. I picked up the fat, square packet, with my first husband's carefully meticulous handwriting. I started undoing the packet, but instead put it in the discard pile. I could always change my mind later, but I didn't really think I would.

Why should I save love letters from my former husband? I didn't really even want to save them for my children to later discover. When I did these sorting operations, I was always stone cold and emotionless. I had never had much storage space and had learned long ago that I had to be ruthless. I seldom regretted my cold-heartedness, and was only rarely sorry.

I turned back to the letters. The second packet contained all the letters Mama had written when we were far from each other. These were the painful years "in the wilderness" I remembered. I would keep those, of course, and read them again when I had more time to dwell in those places of sweet memory. I put the packet aside and turned to the third bundle. These were the letters from Rona, or my brothers, or Betty; a kind of miscellaneous assortment that defied easy cataloguing.

I checked the time and realized I needed to get this whole box out of Joe's office. I put everything back in and carried the box to my desk. I put Philip's discarded letters in my trash container and went back to the task at hand. My goal was to empty the box today and find new homes for all the contents I intended to keep. If I had time later, I would read some of these letters. I put them aside.

I picked up the packet of mixed letters again. I'll just scan a few of these, I decided. Maybe I'll discover something I'd forgotten.

Rona's effusive exuberance leapt off the first letter I picked up in her familiar large scrawl. Much of her stationary was of bright orange daisies on electric blue fields, as psychedelic as the seventies period they came from. Most of the letters were several pages long, paragraph after paragraph of emotion spilling across the page as she reached out to me, the one person she said who could help her understand herself. *She's a good writer but I don't have time for all this...* I caught myself in mid-thought as I remembered that this was a period when the two of us had exchanged long and frequent letters, in an effort to come to grips with the tumult in our hearts. We needed to somehow explain or excuse the "event"—justify it, at least. We had been very close then.

Soon, I was lost in the letters—and the memories. I forgot that it was a hot August day, and that I had planned to do some gardening, or at least pick the fresh bounty of tomatoes from my plants. I didn't notice that the sun was behind the chestnut trees now, providing shade for the whole back yard. Joe's electric eraser whirred in the background and I began to realize I should probably begin thinking about something to put on the grill for dinner. But not yet. One of the envelopes caught my attention.

It was from Papa, and had been forwarded to me by Mama. The envelope was tissue thin airmail paper. It was in his familiar hand—bold, like a lyrical song, a bird wing of expression. Below was the address in Mama's sensible ball-point pen cursive style.

Had I ever seen this letter, or had it been carelessly tucked in with the others, part of one of the many moves of my first marriage? Had this simply escaped my notice? I fingered the envelope hesitantly, then pulled the two paper thin sheets out and opened them carefully. I began to read, then looked at the postmark to get a sense of when this was written—or forwarded: April 27, 1970. I began to read.

Dear Sally Anne,

Your letter touched me very deeply. (I began to remember what I had closed off long ago. I had written to Papa to ask his forgiveness for my role in his exile. I shut this memory away because I thought he never wrote back. Why didn't I know about this letter? Wouldn't it have made a difference in my stone cold heart if I had read these words, back then, when I was hurting so much? Where had this letter been these last thirty years?) How could I have ever invoked God's mercy in the Lord's Prayer, as I so often did in these past few years, if I had not forgiven long ago whatever harm you may think having done to me at a time when passions were too high in our hearts, only human—to act with cool heads?

Love, you see, is the Great Forgiver—and love is God's Way. Our pride makes us believe that we may change someone's destiny by interfering in his path—so short—from birth to death. This is only the ready-made belief that man's life is a one way street, as perfectly and safely traced by his own decisions, from beginning to end, as the ordinated orbit of an Apollo Capsule. I smiled wistfully as I remembered my Papa's gallic way of speaking—my heart filling with love—and longing. But God has other ways to design our life as it passes by. He is the One who forks our path with territories unknown where we learn to grow up through storms, clouds, and brilliant sunshine—ever learning thus to know Him better.

Be reassured, Sally Anne: nobody, but nobody can be taken responsible for having purposely deviated another human being from his path, and changed his destiny. So, be at peace with yourself, and forget about what evil you think you have done to me, not realizing at the time the greater harm you were doing to yourself.

You see, by forcing my hand in such a formidable manner, you only switched on blindly the correction into orbit which bamboozled me into a new way of life in Europe. my heart was breaking as I read his words...In spite of the extreme hardships at times, has also been giving me, ever since, intense hours to live and treasure—together with the unshakeable belief that Love, and only Love is the almighty redeemer of all our weaknesses—the only worthwhile

258

motivation of our acts. For this, I should thank you instead, from the deepest of my heart.

Don't you think that, in turn, I could say much myself about the harm I have done to you—you all this wonderful family of ours—by complacently letting build around me an image too perfect to be human?

My sorrow was complete. I raised my hands upwards, in supplication, as if by doing so I might finally touch my father.

Yes, Sally Anne, no one has the right to judge. What the right of the righteous and those who "know best" consider as evil, hides oftentimes the finest wealth of goodness, tolerance and understanding—that we owe to the bounty of God—finally written as a little four letter word, so innocently powerful as the Bomb, and which most clearly spells His teaching: LOVE

He signed it with words that would reverberate in my soul:

So long, Sally Anne—until His travel bureau unites me (or you) with a ticket across the ocean—and Love, from Papa

I had dragged this box of letters around with me, each packet neatly bundled, unnoticed, forgotten, buried with the pain of my past as I had resolved, over the years, to forget and move on.

I sat still for a long time, looking out the window of my office without seeing.

Finally, I rose and went out to the garden with my market basket. I would pick tomatoes. The sun was softly warm on my back, like a caress, as I reached deep into the plants to let the ripe, red tomatoes fall into my open hand. The vines were fragrant with the singular tomato smell that I loved so much. My bare toes sank into the rich soil around each plant. I pulled a few weeds, while I was there, tossing them into the bucket at the edge of the bed. The August afternoon was redolent with the mingled scents of my Mediterranean garden: piquant rosemary and more complex oregano teamed with the spicy basil I added to my basket. As I picked, memories intruded into the loveliness of the afternoon and began to march forward, first as brilliantly painful scenes, then as the ancient play I had successfully hidden. I went to sit in the shade of the patio umbrella and laid my harvest basket on the table. I allowed the memories to finally overtake my thoughts.

— 26 —

MAMA

Mama's children were all grown and gone. Like an exploding star, the nuclear family became pieces of errant dust floating slowly away from her. She was living alone in the big house, wandering aimlessly from room to room as if possibly expecting one or all of her children to come out from behind one of the doors. But we were all far now, scattered over all corners of the country—even across the ocean—as Paul was in Israel with Audrey and their two children, and Papa was in permanent exile somewhere in Europe... Spain, Italy, France? Mama only knew where he was when she got a letter.

Mama had stopped crying. There were no tears left to fall. The divorce had been finalized years ago, before Sean, my youngest son was born, before we left Houston and moved to Illinois. But memories are pervasive bits of the past, never seeming to let us go.

She would be leaving soon. There was nothing—and no one left for her in Houston. The movers would be coming next week to pack everything up for the long trip to California. Mama had decided on California because at least two of her six children were there: Rona and I. She could make a long journey to spend a few weeks with Paul and his family in Israel. It would be hardest to leave Houston because Betty and her family were living in the Texas hill country—so close—yet too far. She had to not think about Peter and trying to visit him because she was never really sure where he would land next, and John was firmly ensconced in the northeast, teaching computer classes at Boston College.

Mama had a little office downstairs, which she told us she would miss for all the memories it held for her. The room was painted a soft rosy cream, like the inside of a shell. The paned window looked out to the small garden that she had tried to maintain—even in the humid summer heat. Rather than the untidy banana trees, she had tree ferns that shaded the bright impatiens that edged the grassy plot. She had made gauzy curtains for the window, a soft covering that wouldn't obscure the light. Her small desk was at the window. Paintings, pastels, charcoal drawings covered the walls. Most were Papa's landscapes—all in a boldly simple style—almost as if these might be of a mystical foreign land.

Mama sighed as she sat at her desk. She fingered the latest letter she had received from Papa. She would respond later; but first she would write to each of us, whose last letters were in the cubby-hole on her desk. But she opened his letter to read again.

> Dear Liv,
>
> Your letters are a great comfort, as you understand so perfectly my situation and my character that it sometimes scares me that you should be able to see so deeply in myself, when I fail so often to understand my own self.
>
> I received also naturally, the godsend of the money you so generously tucked into your letter. Thank you, from the bottom of my heart—as I was in sore need, as you know. But I think things are looking up. I am painting, I think, quite well—in spite of my state of mind. This, after a great change in technique. I know I shouldn't be painting with an eye to having my paintings sold—but that is my livelihood—isn't it?
>
> Don't worry about me anyway. "Tout vat tres bien, Madame la Marquise..."and I am still the lucky one to be here and I feel confident that it will pay in the end.
>
> Strange also that I have no ill feeling toward Sally Anne. I pity her, that's all. And believe me, it is not being lordly generous or so. Life is so short anyway that it doesn't leave time for grudges. There is so much to construct. We can only ignore the destructive acts and continue to build.

Easy to say, I know. I have been through more than you
may think and am still going strong. Every time I think I have
reached the worst, there is still a little worse yet to come.
It's okay. Thanks so much for your letters.
As ever,
Paul

Even as Mama thought she had no tears left to cry, his letters
always made her heart ache with longing. He said she was the only
one who understood him. Yet she knew that he was the only one
who could ever plumb her depths. He was right: there should be no
bitterness, but it was so very hard to accept all the loss these years
had brought. Only now, as she was selling the house, moving to
California, could she begin to think of a future without him.

But she would continue to send him money, as she could, when
she could. He was destitute, she knew, and was putting on a brave
front for her sake. At some point, she would have to involve all of us,
her children. We would all have to contribute to help him survive—
especially me and my husband—as we had been the instruments
of his exile.

"How like him," she told us often. "He is so trusting—and
when his faith in people is disappointed, he can only accept and
move on."

Mama and I had a strained relationship, even in the passage of
so much time. I had seldom seen her over the past fourteen years,
and though our letters to each other were long and newsy, there
was always an undercurrent of... suspicion. As if we didn't really
know where we stood with each other, as if our show of affection
was just that: a show.

I was looking forward to seeing her, hopeful that since we would
be geographically close, maybe we could also be close as we once
had been—it seemed so long ago.

Our first reunion was over lunch at a Mexican restaurant in
Dana Point.

Mama looked older, a little timid, as she was ushered to the table by our waiter. I stood and moved toward her. She smiled and put her hands out to me, and I saw the magnificent woman I remembered, the woman I had tried to emulate, and the woman I had ultimately disappointed by my actions. I knew that as I begged her for forgiveness, she would dismiss any culpability on my part. It was always my husband.

Mama coughed and winced with the pain of it.

"Mama, are you all right? That's a strange cough you have…"

"I know. Don't worry about it. Now that I'm here, I'll see a doctor. I know it's not an ordinary cold, but I haven't had time to deal with it, what with moving and all. But later. I have too much to do for now to be worried about a chest infection. Rona will have a good doctor that I can see, surely."

"I'm so happy to see you, finally Mama. I've missed you so. You have no idea…"

"Have you really missed me? I thought your life was quite full, quite complete, with Philip and the children."

"Oh, well, full maybe, but really missing being able to spend time with you—as we used to."

"I feel, in a way, that you turned your back on me after Papa left. That it was too difficult for you to be with me when I was going through so much with Papa…"

"I'm so sorry Mama. I've been so immature. Please forgive me. I did such a terrible thing to Papa…I couldn't face you or the others after that. But I wish we could start over again, go back to the times before. I want us to be close again. Can we?"

"It was never about you, dear. I'm sure you would have been quite different without your husband's influence on you."

"What do you mean?"

"I don't think you've been your own person in all the years you've been married. I began to see the change in you when you returned from France, when you were pregnant with Kim. Where was the strong and wise little girl I remembered? You had closed in on yourself, becoming the woman your husband wanted you to be. You bleached your hair, wore too much makeup; you even began to wear clothes that weren't suitable for a woman your age."

I was silent, holding back the tears. She knew me so well. But I had to ignore her assessment.

"Mama, let's start fresh, you and me. I have always valued and trusted your wisdom, your insights. I need you now, Mama, as I never have before. I'm really mixed up, I know. But I want to be better."

"Of course, dear. I'm so glad that I decided to move here. We'll do all the things we've been longing to do together. And I'm sorry to have been so blunt with you about your husband. But he does have a hold on you that's not healthy. I hope you can see that."

"We have our problems, for sure. Most of the time, I wear a mask, I think. But I'm trying to hang in there. I promised Sean a long time ago that I wouldn't leave him."

"Leave him? Sean or your husband? Or both?"

"I don't know, Mama. I'll always be there for my kids. But Philip? I don't know. Maybe not, but we're trying to work things out, I think. After all, this is going to be our twentieth anniversary this year. That must mean something, don't you think?"

"I'm no judge of that. The important question to ask yourself is whether you want to be here twenty years from now."

"You don't like him, do you? You used to, I think."

"I don't like his hold on you. And I know you're a strong person, so I must believe that he has a subtle way of having you behave the way he thinks you should—for him."

We changed the subject, as she saw my discomfort. We talked about her move and began to make plans for all we would do together.

With the sale of her house, Mama had been able to parley that into a condominium in Leisure World. She had a wonderful view of rolling hills and giant sycamores. It was a fresh delight to be in a better climate than Houston.

Best of all, she could now become reacquainted with her grandchildren. Kim was in an art school. She couldn't wait to see what she was painting, or sculpting—or whatever medium she was working in. Mark and Sean she barely knew—but that didn't matter. She would soon discover their unique gifts. And Rona's two lovely children, that had been adopted? She would have time to help her youngest daughter navigate the tumultuous years of raising little children to be strong young adults. Always the strong and wise mother, Mama would know how to counsel Rona.

She coughed again, and sighed impatiently, as I looked on with fresh concern.

— 27 —

LAST ACT

June 1981: I went to Spain, taking a side trip from the publicity tour I was a part of with my job as a manager at Neiman Marcus. We would be writing an article about the embroidered linins of Madeira for Orange County Magazine. I used the savings I had squirreled away since I had started working. Philip didn't know about this money, and that was just as well, or he would have fought me for it in the divorce. I had always feared that he would insist that I put it toward the "budget". After all, if there was enough in the "budget" for a motorcycle for him, surely I could have this for myself. But our divorce was final now and there was no way he could touch me anymore. I wanted to go to Spain to finally see Papa, face to face, to let him know that I loved him, that I had always loved him.

Somehow, it was all so familiar, as if I might still be the very little girl who adored her Papa when we all lived in *le Midi*, with the scent of mimosa drifting through the groves of olive trees. But now I was making new memories, walking through a fishing village, choosing a rough wool sweater, its ivory cables sensuous under my hand. I chose one to bring back, a souvenir of the precious slice of time I could give myself. The salt air from the Mediterranean was a healing balm. The land climbed abruptly up from the beach, dotted with neat olive groves, their dusty leaves grey green against the clear blue sky. Tucked into the rolling landscape I could see the villages, like white dominos thrown against the hills, a patchwork of terra cotta roof tiles and bright white stucco walls.

I would try to find my Papa. This, after all, was the real purpose of my trip. I had gotten a number for him from Mama, and an address. Though I spoke no Spanish, it was easy to be understood—and to understand. I got by with a mix of French and English and eventually found my way to a small side street in the village, the buildings seeming to lean into each other for support over the narrow lane. The windows were all shuttered against the sun, which found its way with blinding directness even in this winding walk. Geraniums spilled out of pots and from window boxes, bright splashes of red and green against the white stucco walls.

I pulled on the knob that was the door knocker and heard a lilting chime echo through the interior. The heavy wood door opened and a man greeted me with a questioning look.

"Mario?" I asked hesitantly, uncertain if I had the right address. He nodded, still puzzled by my presence, a stranger knocking on his door. I hastened to explain who I was.

"I'm Sally Anne—Paul Grillo's daughter." I smiled timidly.

He was slender, almost fragile, while nonetheless exuding a vitality that was electric. His coal black hair fell in a shock over one eye and he flipped it back with a shake. His black eyes smiled a welcome even before he opened his mouth to say *"Hola, señora!"* He extended a strong hand to me and I took it gratefully.

I followed him through the house, my sandaled feet padding on the tiles. He was barefooted and silent in the deep shadows, his white shirt a beacon for me to follow. We made our way to the back of the house, which opened onto an inner courtyard where the bright sun filtered through the leafy green of a jungle profusion of tropical plantings.

He motioned me to one of the white wicker chairs. *"Por favor, Señora,* please, sit. I will get us some tea."

"My father? Paul? Is he here?"

"Oh, *Señora,* I thought you must know. He has gone to the

United States—for a lecture tour. You just missed him. He left this morning."

"Oh, no! That can't be...I've been desperate to see him and now that I am finally here, you're telling me that he's gone..."

"I'm so sorry. If I give you his itinerary, perhaps you can catch up to him somewhere on his tour..."

But I never did catch up to him. I never saw my father again...

* * *

I loved this walk along the bluff. I carried my sandals so that I could better experience my new freedom. The statice bloomed in soft purple clouds, nasturtiums cascaded down the slope, mingled with wildly blooming geranium. And of course, the ubiquitous bougainvillea was everywhere, flaunting its brilliant fuchsia blanket of bloom. The grand old Hotel Laguna, the object of so much mediocre art, seemed to grow out of the crescent beach below. The calm Pacific glistened in the afternoon light.

A year had passed since I tried to see Papa. I moved into a rental house near the beach, in North Laguna. Mark had helped me move in before he went off for basic training in San Diego. He stayed with me, in the beginning, and then was gone. Sean stayed with his father, perhaps recognizing how badly wounded he was. They seemed to be holding each other up in a brokenhearted kind of way. I knew that I was being blamed for the terrible divorce, and that Sean felt betrayed that I had broken my promise to never leave him. So he stayed with his dad and only occasionally came to visit me—usually when Mark or Kim might be there. Kim had gone on to art school, on a scholarship, completely removing herself from the storm of her parents' disintegrated marriage.

My brothers managed to visit with their Papa, once or twice before he died. And Betty and Rona told of the sweet afternoons they had with him when he moved back to Paris and lived in a tiny flat with Mario. Even Philip and his new wife went to see him when they took a trip to Europe soon after they were married. He took a picture of Papa and gave it to me.

I have put the picture away with all the other pieces of Papa's life. Finally, if there is anything left which will move me to tears, it is this photograph of a ravaged old man looking out at the world—still with a smile.

Ultimately I found a measure of peace and was happier than I remembered having been for a very long time. I spent long lovely hours with Mama in her Leisure World condominium. Mama, too, was at peace, having reconciled with Papa many years ago. They exchanged long letters of love and friendship. He was painting with a passion he had never felt before, he told her. Mario, his partner, was loving and patient with all Papa's idiosyncrasies, and encouraged him, even as he cared for him. Paul's heart was failing, Mario wrote to Mama, in halting English, so there was an urgency in the painting.

I also spent time with Rona. The divorce had been grueling, and I wasn't certain I could have stayed strong if I didn't have Mama and my sister faithfully standing by me through the long poisonous year. I tried to see Sean more often and finally gave up, realizing that it would have to be on his terms, when he was ready. I thought he was embarrassed for me. I didn't think that he entirely believed the stories he was hearing, but he could also see how much his dad was hurting, now that I was gone. So through it all, through my new peace and happiness, my heart was broken for my family, now sundered. I knew that Philip, despite his seething anger, loved his family deeply. There was no doubt that he was the most devastated of all, and mourned the loss of the carefully constructed life he thought he had built with me. His roots in his Catholic faith made him frightened of the sin of our divorce. He turned back to the Church, seeking absolution, even as he couldn't admit his own role in the failure of his marriage. His world had crumbled, and he was adrift. As Papa had so wisely said once, Philip was still looking for himself.

The years slid by and bitter memories softened, like the eroding effect of constant wind or water on jagged stones that become smooth over time. I met Joe and was enchanted by his generous spirit and his unabashed love for me; who I was, who I could be. He accepted me and celebrated me and I bloomed in his care, with his love, as he seemed to marvel at his good fortune that God would gift him with such a woman. In my turn, I loved him as the true and constant companion I would treasure "as we grow old together", I told him one night after we had seen "On Golden Pond". Though our fortunes lurched between feast and famine, I knew a security I had never felt in the twenty years I had spent with my first husband.

Mama's serious cough turned out to be lung cancer—virulent and sudden and final. Her six children gathered around her bedside, now taking their turn to care for her, giving back to her the love she had so long lavished on each of us. When she died, we celebrated her passing to God's gracious care with a great party at the beach. We laughed, we cried, we danced, we reminisced and loved the mother who had taught us each so much about life, pain, doubt, and forbearance. And finally, this was the woman who taught us so much about forgiveness.

As if in a last message to us all, I discovered a letter she wrote to Papa just before she died. She was very weak and her lovely handwriting was like a spider web across the page. She began in French, and then lapsed into English as she obviously grew more tired.

Cher Paul, she wrote,

> I write to you as I am surrounded by our grand and beautiful family. I am struck by the knowledge that in all their letters we can find how their thinking has been so richly influenced by our contributions in their individual lives. We, their parents, are far from each other, but their perceptions of us remain intact. Together, I think, we helped them find their values—and they have not strayed from these central truths.
>
> I am surprised to note how valuable—and how often difficult—it is to breathe. Otherwise, all goes well. Each of

the children (I call them children—though we know they are young adults!) has found a particular niche to be helpful in these last days. And each of them has found a way to use their unique gifts to make my passing more comfortable.

And now, each of them is writing to you so that you may know and understand how much you have been loved by your children. Sadly, the theme is the same for them all: they regret the distance and the time that has separated us all so painfully.

I wish we could all see you and tell you how much you have meant—and mean to us. You will always be the one who has given me my most happy moments.

Dearest Paul, I love you. Liv

But sometimes I wonder if this story was not inevitable after all. Would Mama and Papa have stayed together if he had not had to leave? He said my actions pushed him into a change of course. Could his life have been different if he had continued teaching, exploring new ideas and directions, inspiring others to examine the world we all share a little more responsibly? Could he have continued to have an influence on the young minds he was helping to shape and grow? Could he have made a difference? Like a stone thrown into a pool, causing ripples to move outward in an ever-widening circle, his life and his ideas affected us all. Though his book has been out of print for years, it can still be found in odd places, treasured by those who have caught his vision.

Papa followed Mama several years later when his heart finally was too tired to keep pumping. Mario was with him when he died.

Finally, I am struck with a sense of profound loss for what might have been. Just as long ago the cohesion of family was sundered by an act of betrayal, so again, when I turned my back and walked away from my husband, I was the instrument that altered the course of my family. I think of a super nova exploding into the dark galaxy, sending its fractured pieces to drift forever. But are we really like that or do we rejoin and coalesce around a new nucleus?

We six, the children of star-crossed lovers, are the lasting gift of that eternal union. In the same way, my three grown children are the amazing adults they have become because of the crucible of their parents. As I watch Mark's two daughters, my granddaughters, deal with the divorce of their parents, I see them grow in strength and wisdom as they plumb the depths of who they are now that they may grow into the better women they will become.

In the end, many of the masks have come off, as each character in this theater of life closes the curtain on the final act of a play whose story is as old as time itself.

As for me, I still wear a carapace of self-protection. I am afraid that if I try to remove it, I will expose a skin so raw that I fear I might melt away as an open wound.

I have walked away from a marriage. I have left friends behind. But a bond of kinship, as when the same blood courses through us, and we share timeless history—how can that be denied?

So today, I explore the complexity—and the pain of my relationship with my baby sister—who died so suddenly this past year. Was I ever able to tell Rona I loved her, really loved her in a way that she could truly believe, or was I always too selfish, too self-absorbed?

A part of me may always wish I had never explored the boxes of letters. If I had left those mementos of the past in the dust of the attic, would my heart be less broken? Finally, the last mask to come off will have to be to remove the façade that declares I don't hurt anymore. In fact, by writing my story, I am discovering how much I have lost by pretending that everything was always fine.

Maybe someday I will really learn from Mama…and from Papa.